Felicia eventually accepted the harsh reality of her failed romantic relation-ship with Peter, and they reconciled their differences. When the Chameleon temporarily removed Spider-Man's powers, the Black Cat teamed with her old partner to help him regain his abilities.

Felicia now operates on the right side of the law as proprietor of the private-security firm Cat's Eye Investigations. She still dons her Black Cat costume whenever the need arises in the course of her work, most recently teaming with Spider-Man to take down a lethal drug dealer. To enhance her natural strength and training, the Black Cat currently employs a series of custom-made devices created by the Tinkerer to imitate the natural abilities of a cat — gadgets paid for with proceeds from her criminal career.

Although she and Peter are no longer romantically involved, Felicia remains quite fond of Spider-Man — seemingly no less so since he became a married man.

PHYSICAL DESCRIPTION:

Height: 5'10"
Weight: 120 lbs.
Eyes: Green
Hair: Platinum blonde

POWERS & ABILITIES:

Strength Level: Without enhancement, Black Cat possesses the normal human strength of a woman of her age, height, and build who engages in a regular intensive exercise routine. Assisted by the power enhancers in her costume, the Cat's strength reaches peak levels, enabling her to bench press approximately 250 lbs. Her Judo skills enable her to throw opponents who weigh even more than this.

Superhuman Powers: The Black Cat's original "bad luck" powers were nothing more than meticulously planned stunts, executed with the aid of her exceptional gymnastics and unarmed combat skills. Later seeking power to enable her to be a true partner to her lover Spider-Man, she made a secret deal with the Kingpin, whose scientists imbued her with a genuine "bad luck" power. This power enabled her subliminally and psionically to affect probability fields, causing improbable, but not impossible, "unlucky" events to occur to enemies within her line of sight.

Spider-Man eventually realized that his own long-term exposure to this probability field had caused him to become "jinxed". He contacted Doctor Strange, and without notifying Felicity, requested Strange to remotely defuse her bad luck field. This actually mutated the Cat's powers, leaving her instead with infrared vision, superhuman balance and agility, and long extensible claws.

Felicia subsequently lost these while helping Spider-Man regain his own powers. Rays from the Chameleon's power-transferal machine affected her. The device was attuned to Spider-Man's DNA, and the backwash caused the loss of her own super-human abilities. Since then she has relied on her natural human skills and the Tinkerer's high-tech inventions to support her feline antics.

Special Skills: Even without the enhanced abilities which her equipment provides, the Black Cat possesses self-trained gymnastic skills that are Olympic-class. She is extremely agile, able to execute complicated flips, springs and rolls with minimal effort. She is nimble-footed and possesses excellent reflexes. She moves with the grace and stealth of her namesake. She had been known to do standing high jumps of almost six feet and standing broad jumps of nearly ten feet. She also has an uncanny sense of balance.

The Black Cat has earned black belts in karate and judo, as well as being skilled in more brutal and less conventional means of unarmed combat. She is also a world-class lock-picker and safecracker, and has a near-peerless knowledge of both electronic and mechanical security systems.

PARAPHERNALIA:

Weapons: The Black Cat's gloves are metal-mesh, fitted with razor-sharp extensible claws developed by the Tinkerer. They are activated by sensors that detect tension in the tendons of the fingers, and extend up to 3".

Personal Devices: The Black Cat wears earrings of a unique design provided by the Tinkerer. These electronic aids are balance compensators that operate on the inner ear, allowing the Cat to land on her feet from nearly any position.

The Tinkerer also provided her with power-enhancers for her costume which provide a moderate boost to her natural strength, and with contact lenses which enable Felicia to see in non-visible spectra, including UV and IR ranges, giving excellent night vision.

The Cat frequently uses a grappling hook of her own design that contains a built-in release mechanism. Using this, she can swing among urban buildings in a manner similar to Daredevil or Spider-Man, though with marginally less speed than either.

POWER GRID	1	2	3	4	5	6	7
INTELLIGENCE							
STRENGTH							
SPEED							
DURABILITY							
ENERGY PROJECTION							
FIGHTING SKILLS							

CARNAGE

REAL NAME: Cletus Kasady
KNOWN ALIASES: None
IDENTITY: Publicly known
OCCUPATION: Prisoner/patient of Ravencroft, formerly a serial killer
CITIZENSHIP: United States with a criminal record
PLACE OF BIRTH: Brooklyn, New York
MARITAL STATUS: Single
KNOWN RELATIVES: Mother (killed by father), Venom (symbiote parent), Father (deceased), Grandmother (killed by Cletus)
GROUP AFFILIATION: None
EDUCATION: High school

HISTORY: Sentenced to eleven consecutive life terms for the slaughter of numerous innocents, psychopathic serial killer Cletus Kasady shared time with his new cellmate, Eddie Brock. Also known as Venom, Brock had become separated from his symbiotic other half, but the creature sought out Brock in his jail cell and bonded with its host once more. As Venom, the two easily smashed through the cell wall and vanished into the night, failing to notice the trace of alien biomass they left behind.

The symbiote that had possessed Brock — and at one time, Peter Parker — belonged to a less-violent caste of a bloodthirsty race of space-faring parasites. Not so its offspring. Quickly setting about to consume a host, the biomass melded with the murderous Kasady — and the deadly symbiotic duo calling itself Carnage emerged. Far more lethal than Venom, Carnage left jail to embark on a murderous spree, killing a graduate student at Empire State University who happened to be friends with Peter.

Learning of the recent escape of Brock's cellmate, Spider-Man identified Kasady as a former resident of St. Estes Home for Boys — an orphanage destroyed by arson. On a hunch, Peter returned to the ruined scene of that crime. There, Spider-Man battled Carnage — but the powerful entity easily defeated him and disappeared. Along with the Human Torch, Spider-Man traveled to the island on which he had sequestered Brock to inform him of Carnage's

THE OFFICIAL HANDBOOK OF THE
MARVEL UNIVERSE

SPIDER-MAN

BLACK CAT

REAL NAME: Felicia Hardy
KNOWN ALIASES: Felicity Harmon
IDENTITY: Known to legal authorities
OCCUPATION: Private Investigator, former burglar
CITIZENSHIP: United States of America with a criminal record, subsequently granted amnesty
PLACE OF BIRTH: Queens, New York

MARITAL STATUS: Single
KNOWN RELATIVES: Walter Hardy (father, deceased), Lydia Hardy (mother)
GROUP AFFILIATION: Owner of Cat's Eye Investigations, former partner of Spider-Man
EDUCATION: College educated (arts major)

HISTORY: Felicia Hardy grew up as "daddy's little girl," idolizing her father. When Walter Hardy suddenly disappeared, Felicia's mother, Lydia, told her he had died in a plane crash; in reality, he had been incarcerated for his crimes as a notorious cat burglar. Upon discovering the truth about her father, Felicia became determined to follow in his footsteps — embarking on an intense training regimen of martial arts, acrobatics, safe cracking and lock picking. Adopting the masked identity of the Black Cat, Felicia's first mission was not to steal a valuable object, but to free her dying father in a daring prison break. Hired muscle Bruno Grainger and demolitions expert Dr. Boris Korpse aided her. It was during this escape that she first encountered Spider-Man, easily evading the web-slinger with a series of carefully planned traps — as well as the use of her highly suggestive feminine wiles.

Following her father's death, Felicia used her skills to establish herself as New York's premier cat burglar. While Spider-Man attempted to capture the Black Cat a number of times, his efforts were continually thwarted by Felicia's elaborate games of cat and mouse. Although they operated on opposite sides of the law, Felicia had grown increasingly attracted to the heroic Spider-Man; she soon came to desire his heart above all other treasures. To ensnare Spider-Man in her romantic web, Felicia allowed herself to be caught by the crime-fighter and revealed her attraction to him. Spider-Man initially resisted the Black Cat's affections, but he could not hide his own feelings for the seductive beauty for long. After Felicia swore off her criminal activities, the Black Cat and Spider-Man became crime-fighting partners — as well as lovers.

While Spider-Man enjoyed his costumed relationship with Felicia, he also wanted to share his personal life with her. After bringing the Black Cat to his apartment, the web-slinger removed his mask — revealing his secret identity as Peter Parker. Felicia was shocked to learn the hero she idolized was truly just an ordinary guy. Peter eventually realized Felicia was only interested in Spider-Man the super hero, not Peter Parker the man.

Although Felicia had employed artfully designed traps at pre-arranged locations to make others believe she possessed the ability to inflict bad luck, the Black Cat in reality had always relied only on her natural physical skills and training as a costumed adventurer. When she was nearly killed in a battle involving Doctor Octopus and the Owl, for which she was granted amnesty for her past crimes, Spider-Man abruptly ended their working partnership — wracked with guilt for having put her in harm's way with no powers of her own. Distraught, Felicia secretly accepted assistance from the Kingpin, who helped her attain genuine powers through scientific means in exchange for a debt. Armed with the ability to cause others to experience bad luck, Felicia soon returned to her former crime-fighting lifestyle.

Felicia's new powers came with the Kingpin's hidden, heavy price — bringing bad luck to those closest to her. Spider-Man, specifically, received a heavy dose of misfortune. Once he discovered this side effect, the hero enlisted Doctor Strange to strip the Black Cat of her powers without her knowledge, leaving her prey to a vicious beating during a dangerous heist. Bitter over her loss and feeling betrayed by Spider-Man, Felicia briefly struck up a relationship with Flash Thompson — mainly to irritate Peter. Flash ended their affair not long after, believing himself too far afield from Felicia's jet-setting lifestyle.

rampage. Identifying a golden opportunity, Brock agreed to help defeat Carnage — but only in return for his own freedom. Spider-Man had little choice but to consent. True to his word, Venom helped the two heroes incapacitate Carnage. Spider-Man could not live up to the agreement; with help from the Fantastic Four, he ambushed Venom and took him into custody.

Carnage was remanded to Ravencroft Institute. Resisting all treatment, his powers made him nearly impossible to contain; shortly thereafter, he escaped. On the lam from Ravencroft, Carnage teamed with fellow lunatics Shriek, Carrion, Demogoblin and Doppelganger. To battle this threat, a reluctant Venom again joined forces with Spider-Man. Aided by other heroes — including Deathlok, the Black Cat, Captain America and Iron Fist — they returned Kasady to Ravencroft. His incarceration did not last long. During a subsequent jailbreak, Kasady made it his mission to kill the only man who had ever befriended him, Billy Bentine — hoping to perpetuate his message of chaos and explode the conventions dictating that friendship should be repaid in kind. Spider-Man defeated Carnage only after Bentine tricked the creature into returning to human form, rendering Kasady vulnerable to a simple knockout punch.

With other Ravencroft escapes attempted and ultimately foiled, Kasady seemed to be reveling in the thrill of it all. But the symbiote had another trick up its own sleeve: Attempting the unexpected,

it abandoned Kasady and overwhelmed John Jameson, chief of security at Ravencroft. Tracking down Spider-Man — Ben Reilly, at the time — the symbiote allowed the web-slinger to defeat its new host. With Jameson out of the picture, the creature overwhelmed Ben, creating the near-unbeatable Spider-Carnage. But Ben's willpower won out; he was able to contain the symbiote's murderous urges long enough to return it to Ravencroft, where it was subdued once more. The determined symbiote soon adopted another approach: It attempted to possess the space-faring Silver Surfer, creating Cosmic Carnage. Already familiar with the deadly race of symbiotes, the Surfer overcame the creature and encased it in a container of ethereal energy.

The symbiote eventually escaped and returned to its host, only to be forcibly re-absorbed by Venom — leaving Kasady powerless. But just as the world began to believe Carnage was gone for good, Kasady escaped Ravencroft yet again — called into the other-dimensional Negative Zone by a distant voice. The voice belonged to another symbiote. Although not Kasady's original parasitic partner, this creature was every bit as deadly. Merged again with an entity more evil than himself, Kasady battled Spider-Man and Blastaar. Though recaptured, the deadly Carnage had found its way back into the world.

POWERS & ABILITIES:

Strength Level: Without his symbiote, Kasady possesses the normal human strength for a man of his age, height and build who engages in regular exercise, although his psychotic behaviour gives him some enhancement. When combined with his alien symbiote, he has demonstrated super-human strength at least twice that of Spider-Man and Venom combined. It is estimated that Carnage is able to lift (press) approximately 50 tons.

Superhuman Powers: The original Venom "parent" symbiote bonded with its host at a clean juncture to the nervous system. By contrast, the symbiotic "other" that has merged with Kasady was at one stage joined at a much lower cellular level — bonding with the very blood cells of its host. This rendered it impossible for the authorities to remove the symbiote without killing the human within. It is not yet clear if the recently acquired replacement host is bonded at the same low level.

In any case, the symbiote grants its host enhanced strength and speed which are superior to those held by either Spider-Man or Venom, although it is not clear why this is the case. This may possibly be due to this particular spawn being incubated on earth, however it must be noted that the replacement host was not incubated on our planet, possibly implying a recent reduction in power.

Like Spider-Man and Venom, Carnage possesses the power to stick to walls, and to generate "swing lines" or "tendrils", which he uses for travel in a fashion similar to webbing. Like Venom, Carnage generates "snares" to trap and entangle foes, and projects elongated claws. In addition the Carnage symbiote also projects sharp bladed weapons such as axe blades, and sharp sword-like protrusions.

As can Venom, the Carnage symbiote is capable of absorbing bullets from small-arms weapons firing conventional ammunition. However, the symbiote is vulnerable to both sonics (to a much lesser degree than its parent), and to heat-based attacks (to a much greater degree than its parent).

Special Skills: Kasady's symbiote can, like Venom's, mimic any type of clothing, but unlike Venom, Carnage has not been seen using the costume's "chameleon" ability as camouflage.

Carnage is able to deaden Spider-Man's spider-sense to a certain degree, though not neutralize it completely. The Carnage symbiote can apparently also block its parent symbiote's natural ability to track its own offspring.

POWER GRID	1	2	3	4	5	6	7
INTELLIGENCE							
STRENGTH							
SPEED							
DURABILITY							
ENERGY PROJECTION							
FIGHTING SKILLS							

DAILY BUGLE

HISTORY: When Peter Parker found himself in desperate need of money to keep himself and his aunt, May Parker, above the poverty line, he hatched the clever idea to photograph himself as Spider-Man and sell the resulting pictures to the Daily Bugle. With his obsessive hatred of the web-slinging hero, Bugle publisher J. Jonah Jameson was eager to get his hands on Parker's pics and use them to discredit Spider-Man in the public eye. While Peter has abandoned his freelance photography position at the Bugle a number of times throughout the years, he has always remained friendly with the staff of the newspaper — most notably reporters Ben Urich and Betty Brant, and editor-in-chief Joseph "Robbie" Robertson.

Jameson began his journalistic career as a reporter for the Bugle while still in high school and later purchased the newspaper. Under Jameson's control, the Bugle has remained New York City's leading paper, resulting in spin-off publications such as NOW and Woman magazines. More recently, the paper temporarily changed ownership — first to Thomas Fireheart (Puma) and later to Norman Osborn (Green Goblin), who used the Bugle to torment Peter. In both cases, it quickly returned to Jameson's control.

The Bugle's reputation has been harmed by its often sensationalist style, and by Jameson's use of the paper as his own personal platform — unfairly attacking Spider-Man as a menace to the city. However, after a public scandal revealed Jameson's involvement in the Scorpion's creation, JJJ scaled back his editorial role at the newspaper — leaving most of the day-to-day decisions to Robertson.

Another sign of Jameson's increasingly pragmatic approach to the New York super-hero community is his latest pet project, a Bugle supplement called "The Pulse." The team behind The Pulse is headed by Urich and super-powered private investigator Jessica Jones. However, this project should not be misinterpreted as any relaxation of Jameson's loathing of costumed vigilantes. The supplement's mission is to expose the most sensational happenings among the "spandex set" and is nothing more than a cynical ploy to profit from the general public's fascination with the larger-than-life heroes and villains Jameson so despises.

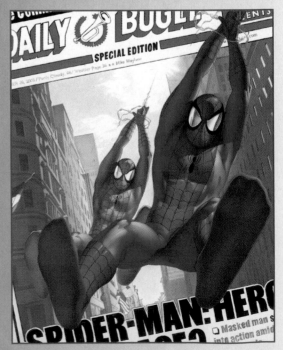

Real Name: Digger
Known Aliases: "The Vegas Thirteen"
Identity: Known to legal authorities
Occupation: Former mobsters
Citizenship: N/A
Place of Birth: Various
Marital Status: N/A
Known Relatives: N/A
Group Affiliation: Various New York City mobs
Education: N/A

PHYSICAL DESCRIPTION:

Height: 7'4"
Weight: 755 lbs.
Eyes: Glowing pink
Hair: None

POWERS & ABILITIES:

Strength Level: Digger's strength is provided by gamma-radiation similar to that which powers the Hulk. Digger possesses strength levels close to that of the Hulk, but is held back by the continual struggle to hold together the 13 various components that make up his composite body. It is estimated that Digger could have lifted (pressed) approximately 100 tons.

Superhuman Powers: The gamma-radiation provides Digger with greatly enhanced strength, speed, and agility. Digger's skin is proof against small arms weapons using conventional ammunition, however he can be harmed and possibly even destroyed by sustained fire of high-velocity ammunition.

The fact that Digger is already dead means he has effectively no critical points to attack. In the end, Spider-Man managed to defeat Digger only by engaging in a protracted fight which did not allow Digger the chance to rest and regain enough energy to hold his unnaturally reassembled form in a coherent state.

HISTORY: On July 3, 1957, seven mafia bosses and their chief lieutenants met at a Las Vegas restaurant to find a peaceful solution to the recent inter-family violence which threatened to damage the business interests of all concerned. As the men took their places at the table they noticed that Morris Forelli from New York was conspicuously absent, even though his right hand man George Sims was reassuringly present.

In fact, Forelli had recently discovered that Sims had betrayed him, arranging the death of one of Forelli's sons. When Forelli's tommy gun-toting killers opened fire they rid Forelli of twelve competitors and one traitor. The bodies were secretly buried in the Nevada desert, and the dead men soon passed into legend, to be known as "The Vegas Thirteen".

Time passed, and the Pentagon came to Nevada seeking to test their latest tactical weapon - a pocket Gamma bomb. When Gamma radiation met long-buried remains, the result was a patchwork monster that dug its way to the surface seeking only one thing... a New York mobster named Forelli.

Having made his way to New York, Digger started doing damage to Forelli's business interests, looking to work his way up the chain of command by sheer brute strength until he came face to face with the long-lived boss himself. Before long, Detective Lamont of the NYPD started picking up a mix of finger-prints from five different long-dead mobsters... all from the same hand-mark. Realizing he needed help, Lamont pulled Spider-Man in on the case.

Lamont wasn't the only man looking for the wall-crawler's assistance in dealing with Digger. Surveying the trail of devastation, Morris Forelli realized that his normal tough-guys were no match for Digger. Calling on Spider-Man for aid, Forelli offered cold hard cash if the web-slinger would protect him and his daughter from Digger's onslaught. Caught in a moral dilemma, Spider-Man decided there could be little harm in accepting money for protecting human lives that he would have protected for nothing. The big question was... how to defeat a gamma-irradiated creature that in terms of pure strength sat not too far below the Hulk.

After a combination of cellular analysis and experimentation, Spider-Man realized that Digger was vulnerable to exhaustion after a protracted battle, leaving him unable to hold his various component parts together, and making him vulnerable to "dismantling". Having little other choice, Spider-Man was forced to destroy Digger, although he took some small comfort from the fact that Digger was not in any real sense, alive.

POWER GRID	1	2	3	4	5	6	7
INTELLIGENCE							
STRENGTH							
SPEED							
DURABILITY							
ENERGY PROJECTION							
FIGHTING SKILLS							

Art by Staz Johnson

REAL NAME: Otto Octavius
KNOWN ALIASES: Formerly Master Planner, Master Programmer
IDENTITY: Publicly known
OCCUPATION: Criminal mastermind, former atomic research consultant
CITIZENSHIP: United States of America with a criminal record
PLACE OF BIRTH: Schenectady, New York
MARITAL STATUS: Single
KNOWN RELATIVES: Torbert Theadore Octavius (father, deceased), Mary Lavinia Octavius (mother, deceased), Hargrove (cousin)
GROUP AFFILIATION: Co-founder of the Sinister Six, frequently heads his own gang of hired thugs. Founded and lead one incarnation of the Masters of Evil.
EDUCATION: Doctorates in nuclear physics, honorary doctorate in biochemistry

---

HISTORY: The son of an overbearing mother and a bullying father, Otto Octavius grew up to become a reclusive but brilliant atomic researcher. To help manipulate radioactive substances from a safe distance, Otto constructed a chest harness controlling four mechanical, tentacle-like arms — earning himself the nickname Doctor Octopus. In a freak laboratory accident, volatile liquids exploded — bombarding the scientist with radiation. The substances left him capable of mentally controlling the arms, but the accident also caused irreversible brain damage — transforming the respected scientist into a megalomaniacal criminal. Waking in a hospital, Otto knew this newfound strength — combined with his awesome intellect — could render him supremely powerful. Holding the medical staff hostage, he easily defeated Spider-Man in their first meeting. Doc Ock then took control of a leading nuclear research facility and again squared off with the wall-crawler, who this time defeated him with one punch to the jaw.

After serving time, Doc Ock attempted to raise funds by springing gangster Blackie Gaxton from prison — assisted by Gaxton's lawyer, Bennett Brant. Spider-Man foiled the scheme, but could not save Bennett from being shot in front of his sister, Betty Brant. Octopus then assembled the first Sinister Six to combat Spider-Man. He plotted to take Betty hostage, knowing Spider-Man had previously rescued her and would likely do so again. May Parker, visiting Betty at the time, was also captured. Otto treated May kindly, and she remained blissfully unaware she had been kidnapped by the charming villain.

Following Spider-Man's defeat of the Sinister Six, Ock assembled another group of criminal underlings and established an undersea base. Calling himself the Master Planner, he embarked on a series of thefts of experimental substances — seeking to further expand his mastery of the atomic sciences. His goal: to develop a radiation ray with which he could rule the world. But his path was fated to entwine with Spider-Man's: When May fell sick, Peter provided her with a blood transfusion — not realizing the radioactivity in his plasma would kill her. The only substance capable of saving her was the experimental ISO-36. Peter man-aged to obtain enough money to fund the operation, but the Master Planner's forces hijacked the shipment for their own deadly research. Spider-Man tracked the Master Planner to his underwater hideout and confronted his foe, revealed to be Doc Ock. After the base was destroyed, Doctor Octopus escaped once more. Spider-Man recovered the ISO-36 and saved Aunt May's life with the aid of Dr. Curt Connors (Lizard).

Doctor Octopus' next scheme involved the theft of a projector that could disable any device. After two failed attempts, Otto finally succeeded on his third. Turning the Nullifier against Spider-Man, he caused the wall-crawler to lose his memory and persuaded him they were allies. He then enlisted Spider-Man's help to steal the remaining components for the device. Though the hero had not regained his memory, his instinctive spider-sense persuaded him not to trust Doc Ock, and he defeated him once more. Now imprisoned, with his arms confiscated, Otto demonstrated that the range of his psionic control over the limbs had increased to a far greater distance than previously believed. The arms freed him from captivity; in the ensuing battle between Doc Ock and Spider-Man, George Stacy was killed while protecting an innocent child.

Free again, Doctor Octopus seized upon the Kingpin's absence to gather his forces and launch an all-out gang war against Hammerhead's thugs. But Spider-Man's involvement quickly resulted in Otto's return to prison. While incarcerated, Doctor Octopus learned May Parker had inherited a small Canadian island containing a commercial nuclear reactor. On his release, he set out to woo and marry May. But Hammerhead interrupted the wedding, and the ensuing chase and brawl led to the destruction of the reactor.

When Doc Ock went to war with the Owl, Spider-Man and the Black Cat attempted to intervene. Devastated that the confrontation had left the Black Cat near death, a cold-hearted Peter said farewell to his friends before entering what he believed to be his final showdown with Doctor Octopus. Spider-Man's victory was remorseless, and Doc Ock developed a morbid fear of his arachnid foe. Imprisoned in a mental institution, Otto struggled with his overwhelming phobia of Spider-Man. Knowing he could not face his foe directly, Ock's next plan involved the use of biological weapons to kill the entire population of New York. Spider-Man was forced to fake a humiliating defeat lest the city be destroyed, restoring Otto's self-confidence.

Still, Otto had clearly changed. As a young scientist, he had fallen in love with a fellow researcher, Mary Alice Burke — but his demanding mother jealously sabotaged the relation-ship. Learning Mary Alice was dying from AIDS, Otto began a desperate search for a cure — stealing research materials to do so. His attempts failed, Mary Alice died, and the villain meekly surrendered to Spider-Man. A world-weary Otto nonetheless escaped from prison. At the time, Spider-Man was dying from a chemical virus. Hoping to one day kill the hero him-self, Doc Ock captured and unmasked his foe. Analyzing the virus, Otto offered him a cure. Daring to trust his enemy, Peter accepted the mixture and was healed.

Art by Mark Brooks

But having found his own salvation in this act, Doctor Octopus did not live to enjoy it. Intending to protect Peter by killing his enemies, Kaine murdered Doc Ock by snapping his neck. But Dr. Carolyn Trainer, Otto's young assistant, had been working with him in the area of solid holographic projection and mind-to-computer communication. Prior to Peter's unmasking, she had created a backup brain-imprint of Doc Ock. With Otto's passing, the backup of his mind became a software projection known as the Master Programmer, and Carolyn used his tentacles to become the second Doctor Octopus. Meanwhile, the Rose (Jacob Conover) employed a cult, the True Believers, to magically resurrect Doctor Octopus as an empty-minded servant. As soon as he was raised, Carolyn uploaded the Master Programmer persona into Octavius' brain. She returned his tentacles to him, and they fled.

With his memories restored from a past snapshot, Otto has forgotten he once knew Spider-Man's true identity. He remains very much the deadly and manipulative criminal genius he was in his heyday.

PHYSICAL DESCRIPTION:

Height: 5'9"
Weight: 245 lbs.
Eyes: Brown
Hair: Brown

POWERS & ABILITIES

Strength Level: Without the use of his artificial tentacles, Doctor Octopus possesses the normal human strength of a man of his age, height, and build who engages in no regular exercise. Each of his tentacles is able to lift approximately 8 tons (provided that Octopus supports his harness with at least one other arm in order to prevent the chest harness/skin interface from bearing any part of the effort). With one arm, Octopus can lift an automobile. With two arms, he can throw an automobile tens of feet, or lift a small bus. The pincers on his arms are capable of gripping with a force of 175 pounds per square inch, sufficient to deform any object made of a thin-walled substance less durable than steel. The pincers can, for instance, crush a handgun. By combining the intrinsic strength of both his tentacles and the pincers, Doctor Octopus can perform such feats as tearing steel doors off bank vaults.

Superhuman Powers: Doctor Octopus' superhuman abilities derive from the four mentally-controlled, electronically-powered, telescoping, prehensile titanium-steel tentacles attached to a stainless steel harness encircling his body from lower chest to waist. Each tentacle, approximately five inches in diameter, terminates in three single-jointed pincers. The pincers are able to rotate in relation to the arm for 360 degrees, in a screwdriver-like twisting motion.

Each tentacle is approximately six feet long at full contraction, but can extend to a maximum of 24 feet. Each tentacle segment contains four high-efficiency electric motors equipped with a clutched, helical-gear train, independently mounted on frictionless gimbals and housed in four thin, overlapping layers of titanium-niobium steel. The titanium-steel alloy is light, has high-tensile strength, a high melting point, and high thin-wall rigidity. The motors get their power from a small nuclear-powered thermo-electric generator, which can provide several hundred watts per hour for up to five years before needing to replace its U-239 core. Each arm is capable of moving at a speed of ninety feet per second and can strike with the force of a jackhammer, or generate a 50 mile per hour wind If spun like a giant fan.

By combining the intrinsic strength of both his tentacles and the pincers, Doctor Octopus can scale stone, brick, or concrete walls by rending "handholds" in the surface of the wall. Octopus is able to use his tentacles for traversing horizontal distances as well. At full extension, he can travel high above the ground as if on stilts, either using two tentacles, or for maximum speed (approximately 50 miles per hour), four tentacles.

Doctor Octopus possesses extraordinary mental abilities and concentration, and through years of practice is able to perform two complex and two simple independent actions, simultaneously, one with each arm. Although there are no nerve endings throughout the length of his artificial arms, Octopus can "feel" basic sensations with them. As a result of mutagenic changes from exposure to radiation during the accident, electrical connections have been made from his chest harness to his spine. Thus, Doctor Octopus can mentally perceive "tactile" sensations by feeling the amount of electrical resistance that the pincer's electric motors feel when the pincers grasp an object.

Octopus can control the actions of his artificial arms psionically even when they have been severed from his body and are separated from him by vast distances (a distance of 900 miles has been recorded). The tentacles have been modified since the time of the original accident to include high-efficiency battery packs (enabling movement when cut off from the central power source) and individual micro-circuit control modules (enabling each arm to perform certain pre-programmed actions when Octopus loses conscious control). In the event that Octopus loses consciousness, the control module of each arm has enough pre-programmed conditional responses in its memory chip to enable it to perform a relatively complex sequence of actions, such as saving his life. The trauma of his arm or arms being separated from the harness causes a period of disorientation in which his arms flail about until the pre-programming takes over.

Special Skills: Doctor Octopus is the world's leading authority on nuclear radiation and its effects on human physiology. He is also a brilliant engineer and inventor.

POWER GRID	1	2	3	4	5	6	7
INTELLIGENCE							
STRENGTH							
SPEED							
DURABILITY							
ENERGY PROJECTION							
FIGHTING SKILLS							

REAL NAME: Maxwell "Max" Dillon
KNOWN ALIASES: None
IDENTITY: Known to legal authorities
OCCUPATION: Professional criminal, former linesman for Consolidated Edison
CITIZENSHIP: United States of America with a criminal record
PLACE OF BIRTH: Endicott, New York
MARITAL STATUS: Divorced
KNOWN RELATIVES: Unnamed mother (deceased), Father (Jonathan, deceased), Ex-wife (Norma Lynn)
GROUP AFFILIATION: Co-founder of the Sinister Six, former member of the Emissaries of Evil and Frightful Four, former partner of Blizzard and the Purple Man
EDUCATION: High school

HISTORY: Max Dillon was a good linesman, but selfish and friendless when not on the job. One day, while he was repairing a downed power line, an unexpected thunderstorm rolled in. Hit by a lightning strike, Dillon foolishly grabbed the power line. The two shocks cancelled each other out; instead of leaving Dillon dead, they granted him extraordinary powers. Upon discovering he possessed the ability to generate, store and project electrical charges, the arrogant Dillon sought a more lucrative profession: crime. Donning a colorful costume, Dillon chose J. Jonah Jameson as his first victim, successfully looting Jameson's safe in front of the newspaperman's very eyes.

An enraged Jameson made the bold claim that Electro was simply Spider-Man in disguise. Spider-Man could hardly resist that challenge, and he set out to fight Electro to prove they were not the same man. Totally unprepared for Electro's attack, Spider-Man was nearly killed when he received a jolt of electricity just from touching the villain. He realized he could defeat Electro only by outsmarting him; spotting a nearby fire-hose, Spider-Man short-circuited his enemy. Seeking revenge, Electro joined the original Sinister Six, but the web-slinger defeated the villian by deactivating his power source. Grounding himself with a steel cable, Spider-Man was able to close in for the knockout punch.

Electro also came into conflict with Daredevil early in his career. He later teamed with the Blizzard to battle Daredevil and Spider-Man together. Ever the team player, Electro joined the Frightful Four in an attack on the Fantastic Four. Following several failed reunions of the Sinister Six, Electro suffered a crisis of confidence. Attempting to go straight, he ended up as a freak show act in a Coney Island carnival. Unable to bear the crowd's laughter, Electro cracked. In a spectacular bid to overcome his self-doubt, he stood on the roof of the Top of New York Hotel and gradually absorbed all the power in Manhattan. Spider-Man arrived, and Electro easily blasted him off the edge of the building. But even Electro has his limits: With his head throbbing near to the bursting point, he attempted to discharge the excess electricity, but found he had overloaded his abilities. In that moment, his self-doubt came flooding back. Returning to the scene, Spider-Man reassured the confused Dillon. Treating Electro as an equal, Spider-Man convinced him his problems were purely psychological. The hero's pep talk worked, and Electro gradually returned the charge to the blacked-out city. In an unexpected mea culpa, the grateful Electro thanked Spider-Man profusely and went willingly to serve his jail sentence.

Art by Steve Ditko

Fearing the murderous Kaine would come for him, Electro escaped and joined the Sinister Seven in self-defense. Afterwards, Electro struggled with his own self-worth — residual damage done to him in childhood after having been abandoned by his violent father and smothered by his overbearing mother. Realizing he had reached a crossroads, and remembering his moment of ultimate power atop the Top of New York Hotel, Electro prepared to take one more gamble in his quest for self-esteem. He allowed the Rose (Jacob Conover) and Delilah to strap him into a super-charged electric chair. The gamble paid off; Electro's powers were temporarily enhanced tenfold. In return, Dillon had promised to aid the Rose

and Delilah in their gangland ambitions. But his drive for vengeance against Spider-Man — and indeed, the whole of Manhattan — took precedence. He created a plan to set off a chain reaction among the New York power stations that would destroy most of the city. Even equipped with an insulated costume, Spider-Man barely managed to defeat him.

Electro remains an ever-present threat — but normally faces defeat despite powers that make him, effectively, a force of nature. It is only Electro's profound lack of judgment that allows him to be beaten by less-powerful yet more prudent foes like Spider-Man.

PHYSICAL DESCRIPTION:

Height: 5'11"
Weight: 165 lbs.
Eyes: Blue
Hair: Reddish-brown

Distinguishing Features: None

POWERS & ABILITIES:

Strength Level: Unenhanced by an immediate power source, Electro possesses the normal human strength of a man of his age, height and build who engages in regular exercise.

Superhuman Powers: Unenhanced by an immediate power source, Electro possesses the normal human strength of a man of his age, height and build who engages in regular exercise. When electrically charged, Electro's physical strength is enhanced, and he is able to lift (press) about 500 pounds at maximum charge.

Superhuman Powers: Electro possesses the ability to bodily acquire, store and manipulate electrostatic energy, which he can release or harness for a number of effects. Typically Electro absorbs this energy from an external power source, but in the absence of an external supply, he can generate a limited amount of electrostatic charge by transforming chemical energy from within his own body, although this will physically weaken him. Electro can also act as a transformer, touching an outside power source (such as a generator) and channeling it through his body for use without intermediate storage.

Electro has been observed generating lightning bolts in air with a range approaching 100 feet. This requires an electrical potential difference of at least 30 million volts compared to the target point. Analysis of the resultant damage caused by Electro's bolts indicates that the current flow can rise as high as 200 amps over short periods. Corresponding analysis of video footage indicates that over the course of a battle Electro can (without recharging) generate around 100 seconds of current (approximately 1000 bolts with an average duration of 1/10 second). Hence, it appears that Electro can store at least 20,000 coulombs (amp-seconds) of charge.

Electro can employ his electrostatic energy in a number of ways. The simplest manifestation is the emission of a lightning-like electric arc from his fingertips, which can propagate through air or other conducting mediums. This discharge, whose total voltage can be regulated within certain limits, travels at the speed of lightning about 1,100 feet per second. The course of the electrostatic bolt, like lightning, does not always follow a straight line since conducting substances like metal or other electrical fields may influence it. If his target is

not grounded, his electrostatic bolt will have little effect. The maximum effective range of his bolts is about 100 feet.

Electro can propel himself along the accompanying magnetic lines of force in objects that have great electric potential, such as high-tension electrical lines. He generates tight, eddying electrical fields around his legs, which develops an intense, opposing magnetic field that can support him above the electric cable's magnetic field. By creating imbalances in his field, he can ride along magnetic ripples at speeds of up to 140 miles per hour, the maximum speed at which he can still breathe unaided. He can sometimes create electrostatic bridges to traverse upon, although the expenditure of energy is enormous.

Electro's electrical powers also grant him certain sensory and manipulative abilities. By "feeling" the course of electricity through the circuitry of any electrically powered device, Electro can override the system and make the device obey his mental commands. Electro can disconnect alarm systems, control computers in a limited way, or overload any electrically controlled system that is insufficiently shielded.

The electric flux of Electro's skin is such that when his electric charge is at its maximum, a person touching him is in danger of being electrocuted. Electro's body is immune to the effects of its electricity and that of other sources as well. Hence, Electro cannot be electrocuted no matter how great the voltage. By using an external electrical power source to recharge his body's energy reserves, he could expend electrical energy indefinitely without diminishing his personal reserves. The electricity coursing through his altered body augments his strength, speed, and recuperative powers.

Note that the preceding statistics apply to "normal" conditions. However, on at least two separate occasions, Electro has been seen to greatly surpass these power levels — in one case absorbing sufficient energy to power a large part of downtown Manhattan. Both scenarios corresponded to extreme states of mental distress and frustration, and hence it could be surmised that Electro's typically observed power limitations are predominantly psychological rather than physical.

POWER GRID	1	2	3	4	5	6	7
INTELLIGENCE							
STRENGTH							
SPEED							
DURABILITY							
ENERGY PROJECTION							
FIGHTING SKILLS							

REAL NAME: Ezekiel Sims
KNOWN ALIASES: None
IDENTITY: Secret
OCCUPATION: Businessman
CITIZENSHIP: Citizen of the United States of America with no criminal record
PLACE OF BIRTH: Unrevealed
MARITAL STATUS: Single
KNOWN RELATIVES: Father (deceased)
GROUP AFFILIATION: Various managed corporations
EDUCATION: College educated (MBA)

HISTORY: The enigmatic Ezekiel appeared seemingly out of nowhere, bearing an intimate knowledge of Peter Parker's powers and history. Ezekiel possessed strikingly similar abilities to those of Spider-Man, although he had used them to a very different end, having built a powerful business empire with international reach. Peter was curious to discover more about Ezekiel's past, but instead it was Ezekiel who asked the questions, suggesting to Peter that perhaps the random accident which gave him his powers was not so random – and causing Peter to examine more deeply his relationship with the world of spiders from which his gifts came.

In return, Ezekiel indicated he wished simply to use his knowledge and resources to aid Peter, as Peter had aided others. This aid was soon given, when the creature named Morlun came seeking to devour Spider-Man's totemistic powers. Soon after, Ezekiel came again to Spider-Man's aid when Shathra the Spider-Wasp came hunting from the astral plane looking to devour her natural enemy. Barely surviving these battles, Spider-Man never sought to question who might have been the true target of these attacks.

To understand more about Ezekiel, it is necessary to hear the story of Kwaku Anansi, inhabitant of Ghana in West Africa, centuries ago. Anansi sought wisdom, but also followed the way of the spider, climbing high on web and line. Anansi climbed high enough to speak to Nyame, the sky-god, and entreat with him for wisdom of the mortal world and the world beyond. Nyame demanded eternal servitude. Anansi agreed, but warned that he could never turn away from those in need, and those he loved and revered. The bargain was struck, and the spirit of Anansi passed down over generations to individuals with the spirit of the hunter, but who also honored Anansi's higher ideals.

Several years ago, the young Ezekiel learned of Anansi's line. Using his wealth to save a Spider-Temple in Peru from planned demolition, Ezekiel demanded that the head priest Miguel should perform the blood-rite and grant the Spider's powers to him. Miguel warned that the true heir of this generation was yet to arrive, and furthermore, that the spirits of the temple would one day learn of the deception, and would not be pleased. Ezekiel insisted. He always planned to first gain more power, in order to help those in need. Instead, the search for "enough" power consumed him, and he never found the moment to act.

When Ezekiel learned of the pending arrival of Morlun, and later of Shathra, he knew that they were coming for him. He sought out Spider-Man, and under cover of "protecting" Peter, guided Spider-Man into unwittingly fighting on his behalf. Learning of the arrival of "The Gatekeeper" and his horde of spiders, Ezekiel saw this foretold the coming of the guardian he had long feared, and no such simple deception would suffice.

Through treachery, Ezekiel subdued Spider-Man and brought him to Peru. A corrupted form of the blood ritual merged his blood with Peter's, and Ezekiel then abandoned Peter to be punished in his place. Unexpectedly, the exchange worked in both directions, and Ezekiel realized the good that Peter had done, in comparison to how he himself had squandered his gifts. Racing back, Ezekiel sacrificed himself to the demonic spider that sought him, leaving Peter to mourn the man with whom he had so much in common, and yet so little.

PHYSICAL DESCRIPTION:

Height: 6'
Weight: 180 lbs.
Eyes: Blue
Hair: Gray

POWERS & ABILITIES:

Strength Level: Ezekiel possesses super-human strength slightly inferior to Spider-Man. He can lift (press) approximately 9 tons.

Superhuman Powers: Ezekiel powers are derived from the same source as Spider-Man, but are acquired through deceit rather than by right. Hence these powers are all held to a marginally inferior level to Spider-Man. Ezekiel possesses all of Spider-Man's powers including his speed, agility, reflexes, and resilience. He also has the power to stick to walls, and a super-human sense. He does not use web-shooters, or any of Spider-Man's other artificial tools. Because of the similar nature of their powers, neither Spider-Man nor Ezekiel can detect each other with their spider-sense.

Special Skills: Ezekiel is a skillful businessman, and has attained a huge level of personal wealth through his own leadership and initiative. He possesses a good understanding of the various mystical ceremonies related to the African/Central American legacy of Kwaku Anansi the founder of the Spider-Clan.

POWER GRID	1	2	3	4	5	6	7
INTELLIGENCE							
STRENGTH							
SPEED							
DURABILITY							
ENERGY PROJECTION							
FIGHTING SKILLS							

GREEN GOBLIN

REAL NAME: Norman Osborn
KNOWN ALIASES: None
IDENTITY: Secret
OCCUPATION: Businessman, professional criminal, leader of "The Order of Goblins"
CITIZENSHIP: United States of America
PLACE OF BIRTH: Hartford, Connecticut
MARITAL STATUS: Widowed
KNOWN RELATIVES: Harold "Harry" Osborn (son, deceased), Norman Osborn Jr. (grandson), Ambrose Osborn (father, deceased), Alton Osborn (grandfather, deceased), Emily Osborn, (wife, deceased), Liz Osborn (daughter-in-law)
GROUP AFFILIATION: The Order of Goblins (splinter group of the Cabal of Scriers)
EDUCATION: College educated (science major, fifth-year degree)

HISTORY: Armed with razor-sharp weapons, empowered by a strength-enhancing serum and driven by a maniacal insanity, the Green Goblin has long been Spider-Man's deadliest opponent. But only two years after Peter Parker first encountered the Goblin did he finally learn his foe's true identity: Norman Osborn — the wealthy, industrialist father of his collegiate roommate and best pal, Harry Osborn.

Norman had risen to prominence after framing his partner, Mendel Stromm, for embezzling funds from their chemical company. With the professor's imprisonment, Norman gained full control of the flourishing Oscorp and acquired access to Stromm's experimental, strength-enhancing formula. Hungry for power, Norman attempted to use the untested serum on himself. The unstable concoction exploded in his face, granting him greatly enhanced physical abilities … at the cost of his sanity. A cunning new persona soon emerged, one of sinister evil.

His body and mind transformed by the Goblin Formula, Norman plotted to become leader of New York City's criminal underworld. He targeted Spider-Man, looking to establish his reputation by murdering the web-slinger. After a failed attempt to use the Headsman to kill Spider-Man, Norman decided to do the job personally. Employing his company's resources and technology, Norman created a grotesque costume based on the goblin-like wraith that had terrorized him in his childhood nightmares. Backed by the muscle of the Enforcers, the Green Goblin faced Spider-Man for the first time; he was soundly defeated in both their initial battle and a subsequent rematch. Even an alliance with the Crime-Master failed to help the Goblin best Spider-Man, but the crafty Norman soon devised a different approach.

Art by John Romita Jr.

Art by Terry Dodson

After concocting a compound that weakened the web-slinger's spider-sense, the Goblin followed him undetected. When Spider-Man assumed his civilian identity, Norman swiftly attacked. Easily overpowering a surprised Peter, the Goblin abducted him and took him back to a secret hideout. There, the Goblin taunted Peter, his mind intoxicated with overwhelming arrogance. While the Goblin indulged in boastful speeches, Peter was able to escape his bindings. During the ensuing battle, Norman was electrocuted with a shock powerful enough to jolt his mind into partial amnesia. With all memories of the Goblin and Peter's true identity seemingly wiped from Norman's mind, Spider-Man decided to protect his friend Harry from the knowledge of his father's maniacal alter ego. To that end, Peter stripped Norman of the Goblin costume and hid the villain's true identity from the authorities.

Against Peter's hopes, Norman's amnesia proved to be as unstable as his sanity. When exposed to stress or images of the Goblin, his madness and memories would return — dominated by an aggressive hatred of Spider-Man. In their subsequent battles, Peter was able to use his knowledge of Norman's unbalanced mind to shock the villain back into brief sanity — but the episodes grew more frequent, and the Goblin's methods became increasingly insidious.

Art by Alex Ross

Knowing Peter's true identity, the Goblin hatched a scheme to attack Spider-Man through the people he loved. The Goblin kidnapped Peter's girlfriend, Gwen Stacy, and brought her to the Brooklyn Bridge. When Spider-Man attempted to rescue her, the Goblin hurled the girl off the bridge. While Spider-Man was able to catch Gwen with a well-placed web-line, the sudden stop snapped her neck. In frenzied grief, Spider-Man fought the Goblin as never before. The hero nearly beat the Goblin to death, but held back his final blow. Bloody, beaten and feigning surrender, the Goblin attempted to spear Spider-Man with the razor-sharp tip of his remote-controlled glider. Warned by his spider-sense, the hero was able to leap away at the last second — leaving the Goblin fatally impaled, the victim of his own final ruse.

Unknown to Spider-Man, Harry had secretly witnessed their final battle. Harry removed the Goblin's costume when Spider-Man departed, preserving his father's identity even after his seeming death. Believing Spider-Man was to blame for Norman's demise, Harry vowed revenge on the web-slinger; soon after, he took up the mantle of his father's criminal identity. Though it was long believed he had been fatally wounded, Norman's death was not what it seemed. The chemicals that granted him enhanced strength and altered his sanity also gifted him with a superhuman healing ability. His impaled chest mended while Norman lay in the morgue, and the clever villain covered his escape by swapping his body with that of a murdered drifter. Returning to his hideout, Norman arrived in time to observe Harry vow vengeance on Spider-Man and don the Goblin costume. Passing the legacy of the Green Goblin to his son, Norman slipped away unnoticed to Europe.

In Europe, Norman joined a secret society known as the Scriers and soon took control of the shadowy cabal. His hatred of Peter still raging as strong as ever, Norman hatched a plan to surreptitiously use the Scriers to psychologically destroy the web-slinger. He dispatched a Scrier to America to aid one of Peter's professors, Dr. Miles Warren (Jackal), in his quest to create clones of both Gwen and Peter. With the Scrier's help, Warren successfully produced a clone of Peter and arranged for him to battle his double at Shea Stadium. Believing his clone had been fatally injured during their fight, Spider-Man cast the

lifeless body into a smokestack. However, the clone was still alive; when he regained consciousness, he assumed the identity of Ben Reilly and lived as a drifter for five years.

After Harry fatally succumbed to the toxic effects of an updated Goblin Formula, Norman returned to the United States. It was at this time that both the Jackal and Ben also resurfaced in Peter's life. Shocked to face his clone after so many years, Peter fell prey to Norman's manipulations — believing he was the clone, and Ben the original. It was Norman's intention to devastate Peter with the false revelation. In fact, the news had the opposite effect: After passing the responsibilities of Spider-Man to Ben, Peter eagerly embraced the idea of a quiet civilian life with his wife, Mary Jane Watson, and moved to Portland. Infuriated by Peter's happiness, Norman was forced to abandon his psychological attacks and finally reveal himself.

The Goblin attacked Ben and Peter in a grand battle, destroying Spider-Man's long-held hope that his greatest foe was dead and buried. During the fight, Ben was killed protecting Peter. When his corpse rapidly disintegrated, it proved Ben had been the clone all along. Peter narrowly escaped death himself, tormented by the fact that he was facing a Green Goblin more driven than ever.

As the Goblin returned to public view, so did Norman. With a carefully contrived story, he resumed his role as a wealthy public figure — regaining control of his industrial empire from his daughter-in-law, Liz Osborn. With his financial control of Oscorp and subsidiary Multivex restored, Norman launched a hostile takeover of the Daily Bugle — using the paper to damage Spider-Man's reputation. Norman's growing lust for power led to his participation in an ancient ritual called the Gathering of Five — in which each undertaker would randomly receive a gift of power, knowledge, immortality, madness or death. Hoping for power, he instead drew mad-ness. Norman was defeated by Spider-Man after a mighty battle that destroyed the Daily Bugle building.

With the aid of his faithful Scriers, Norman escaped the destruction of the Bugle; the use of medicated patches restored some semblance

of his sanity. While Norman recovered, J. Jonah Jameson was able to wrest control of the Bugle from his clutches. Shortly thereafter, Norman came to the realization that Peter was truly the son he had always wanted — studious, inventive, strong-willed and industrious — in contrast to the late Harry, who had always wilted under the pressures of life. Rather than kill his hated enemy, Norman now set out to mold Peter in his own image, an heir to the Goblin legacy. He initiated a mad plan to corrupt Peter and fill him with hatred, pushing him past the point of no return. But Norman had clearly misjudged Peter. No matter how many drugs he employed, the hero's will was too strong for Norman to sway. The time for such tricks was long past.

Relentless in pursuit of retribution, Norman decided to stake everything he had built on one final throw of the dice. Attacking Peter's friends and family, Norman first pressed Flash Thompson into an arranged drunken-driving accident, leaving him in a coma. Then the Goblin forced Spider-Man into battle, threatening to kill every person Peter loved — Mary Jane; his aunt, May Parker; even Norman's own grandson, Norman Osborn Jr. During their heated fight, Peter admitted to Norman that he should hate the Goblin for killing Gwen — but by giving in to that bitterness, he would forever blacken the memory of the first girl he ever loved. Although Norman soon fell to Peter's mercy, Spider-Man refused to give in to his anger and walked away from the fight. Shocked by the strength of Peter's unbreakable spirit, Norman seemed to arrive at the realization that Spider-Man would no longer be willing to continue this deadly cycle of violence. Could the Green Goblin battle a Spider-Man who refuses to fight?

The answer, it seems, is "yes." Peter may refuse to protect himself, but could never refuse to act to protect the innocent. By the simple act of taking a few dozen hostages, the Green Goblin easily demonstrated the battle between the two would continue for as long as Peter accepted the responsibility implied by his powers — which is to say, as long as the two great foes lived.

PHYSICAL DESCRIPTION:

Height: **5' 11"**
Weight: **185 lbs.**
Eyes: **Blue**
Hair: **Reddish-brown**

Distinguishing Features: **None**

POWERS & ABILITIES:

Strength Level: **Norman possesses super-human strength, thanks to his Goblin Formula. However, even enraged, the Goblin's strength is marginally less than that of Spider-Man. The Goblin is capable of lifting (pressing) an estimated 9 tons.**

Superhuman Powers: **In additional to enhanced strength, the Goblin Formula has also granted Norman increased speed, reflexes and endurance to levels which make him a near-equal to Spider-Man. Norman also possesses a regenerative ability that while not as instant as for example that of Wolverine and Sabretooth, nonetheless allowed him to survive and eventually fully recover from the horrific chest-wound inflicted by his own glider.**

The chemical concoction that gave Norman his enhanced physical abilities was also responsible for lifting his intelligence to gifted levels – but at the price of much of his sanity.

Special Skills: **Norman's original talent for ground-breaking electronics and weapon-related chemistry was enhanced by the formula he imbibed, pushing his abilities in this area to exceptional levels, and allowing him to create the extra-ordinary arsenal of weaponry which has become his trademark. Norman is also a cunning businessman, and a masterful strategist.**

PARAPHERNALIA:

Weapons: **Norman created and utilizes various concussive and incendiary grenades, constructed in the form of miniature jack-o'lanterns. The incendiary grenades ignite almost soundlessly and release enough heat to melt through a 3-inch thick sheet of steel. He also carries a variety of smoke and** gas-emitting bombs, which are surrounded by a light plastic mantle that flutter like a wraith when the bomb is thrown. Other gas bombs emit hallucinogenic gases, and others release a specially concocted gas that can neutralize Spider-Man's "spider-sense" for a limited period of time. The Goblin usually carries these in a shoulder bag, nick-named his "bag of tricks." The Goblins gloves are interwoven with microcircuit conducting filaments capable of channeling pulsed discharges of 10,000 volts of high-frequency electrical power from rechargeable power packs in both his glove cuffs and costume tunics. They had the capacity to discharge for up to five minutes of sustained fire before depleting their power supplies.

Personal Devices: The Green Goblin's costume incorporates chain mail in the tunic, giving him some protection from the blows inflicted during his battles with his arch-foe, Spider-Man.

Transportation: The Green Goblin originally rode through the air on a one man, miniature turbo-fan-powered vertical thrust "flying broomstick." He soon re-designed this device into an improved version that he called his "goblin-glider," capable of great maneuverability and speeds of up to 90 miles per hour. It is capable of supporting about 400 lbs including Norman's weight (and far more for very brief moments of time). Top speed and a full normal load will exhaust the fuel supply in about 1 hour. The main microprocessor assisted manual controls are behind the head of the glider, and later modifications added voice-activated radio-linked controls integrated into the Green Goblin's mask. The goblin-glider is steered primarily, however, by the weight and attitude of its rider. The Green Goblin's boots lock into the stirrups of the glider electromagnetically.

POWER GRID	1	2	3	4	5	6	7
INTELLIGENCE							
STRENGTH							
SPEED							
DURABILITY							
ENERGY PROJECTION							
FIGHTING SKILLS							

REAL NAME: Roderick Kingsley
KNOWN ALIASES: None
IDENTITY: Publicly known
OCCUPATION: Retired; former fashion designer, CEO and professional criminal
CITIZENSHIP: United States of America with a criminal record
PLACE OF BIRTH: Unrevealed
MARITAL STATUS: Single
KNOWN RELATIVES: Daniel Kingsley (younger brother)
GROUP AFFILIATION: Ally of the Rose
EDUCATION: College educated (arts major)

HISTORY: Roderick Kingsley began his career as a fashion designer, but harbored ambitions far greater. A ruthless and aggressive businessman, Kingsley was willing to work both sides of the law to parlay his talents into a financial empire. From the outset, Kingsley eliminated his competition either by stealing their ideas or ruining their reputations with brutal smear campaigns. After falling victim to Kingsley's underhanded machinations, designer Narda Ravanna sought vengeance in the guise of Belladonna. Her assault on Kingsley would have killed the designer if not for the timely intervention of Spider-Man. Although Kingsley suffered only broken ribs in the attack, the incident left him with a serious case of wounded pride. Swearing to protect himself from the threat of a future attack, Kingsley became increasingly obsessed with finding a way to enhance his strength and physical power.

Not long after, Spider-Man unwittingly became the catalyst for Kingsley's transformation into one of New York City's most feared criminals. In pursuit of a gang of thieves, Spider-Man was able to nab three, but lost the fourth in New York's maze-like sewer system. During the chase, the crook accidentally discovered a hidden cache of the Green Goblin's weapons and costumes. Knowing of Kingsley's quest for physical power, the criminal sold him the Goblin's long-abandoned arsenal. Kingsley eagerly purchased the weaponry. As the Hobgoblin, Kingsley carved out a piece of the New York underworld. His criminal activities soon brought him into conflict with Spider-Man, and the Hobgoblin was forced to face the hero in battle. Lacking the Green Goblin's original strength-enhancing formula, the Hobgoblin was overpowered by the web-slinger and barely escaped capture.

After tracking down the remainder of Norman Osborn's diaries, Kingsley was able to acquire the Goblin Formula. Using a common street tough named Lefty Donovan as his unwitting guinea pig, Kingsley refined the chemical mixture to remove the portion that had

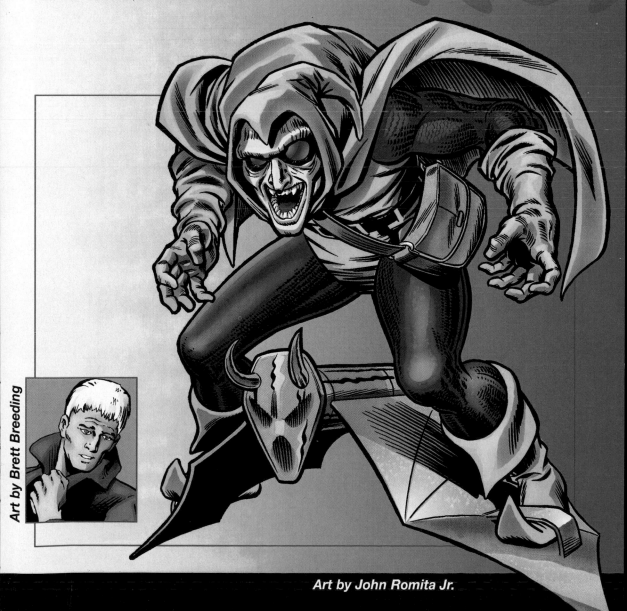

Art by Brett Breeding

Art by John Romita Jr.

cursed the Green Goblin with insanity. Although Kingsley was now almost Spider-Man's equal in terms of strength, the web-slinger still was able to overcome the Hobgoblin in their next battle; the villain nearly drowned making his escape.

Shaken by his brush with death, Kingsley set out to manipulate matters from behind the scenes. By brainwashing Ned Leeds into donning the Hobgoblin costume and acting as his pawn, Kingsley could continue his criminal pursuits while avoiding the increasing danger of physical confrontations with Spider-Man. Under Kingsley's direction, Leeds participated in a brutal gang war that nearly destroyed New York City. When Leeds became increasingly uncontrollable, Kingsley leaked word to the Foreigner that Leeds was the Hobgoblin. Leeds was murdered by the criminal's assassins soon after. With the Hobgoblin's career seemingly ended, Kingsley retired to Europe.

Jason Macendale, formerly known as Jack O'Lantern, later assumed the Hobgoblin's identity. Macendale's impersonation at first amused Kingsley — but when Macendale claimed in court that contrary to public perception, he was not the only Hobgoblin, Kingsley felt threatened and returned to New York to kill him. He quickly murdered the pretender and became the Hobgoblin once more. Despite Kingsley's efforts to conceal his identity, determined sleuthing by Betty Brant uncovered the truth and cleared her late husband Ned Leeds' name. With Spider-Man's help, Kingsley was imprisoned.

Not long after Kingsley's defeat, Norman Osborn publicly re-emerged in an unexpected return from the dead. Kingsley subsequently leaked word he possessed the one surviving journal proving Osborn was the original Green Goblin. Seeking to eliminate a potential witness, Osborn broke Kingsley out of jail — only to discover the journal was merely a ruse to elicit his help in the prison break. After a brief battle between the men ended in a draw, Kingsley fled to the sanctuary of the Caribbean.

PHYSICAL DESCRIPTION:

Height: 5'11"
Weight: 185 lbs.
Eyes: Blue
Hair: Gray

POWERS & ABILITIES:

Strength Level: By obtaining and using a reproduction of the Green Goblin's original formula, Hobgoblin acquired similar strength, being able to lift (press) an estimated 9 tons.

Superhuman Powers: The Hobgoblin's use of Norman Osborn's formula granted him additional speed, reflexes and endurance. It presumably also granted him the same effective though somewhat delayed-action healing factor, although this has never been demonstrated. For some reason, the damage to Kingsley's sanity done by the formula seems to be milder than that suffered by Norman himself.

PARAPHERNALIA:

Weapons: The Hobgoblin uses a large variety of weaponry, most of which he has adapted from the arsenal of the original Green Goblin. He utilizes various concussion and incendiary grenades, constructed in the form of miniature jack o'lanterns. One of the incendiary grenades ignites almost soundlessly, and releases enough heat to melt through a 3-inch thick sheet of steel. He also carries a variety of smoke and gas-emitting bombs, which are each surrounded by a light plastic mantle that flutters like a wraith when the bomb is thrown. The Hobgoblin has improved upon a chemical discovery of the original Goblin's that can neutralize Spider-Man's extrasensory "spider-sense". The Hobgoblin's version can neutralize this power of Spider-Man's for a time period of somewhere over 24 hours, possibly over 36. The Hobgoblin also has a number of casehardened razor-edged throwing blades that are forged into bat-wing shapes. The Hobgoblin carries much of his small, portable weaponry in his shoulder bag.

The Hobgoblin's gloves are interwoven with microcircuit powered conducting filaments capable of channeling pulsed discharges of 10,000 volts of high frequency electrical power from rechargeable power packs in both his glove cuffs and costume tunic. They have the capacity to discharge for up to five minutes of sustained fire before depleting their power supply. The Hobgoblin enhanced the Goblin's original finger blasters by adding a computerized firing mechanism that causes his arm to move about in a random sequence, rapidly firing electrical discharges from his glove, with the goal of stopping Spider-Man from being able to use his spider-sense to evade his blasts.

Personal Devices: Though visually re-designed, the Hobgoblin's costume is functionally equivalent to the Green Goblin's original creation, also incorporating the chain-mail protection in the tunic.

Transportation: The Hobgoblin rides a one-man, miniature turbo-fan powered, vertical thrust "goblin-glider," capable of great maneuverability and speeds of up to 90 miles per hour. It is capable of supporting about 400 lbs., including Hobgoblin's weight (and far more for very brief moments of time). Top speed and a full normal load will exhaust the fuel supply in about 1 hour. The main microprocessor assisted manual controls are behind the head of the glider and there are also voice-activated radio-linked controls integrated into the Hobgoblin's mask. The goblin-glider is steered primarily, however, by the weight and attitude of its rider. Hobgoblin's boots lock into the stirrups of the glider electromagnetically.

The Hobgoblin also uses a heavily armored battle van designed by Norman Osborn, though never actually used by the Green Goblin. The van is built for an average cruising speed of ninety miles an hour. It contains a computerized auto-guidance system. It would take a concussive force equal to an exploding mortar shell to begin to damage the windshield, which is made of a special reinforced jet age plastic, much less the heavier portions of the van. One battle van used by the Hobgoblin was destroyed when its self-destruct mechanism was triggered, but the Hobgoblin presumably has at least one more, or can reconstruct the van.

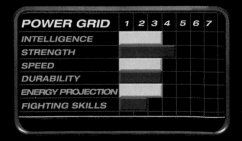

POWER GRID	1	2	3	4	5	6	7
INTELLIGENCE							
STRENGTH							
SPEED							
DURABILITY							
ENERGY PROJECTION							
FIGHTING SKILLS							

REAL NAME: Dr. Curtis Connors
KNOWN ALIASES: None
IDENTITY: Secret
OCCUPATION: Leading researcher in bio-genetics, college professor
CITIZENSHIP: United States of America with no criminal record
PLACE OF BIRTH: Coral Gables, Florida
MARITAL STATUS: Widowed
KNOWN RELATIVES: Martha Connors (wife, deceased), William Connors (son)
GROUP AFFILIATION: None
EDUCATION: Medical school graduate, later earned twin doctorates in biology and biochemistry (mutagenics)

HISTORY: Dr. Curt Connors was a gifted surgeon and biologist who went to war when his country called. He served as a battlefield medic until his arm was wounded in an explosion and was ultimately amputated. His surgical career brought to an abrupt end, Curt returned to his Florida laboratory. Inspired by a reptile's ability to regenerate lost limbs, he pursued a revolutionary study of reptilian molecular biology and DNA manipulation to replicate the process in humans. Curt then drank his untested formula; within seconds, his lost arm miraculously regenerated.

Although the serum worked as predicted, it was more powerful than Curt had expected. The chemical mix transformed him into a human lizard. Overwhelmed by his new reptilian nature, he fled into the dense Florida swamps. From his jungle sanctuary, the Lizard built an army of cold-blooded creatures — aiming to destroy humankind. Rumors of a "giant lizard" soon spread, drawing the attention of New York's Daily Bugle. Viewing the creature as a public menace, J. Jonah Jameson brazenly challenged Spider-Man to face the Lizard.

As a photographer for the Bugle, Peter Parker traveled to Florida. Tracking down Curt's wife, Martha, and young son, Billy, Spider-Man learned the truth. Using Curt's lab notes and equipment, as well as his own scientific knowledge, he was able to concoct an antidote. Battling the Lizard to a standstill, Spider-Man forced the creature to swallow the solution and revert to human form — minus his newly regenerated arm. Spider-Man's aid earned him Curt's undying gratitude, as well as the enmity of his reptilian alter ego.

Curt would soon have the opportunity to repay the favor. When Peter gave his ailing aunt, May Parker, a transfusion, his radioactive blood put her in deadly peril. With doctors powerless, a desperate Spider-Man brought his friend a sample of May's blood. Curt helped the hero develop a formula to save May's life. However, Curt remained unaware of Spider-Man's secret identity.

Art by Damion Scott

Shortly thereafter, Curt and Spider-Man again worked jointly to create a solution that would soften the Rhino's hide. Unfortunately, the chemicals in that solution caused Curt to revert to reptilian form once more. Knowing a cold-blooded creature cannot regulate its internal temperature, Spider-Man trapped the Lizard in a refrigerated train carriage.

For a while, Curt split his time between Florida and New York. A research grant at Empire State University established him for a time in Manhattan, where Peter worked as his teaching assistant. Yet Curt could not escape the Lizard's shadow. More and more frequently, extreme stress or exposure to chemicals would transform him into the horrific creature. Unable to deal with the toll of her husband's relapses, Martha left him and took their son with her. This emotional event triggered another transformation, and Calypso used her voodoo powers to usurp control of the Lizard's mind in pursuit of her own deadly vendetta against Spider-Man.

In the wake of Calypso's defeat, Curt embarked on a search for a permanent cure to his condition. To that end, he created a modified version of his original regeneration formula. This new serum was injected into a severed fragment of the Lizard's tail, with disastrous effects. The tail grew into a completely new Lizard, devoid of any shred of humanity. Curt was forced to trigger his transformation to protect his wife and son.

Following her husband's brave sacrifice, Martha returned to Curt. With his missing arm miraculously restored by Hammerhead, a happy ending for the Connors family seemed assured. However, the cellular structure of Curt's new arm proved unstable, and it soon became use-less. A short time later, Martha and Billy were diagnosed with cancer, a result of pollution from an industrial lab near the Connors' Florida home. The combined efforts of Curt, his reptilian alter ego and Spider-Man were enough to persuade a Monnano Corporation employee to expose the company's misdeeds — but it was too late. Martha's cancer was inoperable, and Curt's long-suffering wife died.

Billy survived, and unwillingly holds his father partly responsible for the tragedies which befell them both. Under the strain of his wife's death and his son's resentment, the line that once existed between Curt Connors and the Lizard has become ever more blurred. It seems Curt can now exert some control over his reptilian alter ego — but in return, the Lizard is ever waiting for those moments of weakness in the man that will allow him to take over Curt's human form.

Most recently, Curt commited a bank robbery, deliberately allowing himself to be imprisoned for the protection of himself and those he loved. This is a false hope, as no simple bars can protect humanity from the menace of the Lizard.

PHYSICAL DESCRIPTION:

Height: 5'11" (6'8 as Lizard)
Weight: 175 lbs. (550 lbs. as Lizard)
Eyes: Blue (red as Lizard)
Hair: Brown (none as Lizard)

POWERS & ABILITIES:

Strength Level: The Lizard has superhuman strength, enabling him to lift (press) approximately 12 tons.

Superhuman Powers: The Lizard possesses a number of superhuman powers endowed by his reptilian form, including his superhuman strength. His powerful leg muscles enable him to clear 12 feet in a standing high jump and 18 feet in a standing broad jump. His alligator-like hide is tougher than human skin and is capable of resisting the penetration of small-caliber billets. His reaction time is about twice that of the normal human being and he can run at speeds of up to 45 miles per hour.

The Lizard possesses a 6.5-foot tail that he can whip at speed up to 70 miles per hour. Like a gegku lizard, his hands and feet have retractable 1-inch hooks growing from the base of his palm and the ball of his foot, and his fingers and toes are covered with scores of tiny claws to create adhesive pads. As a result, the Lizard can support his weight climbing up and down normally intractable surfaces.

When the Lizard emerges, the R-complex of Connors' brain (the most primitive region of the human brain containing the most bestial drives) takes over the cerebellum, causing Connors' mind to become progressively inhuman. The Lizard gains a quasi-telepathic ability to communicate with and command all reptiles within about a one-mile radius of himself.

Special Skills: In his human form, Dr. Curtis Connors is a brilliant biologist and biochemist, and is a leading herpetologist (a scientist who studies reptiles).

POWER GRID	1	2	3	4	5	6	7
INTELLIGENCE							
STRENGTH							
SPEED							
DURABILITY							
ENERGY PROJECTION							
FIGHTING SKILLS							

REAL NAME: Morlun
KNOWN ALIASES: None
IDENTITY: Secret
OCCUPATION: N/A
CITIZENSHIP: Unrevealed
PLACE OF BIRTH: Unrevealed
MARITAL STATUS: Unrevealed
KNOWN RELATIVES: Unrevealed
GROUP AFFILIATION: None
EDUCATION: Unrevealed

POWER GRID	1	2	3	4	5	6	7
INTELLIGENCE							
STRENGTH							
SPEED							
DURABILITY							
ENERGY PROJECTION							
FIGHTING SKILLS							

HISTORY: Morlun is one of the few remaining members of a far-flung group who have walked our world for countless centuries. He and others of his kind draw their great strength by feeding on the totemistic forces of our planet – forces bound to all living things. Such forces are most prevalent in super-beings who have acquired the powers of animals... super-beings such as Spider-Man.

Though Morlun can also find sustenance from the life force of almost any living creature, in order to sustain his long existence, he must periodically consume the pure essence of the four separate strands that comprise the DNA that is unique to his kind. Accompanied by his most recent human servant, Dex, Morlun came seeking to devour Spider-Man.

Following a one-sided series of running battles, Spider-Man knew that he had finally met a foe he could neither escape, nor overcome in open combat. When Ezekiel reluctantly joined the fight against Morlun, he too was overwhelmed.

Taking advantage of Morlun's penchant for toying with his food, Spidey used a respite to analyze the few drops of blood shed by his opponent during the battle. Combining knowledge of Morlun's DNA with hints dropped by Ezekiel, Spider-Man laid a trap in which he himself became the irradiated bait. When Morlun finally moved to take Spider-Man's life force, he fell victim to the radioactive solution with which Spider-Man had poisoned himself. The very nature of Spider-Man's powers made the web-slinger less vulnerable to the radiation to which Morlun was acutely vulnerable.

Weakened, Morlun begged Spider-Man to spare his life, pleading that he was not a creature of evil, but instead was no more than a predator, doing what came naturally. Perhaps Spider-Man would have truly let Morlun survive, but for the intervention of Dex, Morlun's one-time servant. With his powers gone, a single bullet sufficed to destroy Morlun, and to earn Dex freedom from his life of slavery.

PHYSICAL DESCRIPTION:

Height: 6'2"
Weight: 175 lbs.
Eyes: White/red
Hair: Black

POWERS & ABILITIES:

Strength Level: Morlun's strength varies according how recently he has fed, and on what kind of source. Morlun has demonstrated strength capable of lifting (pressing) an estimated 20 tons.

Superhuman Powers: Morlun gains his strength by absorbing the life forces of other beings. While he can feed himself for a while on lesser sources, in order to sustain his centuries long life Morlun must from time-to-time renew himself by consuming pure forms of totemistic (animal-related) super-beings from one of the four categories which make up his own unusually pure DNA – animal, bird, human, and insect.

Art by John Romita Jr.

MAY PARKER

REAL NAME: May Reilly Parker
KNOWN ALIASES: The Golden Oldie
IDENTITY: N/A
OCCUPATION: Retired
CITIZENSHIP: United States of America with no criminal record
PLACE OF BIRTH: Brooklyn, New York

MARITAL STATUS: Widowed
KNOWN RELATIVES: Peter Parker (nephew), Ben Parker (Husband, deceased) Mr. & Mrs. Reilly (parents, deceased), Horace Reilly (paternal uncle, deceased), Richard & Mary Parker (brother & sister-in-law)
GROUP AFFILIATION: Gray Power, Forest Hills Public Library
EDUCATION: High school

HISTORY: May Reilly was the child of a broken home. When her father walked out, her mother raised her begrudgingly — not bothering to conceal the fact that she saw May as nothing more than an unwelcome burden.

When May was a young woman, two men vied for her affection. One was a flashy, wealthy man named Johnny Jerome; the other, a carnival barker named Ben Parker. Preparing to run away with the more exciting Johnny, May changed her mind after he killed a man during a robbery; she chose the wiser course and remained with Ben.

When the two began dating in earnest, they were often saddled with Ben's much younger brother, Richard. So after Ben and May married, they chose to remain childless — free from the worries youngsters can bring. By contrast, the now-grown Richard and his wife, Mary, brought a son into the world. They named him Peter.

Unexpectedly, Ben and May doted on their nephew; the young boy particularly captivated Ben. When Richard and Mary Parker were called overseas on pressing government business, May and Ben happily took Peter into their home until his parents could return.

When word arrived that Richard and Mary had been killed in Algeria, Ben and May had little choice but to raise the child as their own. May at first was overwhelmed with the responsibility, even angry with Richard and Mary for dying and leaving her and Ben with the challenge of bringing up Peter at such a late stage in their life. Yet her heart could not help but be touched by how kind and thoughtful Peter grew to be. Together, the three became a true family.

As he matured into his teens, little did May or Ben realize that the science-loving, socially awkward Peter had by way of a radioactive spider-bite become the daring and colorful Spider-Man they watched on television. To them, those images belonged to another world — a world of crime and violence far from the Parker residence in suburban Forest Hills, Queens ... or so May thought.

One fateful night, a Burglar came seeking a long-lost treasure belonging to a former owner of the Parker home. Surprised by Ben, the Burglar fatally shot May's husband and fled. Though Spider-Man soon tracked down the Burglar and brought him to justice, May was left to continue her life without Ben's strength — a life further complicated by financial woes, her own ever-failing health and the strange new secrecy with which Peter conducted his affairs.

To help Aunt May pay the bills, including the escalating costs associated with her various medications, Peter took a job photographing himself as Spider-Man for the Daily Bugle. May was worried about her fragile nephew, taking pictures so close to the most dangerous of super-powered battles. For Peter, lying to his aunt became a painful — yet seemingly necessary — way of life.

Peter greatly reduced his need to deceive his aunt when he relocated to an apartment in the city, and Mary Jane Watson's aunt, Anna Watson, moved in with May. Though they now lived farther apart, many of Spider-Man's battles still took place dangerously close to May. The wall-crawler's web seemed to be inextricably woven into May's life.

Merely by being in the company of Betty Brant, May was kidnapped by Doctor Octopus during the first attack of the Sinister Six. Though Betty was Doc Ock's intended target, he treated May so well she never realized the charming scientist was actually a deadly villain. The Beetle later took May as a random hostage some time later, and Spider-Man again rescued her. Finally, the Green Goblin (Harry Osborn) captured a con-fused May after he uncovered Spider-Man's secret identity.

Just when life had begun to quiet down, May inherited a Canadian island that was the site of a radioactive mine and small commercial reactor. Doctor Octopus charmed May into a sudden wedding, with the aim of acquiring the island's valuable atomic resources for his own nefarious ends. But the intervention of Hammerhead resulted in the destruction of the island and the apparent death of May's groom-to-be.

Despite her nagging ill health, May maintained an iron will. But while taking part in a Gray Panthers rally, she suffered a serious health threat and required hospitalization. As she continued to convalesce in a nursing home, the Burglar who had killed her husband was freed from prison. Still seeking the unidentified treasure hidden in the Parker home, the Burglar forced the head of the nursing home to fake Aunt May's death so she could be interrogated without the interference of her doting nephew. When Peter discovered the truth, his fury was so terrifying that the Burglar died of a heart attack. More tragic was the fact that all May's suffering was over nothing: Silverfish had long since eaten the treasure.

May returned to Forest Hills after recovering sufficiently and set up her home as a boarding house, taking in half a dozen paying houseguests. Among them was Nathan Lubensky — a charming, wheelchair-bound gentleman she had met at the nursing home. The two were engaged — until a coldly calculating Nathan caused the death of a mugger who had invaded their house, and May called off the wedding. Despite this, Nathan's final act proved his affection for May: He died to prevent her from becoming a hostage of the Vulture.

Peter believed he had lost his aunt when she seemingly died shortly thereafter. But he was unaware of the depths to which the original Green Goblin, Norman Osborn, would sink. Norman had kidnapped May and replaced her with a genetically adapted actress. Even as Norman lost what remained of his sanity taking part in the Gathering of Five, his former agent, Alison Mongrain — aided by Joseph "Robbie" Robertson — revealed May's location to Peter. Peter rescued his aunt and defeated the crazed Green Goblin, whose plans for the real May were never fully revealed.

After May's return, she struggled to regain her place in Peter's life. It was with Mary Jane's disappearance that Peter again realized the strength he and May could give to each other. Then, after Mary Jane's return and subsequent separation from Peter, he relied on May to help him through a time of loss — as they had helped each other many years ago.

But there was one more shock to come. Arriving at Peter's apartment one afternoon, May finally learned the truth he had so long concealed. Battered and bruised, Peter was asleep in bed with his Spider-Man costume and equipment tossed on the floor. After spending a whole day dealing with her newfound knowledge, May finally confronted Peter and began to break through a lifetime of deception.

Seemingly stronger than ever, May is bent on improving Spider-Man's public image and determined to understand Peter's alter ego. Now that the lies are behind them, May and Peter's relationship has been deepened like never before — reborn through a new level of honesty and trust.

PHYSICAL DESCRIPTION:

Height: 5'5"
Weight: 110 lbs.
Eyes: Blue
Hair: White

POWERS & ABILITIES:

Strength Level: May Parker possesses the normal human strength of a woman her age, height and build who engages in occasional mild exercise.

POWER GRID	1	2	3	4	5	6	7
INTELLIGENCE							
STRENGTH							
SPEED							
DURABILITY							
ENERGY PROJECTION							
FIGHTING SKILLS							

SANDMAN

REAL NAME: William Baker
KNOWN ALIASES: Flint Marko, Sylvester Mann, Quarryman
IDENTITY: Known to legal authorities
OCCUPATION: Professional criminal
CITIZENSHIP: United States of America with a criminal record
PLACE OF BIRTH: Queens, New York
MARITAL STATUS: Divorced
KNOWN RELATIVES: Mrs. Baker (mother)
GROUP AFFILIATION: Co-founder of the Sinister Six; former member of the Frightful Four, Outlaws, Silver Sable's Wild Pack; former partner of the Wizard, Mandarin, Hydro-Man; former reserve Avenger.
EDUCATION: High school (incomplete)

HISTORY: When William Baker was 3 years old, his father left him and his mother to live in poverty. To make ends meet, Baker turned to theft at an early age; he went on to cheat and bluff his way through high school. Though he possessed great talent on the football field, he squandered his chance for a legitimate career when he accepted a bribe to throw an important game. His deception revealed, Baker was expelled from school. Forced to find work, Baker became a mob henchman and adopted the underworld alias Flint Marko. Arrested and convicted for his criminal actions, he spent much of his time in solitary confinement. Marko grew bitter and violent — and devoid of hope that his girlfriend, Marcy Conway, would ever marry him.

Released from jail, Marko sought out Marcy, only to discover she had taken up with gangster Vic Rollins. Furious, Marko sought brutal revenge on Rollins and embarked on a one-man, citywide crime spree. Captured and returned to jail, Marko did time in the maximum-security wing of the notorious Rykers Island. An incorrigible inmate, he soon purchased information on an unguarded drainage tunnel, which he used to make his escape. With the FBI and police on his tail, Marko sought refuge in the one place nobody would look for him: an atomic testing site

Art by Mark Bagley

near Savannah, Georgia. As he rested on a nearby beach, the experimental reactor's steam system exploded — bombarding him with a massive dose of radiation. Awaking from a brief period of unconsciousness, Marko discovered his newly acquired ability to transform himself into a sand-like form he could manipulate and reshape at will. On that day, the Sandman was born.

Eager to take full advantage of his newfound power, the Sandman returned to New York and attempted a series of daring robberies — all met with equally bold resistance. Spider-Man employed an industrial vacuum cleaner; the Human Torch, an indoor sprinkler system. The Sandman recovered and regrouped from each of these confrontations, and became a member of the first Sinister Six before joining forces with the Wizard, who provided him with a belt that enabled him to produce a variety of dangerous and deadly effects through the injection of various chemicals. The Sandman and the Wizard then teamed with the Trapster to become core members of the Frightful Four.

Some time later, the Sandman inadvertently merged with Hydro-Man to form the Mud-Thing. After an attack by police helicopters nearly ended his life, the Sandman eventually returned to his usual form, but seemed troubled by his conscience. Striking up a surprising friendship with the Thing of the Fantastic Four, the Sandman soon talked of abandoning crime. When he encountered Spider-Man fighting the Enforcers, the Sandman made good on his intentions and rescued the wall-crawler. Still a wanted man, the Sandman adopted the alias Sylvester Mann. He rented a room with a suburban family, undertook contract work for Silver Sable and joined the Outlaws. When Doctor Octopus blackmailed him into rejoining the Sinister Six, the Sandman turned against his former ally as soon as he had the chance.

His good efforts were recognized when both he and Spider-Man were simultaneously named as reserve Avengers. Granted a pardon for his crimes, the Sandman returned to his birth name, William Baker. Though his undisciplined temperament saw him resign from the Avengers over a minor misunderstanding, his determination to reform survived; he became a permanent agent for Silver Sable, often assisting Spider-Man.

But the good times would not last. Feeling the loss of his former super-powered henchman, the Wizard kidnapped Baker and forcibly subjected him to a machine that would amplify the underlying dark side of its subject's personality. Gone again was William Baker; when the violent Flint Marko regained dominance, much to the Wizard's surprise, he refused to be anyone's lackey.

The now-villainous Sandman re-formed the Sinister Six to seek revenge on Doctor Octopus, but Venom turned on his teammates and took a large bite out of the Sandman. Weakened and poisoned, the Sandman lost control over his form — and his mind. Confused, the villain fell into the sewer and was eventually dumped on a sandy beach, where he merged with the shoreline. Dissolute and confused, the far-flung Sandman was pulled back to consciousness by the presence of a number of minds — a Spring Break live TV broadcast of a popular music compilation show. Sandman absorbed a number of the headline acts, but the massive egos of the pop stars he had swallowed proved too much to contain, and he was forced to disgorge them intact.

Now conscious, though still far from restored, Sandman fractured into four parts — his good side, his evil side, his feminine side and his inner child. Spider-Man attempted to persuade the four independent components of his sandy foe to reunite, but could not save his "good side." Only time will tell if evil is all that remains in the Sandman's silicon soul.

SCORPION

REAL NAME: MacDonald "Mac" Gargan
KNOWN ALIASES: None
IDENTITY: Publicly known
OCCUPATION: Professional criminal, former private investigator
CITIZENSHIP: United States of America with a criminal record
PLACE OF BIRTH: Unrevealed
MARITAL STATUS: Single
KNOWN RELATIVES: Unrevealed
GROUP AFFILIATION: Egghead's Masters of Evil, former partner of Mr. Hyde, former partner of Delilah.
EDUCATION: High school

HISTORY: Unaware his actions would ultimately result in the creation of a monster with an unquenchable lust for vengeance, J. Jonah Jameson hired rough and ready private investigator Mac Gargan to tail Peter Parker and determine how the freelance photographer could capture so many pictures of Spider-Man. But plans changed quickly when Jameson read about a scientist performing groundbreaking experiments in physiological enhancement. The scientist was Dr. Farley Stillwell, whose techniques had been shown to produce great increases in strength and speed in test animals he had subjected to his chemical and radiological bombardment. In return for Jameson's funding, Stillwell agreed to perform the same procedure on a human test subject — one Mac Gargan, who also would be well-paid for his part.

Stillwell modeled Gargan's transformation on a scorpion. He granted Gargan enhanced speed, endurance and strength. In keeping with Gargan's new namesake, Stillwell empowered his guinea pig's hands with the strength of mighty pincers. To cap off the effect, the scientist created a powerful electro-mechanical tail. With the addition of a green costume, Gargan's transformation was complete. Sent to destroy the object of Jameson's hatred, the Scorpion soon

Art by Mark Bagley

met his intended prey. A shocked Spider-Man quickly discovered that the Scorpion possessed strength greater than his own. Back in his laboratory, Stillwell made a shocking discovery, too. Examining the results of his most recent control experiments, he learned that a side effect of the mutation would steadily destroy Gargan's mind — devouring his humanity and transforming him into a cruel psychopath. Stillwell tracked down the Scorpion in the hope of attempting to administer a serum that would reverse the transformation. But while pursuing Gargan, he stumbled and fell from a building. When Stillwell lost his life, Gargan lost hold of his sanity.

Though outmatched physically, Spider-Man's skill and clear thinking proved the edge he needed to overcome the Scorpion in battle. Nothing could save what was left of the man known as Mac Gargan — now, only the Scorpion remained. Arrested and imprisoned, the Scorpion seethed with hatred for Spider-Man for defeating him, and Jameson for creating the monster he had become. Jameson's relief at the Scorpion's incarceration was short-lived. The Scorpion soon escaped and attacked the publisher, who was saved only through Spider-Man's intervention. Jameson watched his two worst enemies battle with mixed emotions. Though he hated Spider-Man passionately, the wall-crawler's loss would have meant Jameson's certain doom. He was grateful Spider-Man won the fight, but only begrudgingly so.

Motivated by revenge, and on the hunt for the power to achieve it, the Scorpion pursued a career as an assassin-for-hire — often seeking payment in the form of more powerful weapons or enhanced strength. Though he fought other heroes, his heart still held a special hatred that only the deaths of Spider-Man and Jameson could ease. Desperate to attain his end goal, the Scorpion ultimately returned to Stillwell's abandoned laboratory and used the equipment there to boost his powers to extreme levels. When the Scorpion learned of Jameson's impending wedding to Dr. Marla Madison, he managed to kidnap his adversary's fiancée — once more leaving Jameson to rely on a humiliating rescue by Spider-Man.

Greedy for even greater power, the Scorpion agreed to become an agent of criminal industrialist Justin Hammer in return for enhanced equipment — including a more flexible, toxin-projecting tail. While carrying out a kidnapping contract, the Scorpion was once more foiled by Spider-Man. The two would cross paths again when the Scorpion teamed first with the Chameleon and later the Tinkerer, who had outfitted him with an electrified tail. This final loss proved to be the Scorpion's breaking point. Overwhelmed by his countless failures, he wandered the sewers — his mind clearer than it had been for years.

But even after he decided to opt out of his life of crime, fate would play a cruel joke at his expense. Spider-Man had been suffering through a private crisis, and he could barely contain his own aggression when he stumbled across the Scorpion. The web-slinger's primal instincts took over, and he beat Gargan to a pulp — ignoring the former villain's sincere protests that he was a changed man. The Scorpion's moment of clarity dissipated, and his chance at redemption was forever destroyed at Spider-Man's hands. The Scorpion's briefly suppressed violence came flooding back, leaving him more psychotic than ever. He has since resumed his place as a deadly, unstable killer-for-hire — even as he awaits one more chance to seek revenge on Spider-Man and Jameson.

The current design consists of an inner woven Kevlar layer, covered with a think layer of insulation/padding, topped with a high-tech composite armor plating. The most notable feature of the suit is always the artificial mechanical tail, which varies in length with each design – from an original 4' version, up to 20' in other implementations. His current tail is approximately 10' in length.

The tail is powered by a self-contained power pack mounted on the back of the costume. Control is via a cybernetic link to the fine muscles of his spinal column when he dons the costume. Internally, the tail consists of a series of separated circular plates connected by a matrix of steel cables. Solenoids contract the cables and manipulate the tail, allowing it to whip at speeds of over 150 feet per second. The tail is also armored, and is tipped with a spike, making it deadly in combat.

The tail is flexible enough to grip large objects, such has people. By coiling his tail behind him and using it as a spring, Scorpion can propel himself a distance of at least 30 feet.

POWER GRID	1	2	3	4	5	6	7
INTELLIGENCE							
STRENGTH							
SPEED							
DURABILITY							
ENERGY PROJECTION							
FIGHTING SKILLS							

SHATHRA

REAL NAME: Shathra
KNOWN ALIASES: Sharon Keller, Spider-Wasp
IDENTITY: N/A
OCCUPATION: N/A
CITIZENSHIP: Inhabitant of the Astral Plane
PLACE OF BIRTH: Unrevealed
MARITAL STATUS: N/A
KNOWN RELATIVES: Brood of babies
GROUP AFFILIATION: None
EDUCATION: N/A

HISTORY: An inhabitant of the Astral plane, Shathra is the "Spider-Wasp" to Peter Parker's "Spider." She learned of Spider-Man when he strayed from the safe path during a visit to the Astral Plane to locate the inter-dimensional kidnapper known as Shade. Shathra immediately realised Spider-Man's true nature, and determined that he would make the perfect meal for her hungry young hatchlings.

Following Spider-Man's scent back to Earth, Shathra quickly engaged her chosen victim in a battle that demonstrated her clearly superior speed and strength. Though Spider-Man was able to use his superior knowledge of New York to find temporary escape, he knew that Shathra would soon locate him once more.

In fact, Shathra turned the game in a new direction, changing to a human form and adopting the name "Sharon Keller." Posing as Spider-Man's jilted lover, she went on live TV to reveal a series of convincing and humiliating details. Spurred by Mary Jane's distress, Peter Parker rose to the taunt, gatecrashed the studio interview, and attacked Sharon Keller in full view. Fortunately, Shathra reverted to her Spider-Wasp form, but her gambit had achieved its goal of pushing Spider-Man to act on pure instinct, bringing the conflict to the simple level of "natural order," in which the Spider-Wasp is the hunter and the Spider is the meal.

Spider-Man managed barely to avoid descending into mindless fury, and though drugged by Shathra's paralyzing agent, managed to escape to brief safety. He was rescued by Ezekiel, who took Spider-Man to a sacred temple in Ghana and helped Peter to set a trap for Shathra. Spider-Man now consciously allowed his arachnid side to take the forefront, or enough so to capture the Spider-Wasp, and to feed her to whatever spider dwelt in the depths of the temple. The food chain, it seems, can run in both directions.

PHYSICAL DESCRIPTION:

Height: 6'2"
Weight: 120 lbs.
Eyes: Glowing white
Hair: Black

POWERS & ABILITIES:

Strength Level: Shathra possesses strength greater than Spider-Man. Evidence indicates that she can lift (press) at least 15 tons, quite possibly more.

Superhuman Powers: Shathra possesses the totemistic powers of the Spider-Wasp. She appears to be almost entirely subsumed by her animal side. Having submitted completely to her spider-wasp nature, Shathra possesses enhanced speed, strength, endurance, resilience, and regeneration well above those of the less "pure" Spider-Man. Shathra has the power of flight. She also has the power to change her shape and take on a human appearance.

Special Skills: Shathra is able to generate warp-holes through space, and even between her home Astral Plane and Earth. She is also able to "smell" her natural foe, the Spider-Man, well enough to track him across continents and dimensions. At either a mystic or psychological level, Shathra is capable of affecting Spider-Man and reducing him to acting at a level of pure instinct.

PARAPHERNALIA:

Weapons: Shathra has natural razor-sharp claws. She can also fire sharp "stingers" with deadly speed and accuracy. These stingers can cut through webbing, and also contain a neural paralyzing agent powerful enough to overcome Spider-Man.

POWER GRID	1	2	3	4	5	6	7
INTELLIGENCE							
STRENGTH							
SPEED							
DURABILITY							
ENERGY PROJECTION							
FIGHTING SKILLS							

Art by John Romita Jr.

burglar. During his third stint in prison, he decided it was time to try a different angle. Employing a hitherto untapped aptitude for invention, Herman used the prison workshop to develop prototype sonic-projection devices designed primarily to shake open bank vaults, but equally devastating when directed at human targets. Herman used the hand-held devices to escape from jail; he then converted the units to wrist-mounted form, complete with thumb-triggers, and created padded body armor that would minimize the painful impact felt when using the devices.

The Shocker first tested his inventions on an office safe; when the ensuing destruction attracted Spider-Man's attention, the vibro-shock devices assured the villain an easy victory. But during their second encounter, Spider-Man simply webbed up the Shocker's hands, ensuring he could not access his thumb triggers. In later battles, Spider-Man defeated the Shocker by blinding him with webbing, or by cleverly webbing his weapon into the "on" position. To counter his continued defeats, the Shocker developed more sophisticated devices.

In style, the Shocker is a creative and flexible villain. Theft, extortion and blackmail — the Shocker has attempted them all. His plans have included such varied schemes as blacking out New York City blocks to spell his name and manipulating the Stock Market to his benefit. Recently he teamed up with Hydro-Man, hoping for one last big heist before retirement. They were foiled as ever by Spider-Man.

REAL NAME: Herman Schultz
KNOWN ALIASES: None
IDENTITY: Publicly known
OCCUPATION: Burglar, hired Assassin
CITIZENSHIP: United States of America with a criminal record
PLACE OF BIRTH: Unrevealed
MARITAL STATUS: Single
KNOWN RELATIVES: Unrevealed
GROUP AFFILIATION: Sinister Seven, former member of the Masters of Evil
EDUCATION: Trained electrical engineer
HISTORY: Herman Schultz started out as a not-so-successful

PHYSICAL DESCRIPTION:

Height: 5'9"
Weight: 175 lbs.
Eyes: Brown
Hair: Brown

POWERS & ABILITIES:

Strength Level: Not enhanced by his uniform, the Shocker's strength is that of a normal man of his age, height and build who engages in moderate exercise.

PARAPHERNALIA:

Weapons: The Shocker's vibro-shock units act much like a pump-action compressed-air gun, creating a series of rapid-succession high-pressure air blasts that result in a series of powerful impacts. These impacts, thrown from a distance, create destructive vibrations that will crumble solid concrete and cause extensive damage to the human body and its internal organs. The Shocker frequently experiments with different ways to mount the vibro-unit control mechanisms, attempting to find a placement for the trigger units that is not subject to being activated by others and turned against him.

His uniform, which contains its own power unit, also establishes a vibrational shield that will deflect normal blows and allow him to slip from any grasp, even that of Spider-Man's webbing.

POWER GRID	1	2	3	4	5	6	7
INTELLIGENCE		2					
STRENGTH		2					
SPEED		2					
DURABILITY			3				
ENERGY PROJECTION				4			
FIGHTING SKILLS		2					

Art by Kyle Hotz

SPIDER-MAN

REAL NAME: Peter Benjamin Parker
KNOWN ALIASES: Formerly Hornet, Dusk, Ricochet, Prodigy, Black Marvel, Captain Universe, Green Hood, Bombastic Bag-Man, Amazing Bag-Man, Scarlet Spider, Spider-Hulk, Spider-Morpohosis, Spider-Boy, Mad Dog 336, Peter Palmer**IDENTITY:** Secret, known to certain government officials
OCCUPATION: Freelance photographer, part-time science teacher, adventurer
CITIZENSHIP: United States of America with no criminal record
PLACE OF BIRTH: New York City

MARITAL STATUS: Married (Mary Jane Watson-Parker)
KNOWN RELATIVES: Richard Parker (father, deceased), Mary Parker (mother, deceased), Benjamin Parker (uncle, deceased), May Parker (aunt), Mary-Jane Watson-Parker (wife), May Parker (daughter, deceased), Ben Reilly (clone, deceased)
GROUP AFFILIATION: None; formerly Avengers, Outlaws, Fantastic Four, Daily Bugle Staff
EDUCATION: College educated (science major), doctorate studies in biochemistry (incomplete)

Art by John Romita Jr.

HISTORY: When Spider-Man first appeared in the Marvel Universe, he was truly unlike any hero who had come before. He was not noble-born like the Sub-Mariner. Unlike the Fantastic Four, he had no headquarters and few resources with which to fight crime. In return for his efforts, he received no money and precious little thanks. Instead, he was just a lonely teenager, a nobody, until fate chose to grant him great power — a power he first squandered at terrible cost to himself and those he loved. Humbled, this ordinary boy grew into a man who could never abandon the responsibility that had fallen upon him. He became Spider-Man, Marvel's most famous super hero.

The only child of Richard and Mary Parker, Peter Parker was orphaned at the age of six when his parents were killed while overseas on government business. Peter was left in the care of his elderly uncle and aunt, Ben Parker and May Parker, who unhesitatingly raised him as the child they never had. Peter was academically gifted, and he displayed an uncanny affinity for science that was nothing short of genius. Socially, however, he was painfully shy and the target of much cruelty. His uncle and aunt compensated with a steadfast love, but they worried privately what lay in store for the fragile boy.

A student at Midtown High School, Peter attended a public evening exhibition demonstrating the safe handling of nuclear laboratory waste materials. A spider, accidentally irradiated by a particle beam, fell onto Peter's hand and bit him. His hand burning from the wound, Peter left the exhibition in a daze and walked into the path of an oncoming car. Without thinking, Peter jumped onto the side of a wall, to which he stuck with his bare hands. Stunned, he realized he had acquired superhuman powers similar to those of a spider: enhanced strength and agility, and the ability to cling to almost any surface. Most incredibly, he had gained a sixth sense that provided him with early warning of impending danger.

To test his new powers, Peter donned a hastily made mask and took part in an all-comers wrestling match against Crusher Hogan, winning with ease. Spotted by a talent scout who promised to arrange a TV appearance, Peter hurried home and created a more elaborate costume, including his unique Web-Shooters. Thus Spider-Man was born. With his new powers and sudden fame, Peter promised himself he would take care of Uncle Ben and Aunt May. But the rest of the world — those who derided lonely science nerd Peter Parker — they were not his concern. So it was that following another TV appearance, when a burglar ran past Spider-Man, pursued by a police officer, Peter did nothing to intervene.

Returning home one evening a few days later, Peter was horrified to learn Uncle Ben had been murdered — shot by an intruder. Spider-Man located the killer, discovering the criminal to be the same man he had failed to stop just days before. Filled with remorse, Peter finally understood that with great power, there must also come great responsibility. That was the first step on his path as a hero, though he did not immediately realize the true nature of his destiny. Unsure how to proceed, Spider-Man attempted to resume his show-business career, but was thwarted by J. Jonah Jameson's crusading editorials in the Daily Bugle.

Failing to find paid employment with the Fantastic Four, Spider-Man battled the Chameleon to protect his reputation. It was not until Jameson offered a reward for photos of the Vulture that Peter recognized he could fulfill his debt to Uncle Ben by fighting crime, while selling photos of the action to pay his bills.

Spider-Man's heroic reputation grew quickly, and he found himself facing a bewildering array of super-villains: the Tinkerer, Doctor Octopus, the Sandman, Doctor Doom, the Lizard, Electro, the Enforcers, Mysterio, the Green Goblin and Kraven the Hunter. Before long, many of these villains turned their attention less to crime, instead seeking revenge on the web-slinger. Through it all, Peter sold photos of Spider-Man's battles to the Bugle, using the money to help Aunt May. Invariably, Jameson would seize on the photos to attack Spider-Man's public image. Although unable to permanently destroy Spider-Man's reputation, Jameson has ensured the wall-crawler will never enjoy the overwhelming popular support he undoubtedly deserves.

With the new confidence his secret identity afforded him, Peter began to throw off his status as "puny" Parker, bookworm. Even the most popular girl in his class, Liz Allan (later Liz Osborn), began to take an interest in him. Jealous, Liz's boyfriend, class bully and sports star Flash Thompson, challenged Peter to a boxing match

and came out second best, leading to a new respect for his former victim. Peter also began dating Daily Bugle secretary Betty Brant. A shy girl, Betty was captivated by the peril that surrounded Peter's photography of Spider-Man. When that dangerous world cost her brother, Bennett Brant, his life at the hands of Blackie Gaxton, Peter understood for the first time the deadly threat Spider-Man presented to those he loved.

Peter struggled daily with the demands of his costumed identity, his part-time job, his Aunt's ever-worsening health and the Parker family's perpetual money woes. These worries left him with little time for friendships — yet he survived, and even flourished. He graduated from Midtown High a far more worldly and independent young man than many had predicted. By that time, he had faced dozens of deadly foes, who little suspected the Amazing Spider-Man to be a mere high-school student.

At Empire State University, Peter found a new life. After a fumbling start, he befriended fellow science majors Harry Osborn and Gwen Stacy. He also resolved his differences with Flash. Together, the four close-knit friends would often hang out at a café called the Coffee Bean.

As Peter emerged from his shell, Spider-Man clashed with ever more deadly opponents. Foremost among them was the Green Goblin, who managed to capture the hero and discover his secret identity. In the wake of a furious battle, the Goblin was revealed to be Norman Osborn, Harry's father. Norman was defeated, suffering amnesia as a result. Shortly after that classic conflict, Peter encountered the lovely Mary Jane Watson, who joined his circle of friends. But love bloomed instead between Peter and Gwen, leaving Mary Jane free to date Harry. While Flash joined the Army and was deployed to Southeast Asia, Peter and Harry moved into a shared apartment downtown.

Life was not so great for Peter's alter ego. With Jonah Jameson fanning the flames of public outcry, Peter resolved to be Spider-Man no more. It was the first time he would abandon his commitment in frustration at his lack of public support, though certainly not the last. Yet his resignation did not last long. More than merely the sheer exhilaration of being a hero, Peter realized Spider-Man was an irrevocable part of the man he had become.

As the bond between Peter and Gwen grew ever stronger, it was observed approvingly by Gwen's father, police captain George Stacy, who also supported Spider-Man's efforts. But tragedy struck when a falling chimney crushed Captain Stacy, even as he saved an innocent child during a battle between Spider-Man and Doctor Octopus. With his dying breath, Captain Stacy told Spider-Man to "be good" to Gwen. The web-slinger had lost a great ally, and Gwen blamed Spider-Man for her father's death. Peter's conscience, already tormented by the ever-present need to lie to Gwen, became even more troubled. Yet their love prevailed through life's challenges — including Harry's drug addiction and Peter's aborted attempt to remove his own powers, which instead resulted in his transformation into the freakish Six-Armed Spider-Man.

In the end, it was death that separated the two lovers. The Green Goblin kidnapped Gwen and dropped her off the Brooklyn Bridge. Spider-Man tried to save her, but failed. In the vicious battle that followed, Norman's Goblin Glider accidentally impaled him. Harry secretly observed his apparent death, swearing revenge on Spider-Man.

Harry soon succumbed to the Osborn legacy, kidnapping those Peter loved most — but Spider-Man prevented him from finishing the work Norman had started. Meanwhile, Peter and Gwen's college professor, Miles Warren, had begun his own deadly schemes as the Jackal. He blamed Spider-Man for the death of Gwen, with whom he had himself fallen in love. The climax of the Jackal's plan involved his creation of a Spider-Man clone — but at the conclusion of their battle, both the Jackal and the clone were believed killed. With their departure, Peter's life returned to normal, as much as it ever could for a college student who was secretly a costumed hero.

In the meantime, Peter and Mary Jane realized their relationship had become far more than just a friendship. Shortly before his college graduation, Peter proposed. But Mary Jane had seen too much pain in her own family, and she turned him down. She left New York to pursue her modeling career in Florida, and Peter moved on to post-graduate studies. It was a time for new challenges and new friends. But one thing would never change: the ever-present responsibility Peter faced as Spider-Man.

Peter's close college friends had begun to find their own lives. Liz Allan was dating a recovering Harry Osborn, and the two would later marry. Flash Thompson was searching for a life after football and the Army with his girlfriend, Sha Shan. Betty Brant had married Daily Bugle reporter Ned Leeds. Even Aunt May had found romance with Nathan Lubensky, a fellow occupant of the convalescent home into which she had moved. With Peter's friends and loved ones forming cozy couples, Mary Jane's departure was all the more unsettling. But it was not long before Peter began socializing again. He enjoyed several dates with Cissy Ironwood. Also, departmental secretary Deborah Whitman was attracted to Peter, but failed to win his heart. Undergraduate student Dawn Starr pretended to date Peter to sneak a peek at an upcoming exam. And Amy Powell tried to use Peter to make her boyfriend, Lance Bannon, jealous.

These women had one thing in common: Peter Parker. But when the Black Cat crossed Spider-Man's path, it was different. Felicia Hardy was beautiful, talented and determined. She was also an unrepentant burglar who harbored a romantic fascination with the web-slinging hero. Spider-Man persuaded Felicia to turn away from crime; the two soon became lovers — and crime-fighting partners. For her part, Felicia urged Peter to spend more and more time in costume. The glamorous Black Cat could never bear to see her hero living the squalid life of a graduate student. Spending swing time as Spider-Man had become easier, though, since Aunt May had recovered enough to return home and open the Parker residence as a boarding house for retired people, aided by Nathan.

There was always plenty of action for Spider-Man in New York, especially given the appearance of the deadly Hobgoblin and Peter's troubles with his symbiotic black costume. Aided by the Black Cat, Spider-Man faced Doc Ock and the Owl — a battle that nearly cost Felicia her life. Peter came crashing down to earth. He realized that without superhuman powers, Felicia was just like the others from his past who had so often paid the price for his activities as Spider-Man. When Mary Jane returned from Florida, she found Peter and the Black Cat embroiled in a shaky and tempestuous relationship. Felicia could not abide Peter's refusal to allow her to accompany him into battle, and she embarked on a secret search for superhuman powers at any price. Tricked by the Kingpin and twisted in her own deceit, the Black Cat finally parted ways with Spider-Man. In contrast, Mary Jane was determined not to let lies come between her and Peter. She finally told him she had known for some time about his secret identity.

With Spider-Man's secret finally out in the open, Peter and Mary Jane's relationship found new depth. As Spider-Man, Peter faced the death of his good friend, police captain Jean DeWolff, at the

hands of the Sin-Eater. He watched as Flash Thompson was taken for a criminal, and Ned Leeds killed, both for their involvement with the Hobgoblin. But life was different now: He had Mary Jane by his side. Peter proposed for a second time, and she accepted. As newlyweds, Peter and Mary Jane shared happiness, but also faced many dangers. Mary Jane was menaced by Kraven the Hunter and imperiled by Venom, who knew Peter's secret identity. She loved Peter and admired his sense of responsibility. But she was unprepared for the loneliness, the fear and the nagging doubt that perhaps he needed Spider-Man far more than he needed her.

Among daily battles with New York's villains and the challenges of marriage, Peter was soon to face the inexplicable return of his parents. Long since believed dead, they claimed to have been held abroad as political prisoners. Aunt May was not ready to accept them, but Peter finally believed them to be who they claimed, even revealing his life as Spider-Man. But Peter's heart had overridden his instincts. The two were eventually exposed as robot agents of the Chameleon, part of a plan prompted by Harry Osborn before his death. Spider-Man was filled with anger at this deeply personal attack. It seemed to him that those he loved were fated to die, while the evil in his life would always return to haunt him. Darkness began to fill his heart, like never before.

Still brooding over Harry's suicidal offensive against both the Osborn and Parker families, and the Chameleon's invasion of his life, Peter was faced with Aunt May's serious heart attack. With May in the hospital, not expected to recover, Peter's frustration at life's injustices boiled over into violence. Encountering the recently reformed and powerless Scorpion, Spider-Man cruelly beat his former foe close to death — ignoring his victim's pleas for mercy. It seemed Peter was beyond even Mary Jane's powers to heal him. In the end, his salvation came in the form of a near-death experience.

Before Doctor Octopus cured him of the Vulture's poison, Peter realized how desperately he wanted to live. His recovery from his dark madness coincided with the return of a figure from Spider-Man's distant past: his clone, created by the Jackal.

The clone had survived his apparent death, wandering the country as Ben Reilly. Learning Aunt May was gravely ill, he returned to New York in time to watch her die. Ben adopted the costumed identity of the Scarlet Spider and portrayed himself as Peter's long-lost cousin. Peter and Ben became friends, almost brothers.

Deceived by Dr. Seward Trainer, they later came to believe that Ben was the original, and Peter the clone. Ben subsequently assumed the role of Spider-Man when Peter temporarily lost his powers, leaving Peter and Mary Jane free to enjoy a normal life. Peter returned to his scientific career, though hampered by the fact that he never completed his doctorate. He and MJ also moved to Portland, until they realized New York was where they truly belonged.

But all too soon, their new world was shattered when Norman Osborn burst back into their lives. He also had survived his apparent death and was revealed to be the mastermind behind the Jackal's schemes. Peter's powers returned, but he could not stop Norman from killing Ben — proving him to be the clone after all. But his machinations ran even deeper: Aunt May was still alive. The woman who died had been an actress, part of a subtle plot never carried to fruition.

Reunited at last, Peter, Mary Jane and Aunt May moved into a luxurious apartment. Furthermore, the appearance of a new Spider-Man — actually Mattie Franklin, Spider-Woman III — allowed Peter to promise Mary Jane he would give up his career as a costumed hero. But Peter could not seem to keep his word. While an anonymous Stalker threatened Mary Jane,

Peter broke his promise and returned to web-slinging. Mary Jane was distraught. She no longer felt needed, no longer felt part of Peter's life. Perhaps matters could have been resolved, but the opportunity vanished when an airplane supposedly carrying Mary Jane exploded.

Peter felt lost. Aunt May returned home, while Peter became reacquainted with old friends Randy Robertson and Glory Grant, now a couple. Randy even allowed Peter to room with him for a while. But with Peter still emotionally adrift, Norman picked the perfect time to drug him and induce him to become his heir. Even lost and confused as he was, Peter proved he could not be tempted so easily.

Meanwhile, Mary Jane was not dead, but had been kidnapped by the Stalker. Spider-Man managed to rescue her, only to learn she had made her choice: She could no longer be with him. Mary Jane relocated to the West Coast, leaving Peter to struggle with a loss almost as traumatic as her apparent death. Stunned, he moved into a place of his own and resumed his bachelor lifestyle.

Peter turned to Aunt May, but she was devastated to discover his greatest secret: Visiting unannounced, she found him asleep following his grueling victory over Morlun — bloodied and battered, his shredded costume piled in a heap on the floor next to his bed. After coming to terms with Peter's double life, May is now his strongest supporter, and the two are closer than ever. May also prompted Peter to take up teaching. He returned to Midtown High — now a poor, urban school — where he teaches science part time.

With renewed hopes, Peter and Mary Jane have agreed to try once more to make their marriage work. After their time apart, Peter earnestly promised Mary Jane he truly needs her in his life.

In truth, it matters little what foes Spider-Man faces, what schemes his enemies concoct to bewilder him or even what he may learn from Ezekiel regarding the nature of his spider-powers. Peter's true strength comes not from a radioactive spider, but from far more enduring sources: the sense of responsibility inspired by Uncle Ben, the unwavering faith of Aunt May and the love he shares with Mary Jane. These are the powers that truly make Peter Parker a hero.

www.kaareandrews.com

Art by Kaare Andrews

Height: **5'10"**
Weight: **165 lbs**
Eyes: **Hazel**
Hair: **Brown**

Distinguishing Features: **None**

POWERS & ABILITIES

Strength Level: Spider-Man possesses superhuman strength enabling him to lift (press) approximately 10 tons.

Superhuman Powers: Spider-Man possesses superhuman strength, reflexes, and equilibrium; the ability to cause parts of his body to stick with great tenacity to most surfaces; and a subconscious premonitional "danger" sense. The irradiated Common House Spider (Achaearanea tepidariorum) that bit Peter Parker was apparently already mutated from prior exposure to certain frequencies of radiation and received a final, lethal dose during Parker's attendance of the exhibition. The radioactive, complex mutagenic enzymes in the spider's blood that were transferred at the time of the bite triggered numerous body-wide mutagenic changes within Peter.

Spider-Man's overall metabolic efficiency has been greatly increased, and the composition of his skeleton, interconnective tissues, muscles, and nervous system have all been enhanced. His reflexes are faster than an average human by a factor of 15 (he is often able to dodge bullets, if he is far enough away). Spider-Man is extraordinarily limber and his tendons and connective tissues are twice as elastic as the average human being's, despite their enhanced strength. He has developed a unique fighting style that makes full use of his agility, strength and equilibrium.

Spider-Man apparently has the ability to mentally control the flux of inter-atomic attraction between molecular boundary layers. This ability to affect the attraction between surfaces is limited to Spider-Man's body (especially concentrated in his hands and feet) and another object, with an upper limit of several tons per finger.

Spider-Man possesses an extrasensory or "spider-sense" which warns him of potential immediate danger by a tingling sensation in the back of his skull. The precise nature of this sense is unknown. It appears to be a simultaneous clairvoyant response to a wide variety of phenomena (everything from falling safes to speeding bullets to thrown punches), which gives him several hundredths of a second's warning — sufficient time for his reflexes to allow him to avoid injury. The sense also can create a general response within several minutes; he cannot judge the nature of the threat by the sensation. He can, however, discern the severity of the danger by the strength of his response to it. Spider-Man's fighting style incorporates the advantage that his "spider-sense" provides him. Spider-Man can use his spider-sense to detect signals emitted by his "spider-tracer" devices.

PARAPHERNALIA:

Personal Weaponry: Spider-Man uses web-shooters that are twin devices worn on his wrists that can shoot thin strands of a special "web fluid" at high pressure. The web fluid is a shear-thinning liquid (virtually solid until a shearing force is applied to it, rendering it fluid) whose exact formula is as yet unknown, but is related to nylon. On contact with air, the long-chain polymer knits and forms an extremely rough, flexible fiber with extraordinary adhesive properties. The web fluid's adhesive quality diminishes rapidly with exposure to air (where it does not make contact with the air, such as the attachment disk of the web-shooter, it remains very adhesive). After about 2 hours, certain imbibed ethers cause the solid form of the web fluid to dissolve into a powder. Because the fluid almost instantly sublimates from solid to liquid when under sheer pressure, and is not adhesive in its anaerobic liquid/solid phase transition point, there is no clogging of the web-shooter's parts.

The spinneret mechanism in the web-shooter is machined from stainless steel, except for the turbine component that is machined out of a block of Teflon and the two turbine bearings that are made of amber and artificial sapphire. The wristlets and web fluid cartridges are mainly nickel-plated annealed brass. Spider-Man's web cartridge belt is made out of brass and light leather and holds up to 30 cartridges. The cartridges are pressurized to 300 pounds per square inch and sealed with a bronze cap which is silver soldered closed. The wristlets have sharp steel nipples that pierce the bronze caps when the cartridges are tightly wedged into their positions. A palm switch, protected by a band of spring steel requiring a 65-pound pressure to trigger, actuates the hand-wound solenoid needle valve. The switch is situated high on the palm to avoid most unwanted firings. A rubber seal protects the small battery compartment. The effect of the very small turbine pump vanes is to compress (shear) the web fluid and force it, under pressure, through the spinneret holes, which cold-draws it (stretches it: the process wherein nylon gains a four-fold increase in tensile strength), then extrudes it through the air where it solidifies. As the web fluid exits the spinneret holes, it is attracted to itself electrostatically and thus can form complex shapes. The spinneret holes have three sets of adjustable, staggered openings around the turbine that permit a single web line, a more complex, spun web line, and a thick stream. The web line's tensile strength is estimated to be 120 pounds per square millimeter of cross section. The 300 p.s.i. of pressure in each cartridge is sufficient to force a stream of the complex web pattern an estimated 60 feet (significantly farther if shot in a ballistic parabolic arc).

POWER GRID	1	2	3	4	5	6	7
INTELLIGENCE							
STRENGTH							
SPEED							
DURABILITY							
ENERGY PROJECTION							
FIGHTING SKILLS							

SPIDER-MAN'S COSTUMES

CLASSIC RED AND BLUE ▶

Spider-Man's original costume was a red-and-blue, screen-printed outfit with black web-lines and a black-spider motif on the chest.

◀ ALIEN SYMBIOTE

Spider-Man's first black costume was actually an alien Symbiote that attempted to bond itself permanently to Peter Parker. Upon discovering his costume's true nature, Peter removed it with the aid of Reed Richards of the Fantastic Four. The alien costume later bonded with Eddie Brock, giving rise to Venom. The costume responded to Peter's mental commands to cover him at will and could generate organic webbing without the need for web-shooters.

CLASSIC BLACK ▶

After removing the alien, Peter created a cloth version of the black costume he alternated with his regular red-and-blue threads. Following Venom's terrifying attack on Mary Jane Watson, Peter permanently retired his black costume at his wife's request.

◀ ELECTRO-PROOF

In response to his numerous clashes with Electro, Spider-Man has developed an insulated costume in defense against the electrically charged villain. The original was a simple rubber outfit, but a modern version included additional padding and styling.

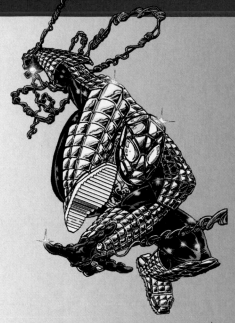

SPIDER-ARMOR

Peter required additional protection against the heavy-caliber firearms wielded by the combined might of the Blood Rose (Richard Fisk), Gauntlet and the New Enforcers. While virtually negating his agility, the costume did provide Spider-Man with increased resistance against gunfire. The armor was destroyed by acid in battle.

SPIDER-MAN REVISED ▶

After Ben Reilly discarded his Scarlet Spider outfit and assumed the role of Spider-Man, he updated Peter's classic look with a revised red-and-blue costume. When Peter returned to the webs, he reinstated his traditional costume.

◀ THE AMAZING BAG-MAN

In times of extraordinary crisis, Peter has been forced to swing into action sans his regular outfit. He has resorted to the use of an ordinary paper bag to conceal his identity.

BEHIND THE MASK ▶

Peter usually wears his costume and belt beneath his regular clothes, with his mask and gloves tucked somewhere handy. The lenses in the mask are made of polarized, one-way reflective material — protecting Peter from glare and helping preserve his identity.

GWEN STACY

REAL NAME: Gwendolyn Stacy
KNOWN ALIASES: None
IDENTITY: N/A
OCCUPATION: College student
CITIZENSHIP: United States of America with no criminal record
PLACE OF BIRTH: Unrevealed, presumably New York City

MARITAL STATUS: Single
KNOWN RELATIVES: George Stacy (father), Helen (mother), Arthur Stacy (uncle), Nancy Stacy (aunt), Paul and Jill Stacy (cousins)
GROUP AFFILIATION: None
EDUCATION: College Educated (Science Major, incomplete)

HISTORY: Everybody remembers their first love. For Peter Parker, it would be impossible to forget Gwen Stacy.

Gwen came to Empire State University from Standard High School, where she had been the resident glamour girl. Arriving at ESU, she and fellow science major Harry Osborn befriended jock Flash Thompson. Flash attempted to introduce Harry and Gwen to Peter, his high-school classmate, during their first chemistry lab. When a preoccupied Peter unintentionally ignored Flash and his new friends, popular Gwen and wealthy Harry did not take kindly to the perceived snub. Spitefully, Harry sabotaged Peter's lab experiment — setting the stage for a rocky start to their eventual friendship.

Peter had too much on his plate to worry about building friendships at school. His aunt, May Parker, was recovering from radiation poisoning; he was still licking his wounds from recent battles as Spider-Man against Kraven the Hunter, the Molten Man, the Looter, Mendel Stromm and the Green Goblin; and he had just broken up with girlfriend Betty Brant.

Over time, Peter reconciled with Gwen, Harry and Flash — transcending his reputation as a standoffish scholarship student. Despite her friends' misgivings about the bookish Peter, Gwen's intuition told her there was more to him than met the eye.

Gwen's emotional breakthrough occurred after Peter turned up at ESU one day on his new motorcycle — a move that greatly surprised her and the rest of the gang. Having just defeated the Green Goblin, Peter was riding high — and for once, free of his many problems. Re-examining her previously held opinion, Gwen found in her heart a true romantic attraction — one Peter clearly returned.

PHYSICAL DESCRIPTION:

Height: 5'7"
Weight: 130 lbs.
Eyes: Blue
Hair: Blonde

POWERS & ABILITIES:

Strength Level: Gwen Stacy possessed the normal human strength of a woman her age, height and build who engaged in moderate regular exercise.

Special Skills: Gwen Stacy was a gifted scholar in the field of biochemistry.

POWER GRID	1	2	3	4	5	6	7
INTELLIGENCE							
STRENGTH							
SPEED							
DURABILITY							
ENERGY PROJECTION							
FIGHTING SKILLS							

Their budding relationship was immediately tested by the arrival of Mary Jane Watson — the glamorous niece of Aunt May's friend, Anna Watson. An aspiring model, Mary Jane quickly fell in with Peter's crowd and took an interest in the young man — causing tension between her and Gwen. But Mary Jane was far too wild and free to settle her heart on any one man, and Gwen knew right away Peter was the one for her. The pair soon surrendered to their irresistible love.

But because of Peter's hidden life as Spider-Man, it was clear their love affair would never run smoothly. Missed dates, unexplained absences, secrets he could never tell — all these things conspired to cast his relationship with Gwen as a roller-coaster of confusion, tears and reconciliation. But Gwen's wise father, police captain George Stacy, warmly approved of Peter and did what he could to help keep the two young lovers together.

Unfortunately, George Stacy was killed protecting an innocent child during a battle between Spider-Man and Doctor Octopus, and a bereaved Gwen held the hero responsible. With the pressures on Gwen and Peter's relationship greater than ever, their love proved true and strong. They swore they could overcome anything. Anything, perhaps, except fate.

Once Norman Osborn, the Green Goblin, recovered his memory of Peter's identity, he burned with a desire for revenge against Spider-Man. Hitting the wall-crawler where it would hurt most, the Goblin kidnapped Gwen and carried her to the top of the Brooklyn Bridge. Spider-Man arrived and was horrified to find the woman he loved in the hands of his nemesis. Peter blazed into battle, but his ferocity was not enough to prevent Norman from pushing Gwen off the bridge.

In his last, desperate act to save the love of his life, Spider-Man fired a slender web-line that caught Gwen by her ankle. Raising her up, Spider-Man discovered she was already dead. The Goblin taunted Peter and told him that Gwen had been killed by the shock of falling. But Peter was tormented by nightmares in which he imagined she had been killed by the sudden jolt of his web-line as it caught her. He was haunted by the thought that maybe he could have saved Gwen's life if he had acted differently.

Even though Spider-Man's subsequent confrontation with the Green Goblin ended in Norman's apparent death at the hands of his own remote-controlled Goblin Glider, Peter's anguish did not die so readily. Peter's love for Gwen lives on in his memory and deep within his heart, even though his love for Mary Jane has long since become the guiding force in his life.

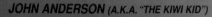

JOHN ANDERSON (A.K.A. "THE KIWI KID")

OCCUPATION: Unknown
MARITAL STATUS: Single
FIRST APPEARANCE: Spectacular Spider-Man Vol. 2 #1 (2003)
HEIGHT: 5'9"
WEIGHT: 265 lbs.
EYES: Brown
HAIR: Blond

Occupant of the apartment directly above Peter's, John Anderson is reputed to be a native of New Zealand, although his primitive social habits suggest a heavy Australian slant to his upbringing. Though clumsy, offensive and barely literate, John is above all well meaning, and he willingly came to Spider-Man's aid, posing as "The Kiwi Kid" to create a diversion against Doctor Octopus.

BETTY BRANT

OCCUPATION: Private investigator
MARITAL STATUS: Widow
FIRST APPEARANCE: Amazing Spider-Man Vol. 1 #4 (1964)
HEIGHT: 5'7"
WEIGHT: 125 lbs.
EYES: Brown
HAIR: Brown

Former secretary to Jonah Jameson at the Daily Bugle, the innocent young Betty Brant eventually married Bugle reporter Ned Leeds. Their life together was devastated when Ned became an unwilling pawn of the Hobgoblin, eventually at the cost of his life. The trauma of being widowed pushed Betty to the brink of madness, where she hovered for some time, until the aid of her friends and her own inner strength eventually saved her. Going from one extreme to another, the formerly meek secretary became a trained investigator. She eventually unmasked the Hobgoblin and sent him to prison by secretly recording his arrogant criminal confession.

CARYN EARLE & BARKER

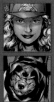

OCCUPATION: Unknown
MARITAL STATUS: Single
FIRST APPEARANCE: Peter Parker: Spider-Man Vol. 2 #30 (2001)
HEIGHT: 5'6" (2'2")
Weight: 120 lbs. (105 lbs.)
EYES: Blue (brown)
HAIR: Blonde (brown)

Peter is unlucky in many respects, but not when it comes to attractive neighbors. The view from his current pad looks across the alley to the apartment occupied by Caryn Earle and her uncannily intelligent rottweiler, Barker. Peter and Caryn enjoyed a friendly date together during Mary Jane's absence, but with the return of Peter's wife, whatever might have happened between the two is now in the past.

GLORIA "GLORY" GRANT

OCCUPATION: Administrative assistant, Daily Bugle
MARITAL STATUS: Single
FIRST APPEARANCE: Amazing Spider-Man Vol. 1 #140 (1985)
HEIGHT: 5'8"
WEIGHT: 120 lbs.
EYES: Brown
HAIR: Black

The glamorous Glory Grant was a former neighbor of Peter. When Betty Brant left the Bugle, Peter suggested Glory apply to replace her as Jonah Jameson's secretary, a highly challenging post Glory performs with ease. A good friend to Peter, Glory has been dragged into several of Spider-Man's tragedies and has established an uneasy relationship with the wall-crawler. Glory is currently dating Randy Robertson.

J JONAH JAMESON

OCCUPATION: Publisher, Daily Bugle
MARITAL STATUS: Married
FIRST APPEARANCE: Amazing Spider-Man Vol. 1 #1 (1963)
HEIGHT: 5'11"
WEIGHT: 210 lbs.
EYES: Blue
HAIR: Gray

J. Jonah Jameson is the publisher of the tabloid-sized newspaper the Daily Bugle and is New York's most vocal opponent of vigilantes, particularly Spider-Man. The Bugle's continuing survival is due in no small part to Jameson's deep-rooted journalistic integrity. However, he is also a bully and a bigot, who clearly has a blind spot when it comes to Spider-Man, producing headlines such as "Spider-Man: Threat or Menace?" Jameson has funded a number of ill-considered private ventures to destroy Spider-Man, including the creation of the Scorpion, the Fly and various mechanical Spider-Slayers. In most cases, these attempts have backfired, often creating new menaces far greater than Spider-Man. The high-profile publisher is married to Dr. Marla Madison, at one time hired by Jameson to create a Spider-Slayer. He is father to John Jameson, former astronaut and perfect example of the kind of human hero Jameson actively promotes. He is uncle to Martha "Mattie" Franklin (a.k.a. Spider-Woman).

JOHN JAMESON

OCCUPATION: Currently unknown; formerly test pilot, astronaut, private pilot to Captain America, head of security at Ravencroft Asylum
MARITAL STATUS: Single
FIRST APPEARANCE: Amazing Spider-Man Vol. 1 #1 (1963)
HEIGHT: 6'2" (6'6")
WEIGHT: 200 lbs. (350 lbs.)
EYES: Brown (Red)
HAIR: Reddish-Brown (White)

John Jameson is a former astronaut and test pilot. He is the son of publisher Jonah Jameson, but the contrast between the two men is great: John, relaxed and easy-going, does not at all share his father's blind loathing of Spider-Man. John became bonded to an alien stone during a lunar flight. This triggered a monthly bestial transformation in him, and he spent many years living a dual life as "Man-Wolf." Leaving the air force, John found work as personal pilot to Captain America. He was later employed as head of security at Ravencroft Asylum, where he fell in love with head psychiatrist Dr. Ashley Kafka. Both lost their jobs when Chameleon escaped from Ravencroft.

LIZ OSBORN

OCCUPATION: Independent means
MARITAL STATUS: Widow
FIRST APPEARANCE: Amazing Fantasy #15 (1962)
HEIGHT: 5'9"
WEIGHT: 135 lbs.
EYES: Blue
HAIR: Blonde

Liz Allan was the most popular girl in Peter's class at Midtown High School and was girlfriend to Flash Thompson. After high school, Liz left to care for her stepbrother, Mark Raxton, a.k.a. the Molten Man. Liz later returned; she dated then married Harry Osborn, until Harry's madness as the Green Goblin eventually led to his death. Liz was left alone to care both for their son, Normie Osborn, Jr., and for the Osborn corporate empire. When Harry's father Norman Osborn returned after years of being believed dead, Liz lost her position at Oscorp and now maintains an uneasy truce with her stepfather. Liz has also taken on the burden of arranging care for Flash Thompson.

JOE "ROBBIE" ROBERTSON

OCCUPATION: City editor, Daily Bugle
MARITAL STATUS: Married
FIRST APPEARANCE: Amazing Spider-Man Vol. 1 #51 (1967)
HEIGHT: 6'1"
WEIGHT: 210 lbs.
EYES: Brown
HAIR: White

At the Daily Bugle, Joseph "Robbie" Robertson is the yin to Jonah Jameson's yang. Robbie is the calming voice that overturns his boss's most outrageous decisions and repairs the damage Jonah's roughshod attitude creates among the staff. Robbie has had his own crises to deal with, most notably when he was unjustly imprisoned for having been frightened into silence concerning a murder committed by Tombstone. Despite the incredible demands of his job, Robbie could scarcely do any other work: Like Jonah, newspaper ink runs in his veins.

RANDY ROBERTSON

OCCUPATION: Part-time student
MARITAL STATUS: Divorced
FIRST APPEARANCE: Amazing Spider-Man Vol. 1 #67 (1968)
HEIGHT: 6'
WEIGHT: 185 lbs.
EYES: Brown
HAIR: Brown

Randy Robertson is the son of Robbie and Martha Robertson, and was also at college with Peter. Randy was something of a rebel when young, joining the protest movement and marrying a white woman in spite of his parent's discomfort. His first marriage failed, although he has recovered well and is now dating Daily Bugle secretary Glory Grant. When Peter was evicted from his expensive apartment following Mary Jane's disappearance, Randy took him in until he could find a place of his own, not far away, both being on Manhattan's Lower East Side.

JILL STACY

OCCUPATION: Unknown
MARITAL STATUS: Single
FIRST APPEARANCE: Spider-Man Vol. 1 #76 (1997)
HEIGHT: 5'9"
WEIGHT: 135 lbs.
EYES: Blue
HAIR: Black

The cousin of the late Gwen Stacy, Jill moved to New York City with her father and brother, Arthur and Paul. She befriended Peter and Mary Jane, taking classes with Mary Jane at ESU. Jill sought to understand the events surrounding Gwen's death; though hesitant, Peter eventually told Jill his side of the story. Jill was nearly killed when caught in the crossfire during an attack by one of Norman Osborn's operatives on the Parker's home. When it appeared Mary Jane was dead, Jill made romantic advances upon him, but withdrew when MJ was found to be alive.

EUGENE "FLASH" THOMPSON

OCCUPATION: Unemployed
MARITAL STATUS: Single
FIRST APPEARANCE: Amazing Fantasy #15 (1962)
HEIGHT: 6'2"
WEIGHT: 185 lbs.
EYES: Blue
HAIR: Reddish-blond

At Midtown High School, Flash Thompson was the big man on campus. His three favorite past-times were playing football, persecuting Peter and running the Spider-Man fan club. Flash and Peter ended up at Empire State University together and eventually became close friends. Flash went to war in Asia, where he met a woman named Sha Shan, who later came back to the U.S. When Flash and Sha Shan broke up, Flash pursued an affair with Betty Brant, while she was married to Ned Leeds, and later entered into a short-lived relationship with Felicia Hardy, unaware she was the Black Cat. But when Flash finally found himself single once more, he realized that somehow, the life he had imagined had passed him by. His glory days as college athlete and dashing uniformed soldier were behind him. He fell into alcoholism, as his abusive father had done many years before. In such a state, his attempts to rekindle his relationship with Betty were doomed to failure. Norman Osborn entered the scene, offering a steady job at Oscorp. But of course, Osborn's actions were designed only to needle Spider-Man. His plan concluded with an engineered accident framing Flash as a drunk driver and leaving him crippled. Flash's face was unharmed, but his body and mind were both broken. Liz Osborn took it upon herself to arrange for a full-time nurse to care for Flash in an apartment near to Peter's.

DET. NEIL GARRETT & LT. WILLIAM LAMONT
Lt. William Lamont

OCCUPATION: NYPD
MARITAL STATUS: Married
FIRST APPEARANCE: Amazing Spider-Man Vol. 2 #41 (2002)
HEIGHT: 5'10"
WEIGHT: 175 lbs.
EYES: Blue
HAIR: White

Det. Neil Garrett

OCCUPATION: NYPD
MARITAL STATUS: Married
FIRST APPEARANCE: Spectacular Spider-Man Vol. 2 #1 (2003)
HEIGHT: 5'9"
WEIGHT: 165 lbs.
EYES: Brown
HAIR: Sandy Brown

Though the relationship between Spider-Man and New York's fine police force is often strained, there are a few cooler heads among the NYPD who recognize that they would be foolish not to take advantage of the web-slinger's assistance from time to time. Detective Neil Garrett and Lieutenant William Lamont are prominent among those members of the police department with whom Spider-Man maintains a quietly constructive relationship, both on and off the record.

VENOM

REAL NAME: Edward Charles Brock
KNOWN ALIASES: None
IDENTITY: Known to legal authorities
OCCUPATION: Vigilante; former Daily Globe reporter, government operative
CITIZENSHIP: United States of America with a criminal record
PLACE OF BIRTH: New York City
MARITAL STATUS: Divorced
KNOWN RELATIVES: Carol Brock (father), Anne Weying (ex-wife, deceased), Mary Brock (younger sister)
GROUP AFFILIATION: Briefly member of Sinister Six, former ally of convenience to Spider-Man
EDUCATION: College educated (journalism major)

HISTORY: Devout Catholic Eddie Brock entered what he thought was an empty church seeking absolution from God for his forthcoming mortal sin: suicide. Before arriving at this desperate point in life, Eddie had been a successful columnist for the Daily Globe. When a man approached him and confessed to the killings committed by the Sin-Eater, Eddie knew he had a career-defining story on his hands. Protecting the killer's identity under his Constitutional right to do so, Eddie wrote a series of articles detailing their dialogues.

Eddie's articles were a hit, and the climax of his exclusive story sold out immediately. But after its publication, Spider-Man identified the true killer; the man who had confessed to Eddie was revealed to be a fraud. Fired from his job, disowned by his father and deserted by his wife, Eddie was forced to scratch a living writing venomous stories for scandal sheets. Blaming Spider-Man for his ruin, Eddie focused on developing his physique and fixated on his hatred for the wall-crawler. But he found solace in neither. Only one, final option beckoned.

Just before Eddie entered the peaceful Our Lady of Saints Church to beg God's forgiveness for his planned suicide, Spider-Man had rid himself of the parasitic alien Symbiote that had masqueraded as his black costume by subjecting them both to the overwhelming sound of the church's bells. Amid the pealing, ear-splitting cacophony, the Symbiote realized Spider-Man would never act as its host. Perhaps having learned a measure of human empathy during its time with Peter Parker, the Symbiote saved Spider-Man from painful death by dragging him to safety. The wall-crawler staggered away, assuming the parasite had crawled off to die. Instead, the weak and dying creature entered the church proper — where it eventually encountered the broken, despairing Eddie. With nothing left to lose, Eddie gave himself over. Gone forever in that moment of absolute abandon was the man known as Eddie Brock. What emerged from the terrible union of lost souls was something else. Something evil. Something unstoppable. Venom. And any humanity the creature had learned from Spider-Man was overwhelmed in the torrent of loathing that drove Eddie. Now possessing the power to destroy Spider-Man, the twin minds were united in a single purpose.

Imparting to Eddie the knowledge of Spider-Man's identity, the alien could also neutralize Peter's spider-sense — which left the web-slinger vulnerable to Venom's attack. Stalking Spider-Man from a distance, Venom threatened his life undetected — pushing Peter into the path of a subway train. Venom then approached Mary Jane Watson, terrifying her so much that Peter subsequently abandoned his black costume. The message to Peter was clear. After arming himself with a sonic blaster courtesy of the Fantastic Four, Spider-Man immediately tracked down Venom. But the bond between Eddie and the Symbiote was nearly perfect, and Spider-Man could not defeat the alien without killing its host in the process — something the hero was not prepared to do. With Venom seemingly in command, the web-slinger eventually managed to trick his adversary into expelling so much organic webbing that he became physically weakened. Defeating his foe, Spider-Man had him imprisoned in the Vault, a high-security holding facility for super-villains.

Using the Symbiote to act as a fallen prison officer, Eddie escaped from captivity. He was recaptured when Spider-Man persuaded the Symbiote to leave Venom and return to him. Eddie again managed to gain freedom, this time by using the Symbiote to appear as a cold layer of skin that convinced authorities he had killed himself — but Styx's plague virus rendered the Symbiote comatose. Without his alien other half, Eddie was placed in a conventional prison, from which he was later rescued by the revived Symbiote. During the escape, the Symbiote left behind the spawn that would transform Eddie's psychopathic cellmate, Cletus Kasady, into the deadly Carnage. Following that escape,

Art by Mark Bagley

Spider-Man and Venom wound up on a deserted island. The wall-crawler faked his own death, leaving Eddie with little reason to return to civilization. But Peter was forced to return to Venom after Carnage embarked on a bloody rampage, asking him to help bring his offspring to justice. Unexpectedly, Venom was willing to do so. For all his bloodthirsty hatred of Spider-Man, Eddie bears no grudge against society in general. To the contrary, Venom sees himself as a lethal protector of the innocent. Their collaboration helped defeat Carnage, but Spider-Man reluctantly went back on his word and helped the Fantastic Four capture Venom.

Venom has taken extreme steps to protect those he saw as blameless and equally violent measures to punish those he viewed as evil — first and foremost, Carnage. When Venom's spawn gathered a ragtag army of criminally insane beings to spread his message of chaos and hostility, Venom sided with Spider-Man against the evils of Carnage, Shriek, Doppelganger and Carrion. While at times Venom and Spider-Man would accept each other as necessary evils and join forces to fight clear and-present dangers, Venom's deadly instincts began over time to dominate his desire to protect the innocent. Seeing potential in this deadly demon, the government attempted to employ Venom to intimidate J. Jonah Jameson, whose editorials spoke out against sensitive policy. When it became clear that for Venom there existed no line between intimidation and murder, only Spider-Man's intervention saved the publisher from death.

Abandoned by the government and suffering partial amnesia after nearly dying in an explosive blast, Eddie appeared to have forgotten Spider-Man's true identity and lost his grip on the last threads of his sanity. Even after Venom joined the Sinister Six, he rapidly turned against his teammates — nearly killing the Sandman and Electro. In his unhinged state, Venom made peace with Spider-Man, and Eddie attempted to return to his wife, Ann Weying. But Ann committed suicide rather than face life with the Symbiote, leaving Eddie to once again blame Spider-Man for his loss in life. With his mind and life in tatters, Venom was abducted by Senator Stewart Ward, who forcibly separated Eddie from his Symbiote so he could perform research on the entity to help him better understand his own alien infection.

Senator Ward released the Symbiote to return to Brock once more, but something had changed. Where formerly Eddie Brock was in control, now the Symbiote itself had become the master of their relationship. The alien creature began abandoning Brock to seek and attack innocent victims, leaving them with uncanny puncture marks on their bodies. Investigating, Spider-Man learned that the victims were all cancer patients. The Symbiote sought the unusual adrenaline present in their systems, the same adrenaline that was also released in Spider-Man's body when he used his spider-sense. Brock then revealed that he was suffering from cancer on that fateful day in the church where he first encountered his "other", and that his suicide had as much to do with his impending suffering as with the humiliation caused by his journalistic blunder.

Now frustrated with the meager meal that Brock provided, the Symbiote had enough strength to merge just one last time, and his chosen "mate" was Spider-Man. Naturally, Spider-Man had other ideas, and he maneuvered the alien being into joining with the near-dead Brock. The two were now inexorably bound to a shared lifetime of sickness and pain.

In a separate series of events, it appears that following one of Venom's battles, agents of an independent research outfit recovered a fragment of severed tongue. This tissue was grown into a full, second Symbiote by persons as yet identified. Taken to the Arctic Circle in Northern Canada for experiments, the creature escaped, and is now the target of various groups attempting to respectively destroy and recover the unhosted second Symbiote.

POWERS & ABILITIES:

Strength Level: Without his Symbiote, Brock's muscular but cancer-ridden body possesses minimal strength. When combined with his life-giving alien Symbiote, he has super-human strength enabling him to lift (press) almost 11 tons.

Superhuman Powers: The costume which has grafted itself to Brock's nervous and adrenal systems has enhanced Brock's physical strength and speed to levels similar to those possessed by Spider-Man. In addition, the costume learned to emulate some of Spider-Man's powers during the period it was hosted by the web-slinger, and it allows Eddie to replicate Spider-Man's ability to cling to walls by controlling the flux of inter-atomic attraction between molecular boundary layers.

Venom can also shoot strands of the alien's substance in the form of "webbing" at high pressure up to a distance of 70 feet. The alien's substance seems to be composed of tough, flexible fibers of organic polymers that regenerate swiftly after "shedding." The strands have extraordinary adhesive properties that diminish rapidly once they abandon their living source. After about three hours, with no source to nourish them, the strands dry up like dead skin and dissolve into a powder. The strands possess a tensile strength of 125 pounds per square millimeter of cross section. Venom also extends "snares" from his body to entrap and hold his foes.

When distributed at typical thickness over Brocks' body, the Symbiote is capable of absorbing bullets from small-arms weapons firing conventional ammunition. The Symbiote is ,however, particularly vulnerable to both sonic and heat-based attacks.

Special Skills: The Symbiote costume is able to morph and appear as any form of clothing of roughly equal mass. In addition, it is able to act as a chameleon, and effectively camouflage the wearer, rendering them nearly invisible.

Also, because of its previous attachment to Spider-Man, the Symbiote has the peculiar ability to neutralize the web-slinger's spider-sense, allowing it to launch a deadly ambush on the unsuspecting Spider-Man.

The Symbiote has generated several offspring over time, but it possesses a natural ability to track such spawn. The Carnage spawn appears to be an unusual exception to this case.

POWER GRID	1	2	3	4	5	6	7
INTELLIGENCE							
STRENGTH							
SPEED							
DURABILITY							
ENERGY PROJECTION							
FIGHTING SKILLS							

VULTURE

REAL NAME: Adrian Toomes
KNOWN ALIASES: None
IDENTITY: Publicly known
OCCUPATION: Professional criminal, former electronics engineer
CITIZENSHIP: United States of America with a criminal record
PLACE OF BIRTH: Staten Island, New York
MARITAL STATUS: Widower
KNOWN RELATIVES: Malachi Toomes (nephew, deceased)
GROUP AFFILIATION: Co-founder of the Sinister Six
BASE OF OPERATIONS: New York City
EDUCATION: College educated (science major)

HISTORY: A brilliant engineer and inventor, Adrian Toomes partnered with Gregory Bestman to form B+T Electronics. For years, Toomes labored over the creation of an electromagnetic harness that would allow its wearer to fly. Finally creating a working prototype, Toomes rushed into Bestman's office to break the news. His partner was out, but lying on his desk were the real company accounts — proof that Bestman had been robbing the firm blind.

In shock, the elderly Toomes confronted Bestman. Using the mechanically enhanced strength granted by the harness, Toomes easily overpowered his partner. But the treacherous Bestman

Art by Mark Brooks

had a plan: Years earlier, Toomes had signed paperwork that allowed his partner to take complete control of B+T Electronics. Expelled from his own company, Toomes returned to his Staten Island farm to complete the harness — adding wings and crafting his criminal identity. Clad as the Vulture, Toomes wrecked his old company's headquarters, discovering a cache of cash hidden in Bestman's office. Helping himself to the loot, Toomes was intoxicated by the ease of the theft and soon embarked on a wild crime spree — striking swiftly and silently from the skies.

After J. Jonah Jameson's NOW magazine offered a reward for photos of this new criminal, Peter Parker was inspired to pick up a camera for the first time. As Spider-Man, Peter was able to get close enough to the Vulture to snap his picture. When the Vulture noticed the young web-slinger, he attacked — defeating Spider-Man with ease. Recovering from their first encounter, Peter deduced the nature of the Vulture's flying apparatus and developed an Anti-Magnetic Inverter. This device allowed Spider-Man to down his flying foe, making the Vulture easy pickings for police.

Far too crafty for any traditional prison, Toomes soon broke free to resume his criminal ways. The Vulture was a founding member of the Sinister Six and has participated in every incarnation of the criminal sextet, including the latest Sinister Seven.

For a time, Toomes briefly relocated to a retirement village in the Southwest. His short hiatus lasted only until he read of Bestman's resurrection of B+T Electronics. Returning to New York, the Vulture attacked Bestman — but Spider-Man's intervention prevented any bloodshed. The Vulture's actions were successful enough to publicly expose Bestman's treachery, leaving him in financial ruin.

Rebounding from his brief retirement, the Vulture was more active than ever. Following a failed attempt to gain control of New York City's criminal underworld by arranging the assassinations of several top mobsters, he confronted the Vulturions, a trio of criminals who had stolen his designs during his absence. The Vulture was also responsible for the accidental death of Nathan Lubensky, who sacrificed his life preventing Toomes from kidnapping his fiancée, May Parker.

When Toomes was diagnosed with cancer as a result of his prolonged use of the harness, he decided that none of his enemies should outlive him. After killing Bestman, the Vulture faced Spider-Man in what Toomes believed to be their final battle — but the web-slinger again defeated him. Toomes' illness did inspire him to undertake one unexpected act of kindness: He apologized to May for his role in Nathan's death.

Toomes' desperate search for a cure led him to Empire State University, where he used the experimental Rejuvenator to steal Spider-Man's life force and restore his own. Spider-Man eventually regained his vitality, leaving the Vulture to co-opt the life essence of the Chameleon's android simulacra of Mary Parker. Young once more and free of cancer, the Vulture soon discovered his newfound youth required constant renewal. Toomes was forced to prowl the streets seeking victims to drain.

Returned to his rightful age following an encounter with D.K., the Vulture remains as crafty and powerful as ever. He may appear elderly, but his twin goals of personal wealth and revenge on Spider-Man will surely sustain him for years to come.

PHYSICAL DESCRIPTION:

Height: 5'11"
Weight: 175 lbs.
Eyes: Hazel
Hair: Bald

POWERS & ABILITIES:

Strength Level: Ordinarily, without his electromagnetic harness, the Vulture possesses the normal human strength of a man of his age, height and build who engages in moderate regular exercise. However, the harness, in some as yet unknown way, augments the Vulture's strength while he is wearing it. After he removes the harness, the Vulture's superhuman strength gradually fades. At peak strength while wearing the harness, the Vulture can lift 700 lbs.

Superhuman Powers: While wearing his electromagnetic harness, the Vulture possesses strength, vitality and athletic prowess that are at superhuman levels for a man of his age. It is not known exactly how the harness induces these superhuman abilities in the Vulture. After he removes the harness, his superhuman abilities gradually fade. It is not known precisely how long it takes for his superhuman abilities to dwindle to normal human levels.

Special Skills: The Vulture is a brilliant electronics engineer with a great talent for invention.

PARAPHERNALIA:

Weapons: The Vulture flies by means of an electromagnetic anti-graviton generator device worn on his body by means of a tailored body harness. It enables him to fly, completely silently, by flapping the bird-like wings that he wears attached underneath his arms. He can fly at speeds of up to 95 mph for up to 6 hours without tiring appreciably. He can attain a maximum altitude of 11,000 feet (the limit at which he can still breathe).

The Vulture can glide for long distances. He can maneuver with a high degree of precision; for example, he can fly into buildings through narrow windows, up and down narrow staircases, and through narrow corridors in the course of the execution of crimes. He can turn, spin, fly upside-down and perform mid-air acrobatics.

POWER GRID	1	2	3	4	5	6	7
INTELLIGENCE							
STRENGTH							
SPEED							
DURABILITY							
ENERGY PROJECTION							
FIGHTING SKILLS							

MARY JANE WATSON

REAL NAME: Mary Jane Watson-Parker
KNOWN ALIASES: Crimson She-Devil
IDENTITY: N/A
OCCUPATION: Fashion model and "B" movie actress, former star of daytime TV drama.
CITIZENSHIP: United States of America with no criminal record
PLACE OF BIRTH: Montoursville, PA
MARITAL STATUS: Married
KNOWN RELATIVES: Peter Parker (husband), Anna May Watson (Aunt), Philip (father), Madeline (mother, deceased), Gayle Watson-Byrnes (sister), Timothy Byrnes (ex-brother-in-law), Kevin and Tommy Byrnes (nephews), Judge Spenser Watson (uncle), Frank Brown (mother's cousin), Kristy (cousin), Lou and Lorraine Watson (uncle and aunt, parents of Kristy)
GROUP AFFILIATION: None
EDUCATION: High School, partially completed college studies as an adult student

HISTORY: Mary Jane Watson's parents met in high school and married at age 18. Madeline Watson followed her husband, Philip Watson, across the country as he began his academic career in modern American literature; by age 20, they had one daughter, Gayle Watson. Mary Jane arrived four years later.

Philip became a popular college professor, and Madeline devoted her life to their children. When Philip began to harbor visions of himself as the next great American novelist — another Faulkner, perhaps — their marriage unraveled. Possessing no such talent, Philip turned his fury on his family. Dragging his wife and children from college to college, he searched in vain for inspiration.

The family's turmoil caused Gayle to turn inwards, seeking solace in ballet. Mary Jane hid behind the façade of a bubbly personality. In public, MJ was the popular class clown and party animal; in private, little was ever right. Eventually, Philip's frustrations boiled over, and he struck Gayle over the cost of her dancing lessons. Madeline had had enough.

A few weeks later, as Philip received honors during a college awards ceremony, Madeline left home with her daughters and two suitcases. She received nothing from the divorce and was left to shuffle from one resentful relative to the next, with one exception: her ex-husband's elderly sister, Anna Watson, who lived in Forest Hills.

Thirteen-year-old Mary Jane loved to visit her aunt — even though Anna and her neighbor, May Parker, attempted on more than one occasion to set MJ up with May's nephew, 14-year old Peter Parker. Mary Jane had other priorities — and other worries.

Madeline uprooted her family again and settled in Pittsburgh, staying with her cousin, Frank Brown. A widower with three children of his own, Frank paid the bills, and Madeline looked after the household. While Mary Jane broke hearts as a freshman, Gayle ignored her mother's warnings and married her high-school sweetheart, football star and honors student Timothy Byrnes. When Timmy was 19, Gayle became pregnant.

In Timmy's trapped eyes, Mary Jane saw the roots of the desperation that had destroyed her father. Turning away from Gayle's impending misery, Mary Jane buried herself in acting, parties and the nation's newest celebrity sensation — Spider-Man. MJ knew she and Spider-Man shared at least two things in common: a determination to enjoy life and a mask that hid their true faces.

The following Thanksgiving break, Mary Jane went to stay with Aunt Anna. After Ben Parker's murder, May Parker had come to Anna's house. But Mary Jane had little stomach for the misery of others. Ignoring the woman, MJ watched outside as Peter arrived home and rushed inside. Only a minute later, she saw Spider-Man emerge from an upstairs window.

Burying what she had witnessed, Mary Jane grappled not only with Timmy's abandonment of the again-pregnant Gayle, but also her mother's death. Gayle assumed Mary Jane would stay and help raise the two young children, but MJ saw only a cage. She ran from Gayle's life, all the way to New York.

Staying briefly with Aunt Anna, Mary Jane found work waiting tables and dancing on stage in discos. Soon, she earned enough money to afford a cheap downtown studio apartment. Though she managed for a time to avoid the date with Peter that their respective aunts were so keen to arrange, MJ could not put it off forever.

Expecting a dowdy girl, Peter was stunned by Mary Jane's beauty and charm. He had hit the jackpot. Remembering a bookish, bespectacled nerd, MJ never imagined the confident young college student Peter had become. Nor, when a TV bulletin announced that the Rhino was at large in the city, did she expect him to suggest they ride into town on his motorcycle and catch the action. When Peter immediately disappeared to take photos, and Spider-Man turned up moments later, Mary Jane bit her tongue and feigned surprise at the coincidence.

Mary Jane dated Peter a couple more times and became part of his circle of friends — joining Harry Osborn, Gwen Stacy and Flash Thompson. When Peter and Gwen fell deeply in love, Mary Jane casually dated Harry until his drug addiction ended the relationship.

Mary Jane's friendship with Peter remained true, and she comforted him through the loss of Gwen. Over time, Peter began to realize there was more to Mary Jane than the party-girl persona she affected. Before Peter departed on a trip to Europe, he left MJ with a kiss that at last reflected the depth of feeling that had developed between them. The two eventually became lovers, although Peter's commitments as Spider-Man caused no less grief with Mary Jane than they had when he dated Gwen or Betty Brant. Even though she secretly knew the reasons for his erratic behavior, Mary Jane still felt the need to punish him — occasionally dating jocks like Flash Thompson to get her point across.

Peter eventually proposed to Mary Jane — but she declined, claiming she wasn't the sort of girl who could be happy with just one man. Uncomfortable, Mary Jane left New York to further her modeling career in Florida. Peter dated several women during her absence, including the Black Cat, with whom he shared a particularly tempestuous relationship.

When Mary Jane returned, both she and Peter relied on one another as good friends. But following another round of the usual Peter Parker lies in the wake of a battle with Puma, Mary Jane emotionally revealed to Peter that she knew he was Spider-Man. His mask now gone, she felt free to remove her own and told Peter about her difficult past. In their shared honesty, the two realized how close they had become in their lives. A few months later, Peter proposed again. Mary Jane accepted.

They married, but the reality of being wed to a super hero was far more demanding than Mary Jane had ever imagined. Villains like Venom invaded their personal lives, and MJ struggled with Peter's extended absences — and the very real fear that one day, she might receive a phone call saying her husband was in a morgue, inexplicably dressed in a Spider-Man costume.

Her own career presented its share of problems, too, when Jonathan Caesar, a wealthy admirer, kidnapped Mary Jane. After MJ escaped, the incarcerated Caesar managed to use his influence to ensure that she was forced out of the modeling business. Down but not out, MJ found high-paying work in the daytime drama Secret Hospital.

Whether at home or out being the social animal her soap-opera fans expected her to be, the young bride found herself increasingly alone — like a super-hero widow. Seeking respite, MJ took up — but later quit — smoking and nearly entered into an affair with smooth-talking actor Jason Jerome. Miserable and tense, Mary Jane did at least manage to reconcile with her father.

Life started looking up when Mary Jane became pregnant, and Peter's long-lost clone, Ben Reilly, assumed the role of Spider-Man. After Norman Osborn's plans caused the loss of her unborn child and Ben's death, Mary Jane enrolled at Empire State University and eventually resumed modeling, for which she was richly paid. Though uncomfortable with his wife's higher paycheck, Peter soon moved into an expensive apartment with MJ and Aunt May. Peter even told Mary Jane he was done being Spider-Man, once and for all. But the

spider-bite ran deeper in his blood than his own resolve. With MJ's busy modeling schedule already straining their relationship, the truth came out that Peter was still fighting crime as Spider-Man.

Mary Jane had never resented Peter's double life. His incredible sense of responsibility was a key factor in her love and respect for him. But the one fact she could never accept was the growing feeling that Spider-Man was more important to Peter than she was. Peter's lies only served to foster that sentiment, and their marriage hit the rocks. Mary Jane faced further problems as a Stalker harassed her constantly on the phone — a secret she withheld from Peter.

With their love hanging in the balance, Mary Jane took off on a plane trip. Peter was supposed to meet her before she left, but could not get to her in time. The Stalker, on board the same flight, had other plans. When the plane exploded in mid-air, Peter at first refused to believe his wife dead. He was eventually convinced otherwise by the weight of evidence.

But his first instincts had been correct: The Stalker, who had begun to mimic Peter after absorbing his memories through superhuman means, was holding Mary Jane captive. Peter rescued MJ, but she had already made up her mind: She would not return to New York to run second place to Spider-Man. The two separated, and Mary Jane moved to the West Coast.

Following a painful time apart, both Peter and MJ decided to make one last move. As Mary Jane flew to New York, Peter flew to Los Angeles. Each finding the other absent, they left for home. When Peter's return flight encountered an electrical storm, the pilot made an unscheduled stop in Denver — where Mary Jane's plane had touched down for a layover. The two met in the airport.

Their reunion was nearly sabotaged when Doctor Doom arrived, and a Latverian resistance group launched an all-out attack in the waiting lounge. As Spider-Man aided Captain America to defend Doctor Doom, Mary Jane could have no clearer proof that loving Peter meant accepting the wall-crawler, too. In the aftermath of the fight, Peter told Mary Jane he needed her, that he loved her, and that he was nothing without her. Watching them, Captain America could see the truth and offered Peter a word to the wise: "The mask is supposed to hide your face. Don't let it hide your heart."

Peter and Mary Jane know things between them will never be easy, but they believe the love they share is worth the heartache.

POWER GRID	1	2	3	4	5	6	7
INTELLIGENCE							
STRENGTH							
SPEED							
DURABILITY							
ENERGY PROJECTION							
FIGHTING SKILLS							

BIBLIOGRAPHY

BLACK CAT

First Appearance: Amazing Spider-Man Vol. 1 #194 (1979)
Origin: Amazing Spider-Man Vol. 1 #205 (1980)
Significant Issues: revealed to be in love with Spider-Man (Amazing Spider-Man Vol. 1 #204, 1980); origin (Amazing Spider-Man Vol. 1 #205, 1980); nearly killed by Doctor Octopus and The Owl (Spectacular Spider-Man Vol. 1 #75, 1983); Black Cat Meets Peter Parker (Spectacular Spider-Man Vol. 1 #87, 1984); Black Cat gains real powers (Spectacular Spider-Man Vol. 1 #89, 1984); splits with Peter (Spectacular Spider-Man Vol. 1 #100, 1985); powers are mutated (Spectacular Spider-Man Vol. 1 #115, 1986); discovers Peter was responsible (Spectacular Spider-Man Vol. 1 #116, 1986); confronts Dr. Strange, joins the Foreigner (Spectacular Spider-Man Vol. 1 #117, 1986); skirmish with Peter, relationship with Foreigner discovered (Spectacular Spider-Man Vol. 1 #129, 1987); loses her natural powers (Amazing Spider-Man Vol. 1 #343, 1991); gets new gear from Tinkerer (Amazing Spider-Man Vol. 1 #370, 1992); first Cat's Eye Investigations (Felicia Hardy: The Black Cat #1, 1994); joins Spider-Man in fighting Mister Brownstone (Spider-Man/Black Cat: The Evil That Men Do #1, 2002)

CARNAGE

First Appearance: Amazing Spider-Man Vol. 1 #344 (as Cletus Kasady, 1991); Amazing Spider-Man Vol. 1 #361 (as Carnage, 1992)
Origin: Amazing Spider-Man Vol. 1 #345 (1991)
Significant Issues: acquired spawn of Venom Symbiote (Amazing Spider-Man Vol. 1 #345, 1991); became Carnage, went on killing spree, battled Spider-Man & Venom. (Amazing Spider-Man Vol. 1 #361, 1992); Maximum Carnage starts (Spider-Man Unlimited #1, 1993); Planet of the Symbiotes (Amazing Spider-Man Annual, 1995); Web of Carnage (Sensational Spider-Man Vol. 1 #3, 1996); steaks Silver Surfer's powers (Amazing Spider-Man Vol. 1 #430, 1997); Venom *absorbs* Carnage Symbiote (Peter Parker: Spider-Man Vol. 2 #10, 1999); Cletus Kasady without Carnage Symbiote (Peter Parker: Spider-Man Vol. 2 #13, 2000); gains new Symbiote (Web-Spinners #14, 2000)

DAILY BUGLE

First Appearance: Fantastic Four #2 (1962)
Significant Issues: first building destroyed by Graviton (Amazing Spider-Man Vol. 1 #326, 1989); second building destroyed by Green Goblin (Spider-Man Vol. 1 #98, 1998); third Building appears (Amazing Spider-Man Vol. 2 #1, 1999)

DIGGER

First Appearance: Amazing Spider-Man Vol. 2 #51 (2003)
Origin: Amazing Spider-Man Vol. 2 #52 (2003)
Significant Issues: Destroyed (Amazing Spider-Man Vol. 2 #54, 2003)

DOCTOR OCTOPUS

First Appearance: Amazing Spider-Man Vol. 1 #3 (1963)
Origin: Amazing Spider-Man Vol. 1 #3 (1963)
Significant Issues: Second appearance (Amazing Spider-Man Vol. 1 #11, 1964); Founds Sinister Six (Amazing Spider-Man Annual #1, 1964); Master Planner story (Amazing Spider-Man Vol. 1 #30, 1965); Spider-Man joins Doctor Octopus (Amazing Spider-Man Vol. 1 #53, 1967); Death of Captain Stacy (Amazing Spider-Man Vol. 1 #88, 1970); Gang War (Amazing Spider-Man Vol. 1 #113, 1972); nearly marries Aunt May (Amazing Spider-Man Vol. 1 #131, 1974); creates Adamantium arms (Daredevil #165, 1980); becomes terrified of Spider-Man (Spectacular Spider-Man Vol. 1 #78, 1983); significant role in Secret Wars (Secret Wars #1, 1984); first uses Adamantium arms (Marvel Fanfare #22, 1985); recovers from fear of Spider-Man (Amazing Spider-Man Vol. 1 #296, 1988); return of the Sinister Six (Amazing Spider-Man Vol. 1 #334, 1990); attacked by former Sinister Six allies (Spider-Man Vol. 1 #18, 1992); Adamantium arms destroyed (Spider-Man: Lethal Foes (of) #1, 1993); saves Spidey from poisoning, killed by Kaine (Spectacular Spider-Man Vol. 1 #221, 1995); reborn (Amazing Spider-Man Vol. 1 #426, 1997)

ELECTRO

First Appearance: Amazing Spider-Man Vol. 1 #9 (1964)
Origin: Amazing Spider-Man Vol. 1 #9 (1964)
Significant Issues: Joins Emissaries of Evil (Daredevil Annual #1, 1967); hired by J.J.J. to defeat Spidey (Amazing Spider-Man Vol. 1 #82, 1970); joins Frightful Four (Spectacular Spider-Man Vol. 1 #39, 1980); return of the Sinister Six (Amazing Spider-Man Vol. 1 #334, 1990); revenge of the Sinister Six (Spider-Man Vol. 1 #18, 1992); blacks out New York to prove self-worth (Spider-Man Vol. 1 #38, 1993); joins Sinister Seven to kill Kaine (Spider-Man Unlimited #9, 1995); temporary power boost (Amazing Spider-Man Vol. 1 #422, 1997); Sinister Six again (Amazing Spider-Man Vol. 2 #12, 1999); apparently killed by Venom (Peter Parker: Spider-Man Vol. 2 #17, 2000); reappears unharmed (Spider-Man: Tangled Web #10, 2002)

EZEKIEL

First Appearance: Amazing Spider-Man Vol. 2 #30 (2001)
Origin: Amazing Spider-Man Vol. 2 #32 (2001); Amazing Spider-Man Vol. 1 #507 (2004)
Significant Issues: Origin in flashback (Amazing Spider-Man Vol. 2 #32, 2001); seemingly killed by Morlun (Amazing Spider-Man Vol. 2 #34, 2001); revealed to have survived (Amazing Spider-Man Vol. 2 #35, 2001); aids Spider-Man against Shathra (Amazing Spider-Man Vol. 2 #48, 2003); plans to kill Spider-Man (Amazing Spider-Man Vol. 1 #506, 2004); death (Amazing Spider-Man Vol. 1 #508, 2004)

GREEN GOBLIN

First Appearance: Amazing Spider-Man Vol. 1 #14 (as Green Goblin, 1964); Amazing Spider-Man Vol. 1 #40 (as Norman Osborn, 1966)
Origin: Amazing Spider-Man Vol. 1 #40 (1966)
Significant Issues: First gangland plans (Amazing Spider-Man Vol. 1 #23, 1965); First Norman Osborn (Amazing Spider-Man Vol. 1 #37, 1966); discovers Spider-Man's identity. (Amazing Spider-Man Vol. 1 #39, 1966); face revealed, origin told (Amazing Spider-Man Vol. 1 #40, 1966); first regains Green Goblin memories. (Spectacular Spider-Man Magazine #2, 1968); regains memories second time (Amazing Spider-Man Vol. 1 #96, 1971); kills Gwen Stacy before his own accidental "death" (Amazing Spider-Man Vol. 1 #121, 1973); returns to New York, revealed to be behind Clone Saga (Spectacular Spider-Man Vol. 1 #240, 1996); kills Ben Reilly (Spider-Man Vol. 1 #75, 1996); frames Spider-Man for the death of Joey Z (Spider-Man Vol. 1 #88, 1998); battles Kingsley (Spectacular Spider-Man Vol. 1 #261, 1998); begins search for increased power in Gathering of Five (Sensational Spider-Man Vol. 1 #32, 1998); revealed to have received madness from the Gathering (Amazing Spider-Man Vol. 1 #441, 1998); forms Order of the Goblin, plots to turn Peter Parker into his new heir (Spider-Man: Revenge of the Green Goblin #1, 2000); kidnaps Peter Parker (Amazing Spider-Man Vol. 2 #25, 2001); fails to convert Peter into his heir (Peter Parker: Spider-Man Vol. 2 #25, 2001); resumes attempts to push Spider-Man to violence (Peter Parker: Spider-Man Vol. 2 #44, 2002); Spider-Man refuses to fight (Peter Parker: Spider-Man Vol. 2 #47, 2002); kidnaps church-goers, defeated by Spider-Man (Spider-Man: Marvel Knights #1, 2004)

HOBGOBLIN

First Appearance: Spectacular Spider-Man Vol. 1 #43 (1980); Amazing Spider-Man Vol. 1 #238 (as Kinglsey, 1983)
Origin: Spider-Man: Hobgoblin Lives #3 (1997)
Significant Issues: First appearance as Hobgoblin (Amazing Spider-Man Vol. 1 #238, 1983); search for Osborn Formula (Amazing Spider-Man Vol. 1 #244, 1983); gains Super-Powers (Spectacular Spider-Man Vol. 1 #85, 1983); battered by Spider-Man, all subsequent appearances until #276 may be Flash (Amazing Spider-Man Vol. 1 #251, 1984); Flash framed as Hobgoblin (Amazing Spider-Man Vol. 1 #276, 1986); gang war, Hobgoblin vs. Jack O' Lantern (Amazing Spider-Man Vol. 1 #284, 1987); presumed murdered, later revealed his brother was actually shot and survived (Web of Spider-Man Vol. 1 #29, 1987); returns, kills Jason Macendale (Spider-Man: Hobgoblin Lives #1, 1997); Peter/MJ/Betty/Flash attempt to solve Hobgoblin mystery (Spider-Man: Hobgoblin Lives #2, 1997); true Hobgoblin revealed at last (Spider-Man: Hobgoblin Lives #3, 1997); broken out of jail by Norman Osborn's agent (Spectacular Spider-Man Vol. 1 #259, 1998); loses Kingsley Ltd. to Norman, flees to the Caribbean (Spectacular Spider-Man Vol. 1 #261, 1998)

LIZARD

First Appearance: Amazing Spider-Man Vol. 1 #6 (1963)
Origin: Amazing Spider-Man Vol. 1 #6 (1963)
Significant Issues: Helps vs. Rhino (Amazing Spider-Man Vol. 1 #43, 1966); Kidnapped during Petrified Tablet saga (Amazing Spider-Man Vol. 1 #73, 1969); vs. Spidey and Human Torch (Amazing Spider-Man Vol. 1 #76, 1969); vs. Spidey and Morbius (Amazing Spider-Man Vol. 1 #101, 1971); Stegron & Lizard (Amazing Spider-Man Vol. 1 #166, 1977); begins teaching at ESU (Spectacular Spider-Man Vol. 1 #32, 1979); Iguana vs. Lizard (Spectacular Spider-Man Vol. 1 #34, 1979); Spider-Lizard (Spectacular Spider-Man Vol. 1 #40, 1980); Lizard/Curt Connor personas fully merge, vs. the Owl (Spectacular Spider-Man Vol. 1 #127, 1987); Lizard Monster (Spectacular Spider-Man Vol. 1 #237, 1996); second Petrified Tablet story (Spider-Man: Lifeline #1, 2001); wife and son struck with cancer (Spider-Man: Quality of Life #1, 2002); Lizard and Connors personalities overlap once more (Spectacular Spider-Man Vol. 2 #11, 2004)

MORLUN

First Appearance: Amazing Spider-Man Vol. 2 #30 (2001)
Significant Issues: Death (Amazing Spider-Man Vol. 2 #35, 2001)

MAY PARKER

First Appearance: Amazing Fantasy #15 (1962)
Origin: Spectacular Spider-Man Annual #4 (1984); Amazing Spider-Man Vol. 1 #370 (1992)
Significant Issues: Kidnapped by Sinister Six (Amazing Spider-Man Annual #1, 1964); Meets Ock Again (Amazing Spider-Man Vol. 1 #54, 1967); goes to live with Ock (Amazing Spider-Man Vol. 1 #110, 1972); nearly marries Doctor Octopus (Amazing Spider-Man Vol. 1 #131, 1974); heart attack while protesting (Amazing Spider-Man Vol. 1 #176, 1978); relapse (Amazing Spider-Man Vol. 1 #178, 1978); believed dead (Amazing Spider-Man Vol. 1 #196, 1979); discovered safe (Amazing Spider-Man Vol. 1 #200, 1980); announces engagement to Nathan Lubensky (Spectacular Spider-Man #49, 1980); Aunt May, rest home detective (Amazing Spider-Man Vol. 1 #220, 1981); leaves rest home, opens boarding house (Marvel Team-Up #124, 1982); May Reilly's former love revealed (Spectacular Spider-Man Annual #4, 1984); breaks off engagement to Nathan (Spectacular Spider-Man Vol. 1 #113, 1986); story of early years told (Amazing Spider-Man Vol. 1 #370, 1992); supposedly suffers a stroke (Web of Spider-Man Vol. 1 #115, 1994); death of 'Genetic Construct' Aunt May (Amazing Spider-Man Vol. 1 #400, 1995); 'real' Aunt May discovered and returns (Spider-Man Vol. 1 #97, 1998); discovers Peter's identity (Amazing Spider-Man Vol. 2 #35, 2001); confronts Peter (Amazing Spider-Man Vol. 2 #38, 2002)

SANDMAN

First Appearance: Amazing Spider-Man Vol. 1 #4 (1963)
Origin: Amazing Spider-Man Vol. 1 #4 (1963)
Significant Issues: Joins Sinister Six (Amazing Spider-Man Annual #1, 1964); Hydro-Man & Sandman (Amazing Spider-Man Vol. 1 #217, 1981); first pangs of conscience (Marvel Team-Up #138, 1984); aids Silver Sable and Spider-Man (Amazing Spider-Man Vol. 1 #280, 1986); joins Silver Sable's "Wild Pack" (Amazing Spider-Man Vol. 1 #303, 1988); joins the "Outlaws" (Web of Spider-Man Vol. 1 #50, 1989); forced to rejoin Sinister Six (Amazing Spider-Man Vol. 1 #334, 1990); joins Avengers (Avengers #329, 1991); quits Avengers (Amazing Spider-Man Vol. 1 #348, 1991); returns to Avengers (Avengers #332, 1991); joins Sinister Six against Doc Ock (Spider-Man Vol. 1 #18, 1992); Wizard's machine restores criminal psyche (Peter Parker: Spider-Man Vol. 2 #12, 1999); becomes sick when bitten by Venom (Peter Parker: Spider-Man Vol. 2 #16, 2000); body disintegrates (Peter Parker: Spider-Man Vol. 2 #22, 2000); recovers strength by eating pop stars (Peter Parker: Spider-Man Vol. 2 #42, 2002); personality split (Peter Parker: Spider-Man Vol. 2 #56, 2003);

SCORPION

First Appearance: Amazing Spider-Man Vol. 1 #19 (as Gargan, 1964); Amazing Spider-Man Vol. 1 #20 (as Scorpion, 1965)
Origin: Amazing Spider-Man Vol. 1 #20 (1965)
Significant Issues: Becomes Scorpion (Amazing Spider-Man Vol. 1 #20, 1965); escapes jail, attacks JJJ (Amazing Spider-Man Vol. 1 #29, 1965); paroled, attacks Aunt May's hospital (Amazing Spider-Man Vol. 1 #145, 1975); escapes, kidnaps JJJ's bride (Amazing Spider-Man Annual #18, 1984); hired by Justin Hammer, new costume and tail (Amazing Spider-Man Vol. 1 #318, 1989); hired by Chameleon vs. Spider-Man and Black Cat (Amazing Spider-Man Vol. 1 #342, 1990); regains sanity and quits crime, battered by Spider-Man regardless (Spectacular Spider-Man Vol. 1 #215, 1994); returns meaner and madder than ever (Spider-Man Unlimited #13,

1996); briefly stint as government agent (Spider-Man Unlimited #22, 1998)

SHATHRA

First Appearance: Amazing Spider-Man Vol. 2 #46 (2002)
Significant Issues: Death (Amazing Spider-Man Vol. 2 #48, 2003)

SHOCKER

First Appearance: Amazing Spider-Man Vol. 1 #46 (1967)
Origin: Amazing Spider-Man Vol. 1 #46 (1967)
Significant Issues: Steals Petrified Tablet (Amazing Spider-Man Vol. 1 #72, 1969); holds New York City to ransom (Amazing Spider-Man Vol. 1 #151, 1975); manipulates the stock market, makes $1m (Defenders #64, 1978); joins Masters of Evil (Avengers #228, 1983); crisis of confidence (Spider-Man: Deadly Foes (of) #1, 1991); begins to recover confidence (Amazing Spider-Man Vol. 1 #364, 1992); temporarily acquires super-human powers (Web of Spider-Man Vol. 1 #109, 1994); joins the Sinister Seven (Spider-Man Unlimited #9, 1995); confronts a helpless Spider-Man and lets him go (Spider-Man Vol. 1 #83, 1997); fired by Justin Hammer, teams with Hydro-Man (Peter Parker: Spider-Man Vol. 2 #51, 2003)

SPIDER-MAN

First Appearance: Amazing Fantasy Vol. 1 #15 (1962)
Origin: Amazing Fantasy Vol. 1 #15 (1962); Amazing Spider-Man Vol. 1 #50 (1967); Spectacular Spider-Man Magazine #1 (1968); Amazing Spider-Man Vol. 1 #94 (1971); Amazing Spider-Man Vol. 1 #181 (1978); Amazing Spider-Man Vol. 1 #200 (1980); Spectacular Spider-Man Vol. 2 #60 (1981); Amazing Spider-Man Vol. 1 #248 (1984); Spectacular Spider-Man Vol. 2 #87 (1984); Marvel Graphic Novel: The Amazing Spider-Man "Parallel Lives" (1989); Spectacular Spider-Man Vol. 2 #189 (1992); Web of Spider-Man #90 (1992); Amazing Spider-Man Vol. 1 #365 (1992), Spider-Man Vol. 1 #26 (1992)
Significant Issues: Attempts to join Fantastic Four (Amazing Spider-Man Vol. 1 #1, 1963); first Doctor Octopus (Amazing Spider-Man Vol. 1 #3, 1963); first Lizard (Amazing Spider-Man Vol. 1 #6, 1963); first Electro (Amazing Spider-Man Vol. 1 #9, 1964); first Green Goblin (Amazing Spider-Man Vol. 1 #14, 1964); first Kraven the Hunter (Amazing Spider-Man Vol. 1 #15, 1964); graduates high school (Amazing Spider-Man Vol. 1 #28, 1965); unmasked by Green Goblin (Amazing Spider-Man Vol. 1 #39, 1966); first Kingpin (Amazing Spider-Man Vol. 1 #50, 1967); death of Captain Stacy (Amazing Spider-Man Vol. 1 #90, 1970); death of Gwen Stacy (Amazing Spider-Man Vol. 1 #121, 1973); cloned by Jackal (Amazing Spider-Man Vol. 1 #149, 1975); graduates college (Amazing Spider-Man Vol. 1 #185, 1978); first Black Cat (Amazing Spider-Man Vol. 1 #194, 1979); first black costume on Earth (Amazing Spider-Man Vol. 1 #252, 1984); breaks up with Black Cat (Spectacular Spider-Man Vol. 1 #100, 1985); marries MJ (Amazing Spider-Man Vol. 1 Annual #21, 1987); first Venom (Amazing Spider-Man Vol. 1 #300, 1988); death of Harry Osborn (Spectacular Spider-Man Vol. 1 #200, 1985); Ben Reilly returns (Web of Spider-Man #117, 1994); Green Goblin returns (Peter Parker: Spider-Man Vol. 1 #75, 1996); MJ's plane explodes (Amazing Spider-Man Vol. 2 #13, 2000); reunites with MJ (Peter Parker: Spider-Man Vol. 2 #29, 2001); unmasked by Aunt May (Amazing Spider-Man Vol. 2 #35, 2001); reconciles with MJ (Amazing Spider-Man Vol. 2 #500, 2003); encounters Uncle Ben following otherdimensional adventure (Amazing Spider-Man Vol. 2 #500, 2003)

SPIDER-MAN'S COSTUMES

First Appearance: Amazing Fantasy Vol. 1 #15 (1962)
Origin: Amazing Fantasy Vol. 1 #15 (1962);
Significant Issues: First insulated costume (Spectacular Spider-Man Vol. 1 #66, 1982); Symbiotic Costume (Secret Wars #8, 1984); Amazing Bag-Man, Red and Blues return (Amazing Spider-Man Vol. 1 #258, 1984); Spider-Armour (Web of Spider-Man Vol. 1 #100, 1993); Ben's Costume (Sensational Spider-Man #0, 1996); Original Red and Blues return (Spectacular Spider-Man Vol. 1 #241, 1996)

GWEN STACY

First Appearance: Amazing Spider-Man Vol. 1 #31 (1965)
Significant Issues: first Captain Stacy (Amazing Spider-Man Vol. 1 #56, 1968); Peter reveals he is Spider-Man, isn't believed (Amazing Spider-Man Vol. 1 #87, 1970); death of Capt. Stacy (Amazing

Spider-Man Vol. 1 #90, 1970); Gwen in London with Uncle Arthur (Amazing Spider-Man Vol. 1 #95, 1971); Gwen in the Savage Land (Amazing Spider-Man Vol. 1 #103, 1971); death (Amazing Spider-Man Vol. 1 #121, 1973)

VENOM

First Appearance: Secret Wars #8 (as Symbiote, 1984); Amazing Spider-Man Vol. 1 #298 (as Venom, 1988); Amazing Spider-Man Vol. 1 #300 (as Brock, 1988)
Origin: Secret Wars #8 (1984); Amazing Spider-Man Vol. 1 #258 (1984); Amazing Spider-Man Vol. 1 #300 (1988)
Significant Issues: Spider-Man discards costume (Amazing Spider-Man Vol. 1 #258, 1984); Spider-Man battles costume (Amazing Spider-Man Vol. 1 #1, 1985); Brock pushes Peter Parker in front of train (Web of Spider-Man Vol. 1 #18, 1986); first Venom sighting (Amazing Spider-Man Vol. 1 #298, 1988); Venom confronts Mary Jane (Amazing Spider-Man Vol. 1 #299, 1988); Venom battles Spider-Man, origin (Amazing Spider-Man Vol. 1 #300, 1988); escapes "The Vault" (Amazing Spider-Man Vol. 1 #315, 1989); visits Aunt May's house (Amazing Spider-Man Vol. 1 #317, 1989); Symbiote diseased by Styx (Amazing Spider-Man Vol. 1 #333, 1990); Symbiote finds Brock, drops "Carnage" spawn (Amazing Spider-Man Vol. 1 #345, 1991); transports Spidey to a deserted island (Amazing Spider-Man Vol. 1 #347, 1991); returns to New York to battle Carnage (Amazing Spider-Man Vol. 1 #362, 1992); neutrality pact with Spider-Man (Amazing Spider-Man Vol. 1 #375, 1993); Maximum Carnage (Spider-Man Unlimited #1, 1993); defeated by Scarlet Spider (Spider-Man Vol. 1 #53, 1994); Symbiote Race visits Earth (Amazing Spider-Man Annual #1995, 1995); first solo title (Venom: Lethal Protector #1, 1993); Venom *absorbs* Carnage Symbiote (Peter Parker: Spider-Man Vol. 2 #10, 1999); ex-wife commits suicide (Amazing Spider-Man Vol. 2 #19, 2000); loses Symbiote to Senator Ward (Amazing Spider-Man Vol. 2 #22, 2000); Symbiote seeks new host (Spectacular Spider-Man Vol. 2 #1, 2003); Brock revealed as having cancer (Spectacular Spider-Man Vol. 2 #4, 2003); Brock and Symbiote permanently re-attached (Spectacular Spider-Man Vol. 2 #5, 2003)

VULTURE

First Appearance: Amazing Spider-Man Vol. 1 #2 (1963)
Origin: Amazing Spider-Man Vol. 1 #240 (1983)
Significant Issues: Second appearance (Amazing Spider-Man Vol. 1 #7, 1963); joined Sinister Six (Amazing Spider-Man Annual #1, 1964); believed self dying, revealed Vulture secrets to cellmate (Amazing Spider-Man Vol. 1 #48, 1967); came out of retirement for revenge, also origin told (Amazing Spider-Man Vol. 1 #240, 1983); confronted Vulturians who stole his design (Web of Spider-Man Vol. 1 #3, 1985); rejoined Sinister Six, killed Nathan Lubensky (Amazing Spider-Man Vol. 1 #336, 1990); revenge of the Sinister Six (Spider-Man Vol. 1 #18, 1992); discovers has cancer, decides to kill all his enemies (Spectacular Spider-Man Vol. 1 #186, 1992); aids Chameleon in revenge on Spider-Man, youth and health restored, donned redesigned costume and weapons (Amazing Spider-Man Vol. 1 #386, 1994); poisoned Spider-Man (Amazing Spider-Man Vol. 1 #396, 1994); becomes old once more (Sensational Spider-Man Vol. 1 #18, 1997); returns to burglary (Web-Spinners #15, 2000)

MARY JANE WATSON

First Appearance: Amazing Spider-Man Vol. 1 #15 (first mentioned – not shown, 1964); Amazing Spider-Man Vol. 1 #25 (first appears – face not shown 1965); Amazing Spider-Man Vol. 1 #42 (full appearance, 1966)
Origin: Marvel Graphic Novel: The Amazing Spider-Man "Parallel Lives" (1989); Amazing Spider-Man Vol. 1 #259 (1984)
Significant Issues: Face first seen (Amazing Spider-Man Vol. 1 #42, 1966); first date with Peter (Amazing Spider-Man Vol. 1 #47, 1967); falls in love with Peter (Amazing Spider-Man Vol. 1 #143, 1975); Peter first proposes, is rejected (Amazing Spider-Man Vol. 1 #182, 1978); Peter and Mary Jane break up (Amazing Spider-Man Vol. 1 #193, 1979); last appearance before going to Florida (Amazing Spider-Man #201, 1980); returns to New York (Amazing Spider-Man Vol. 1 #242, 1983); reveals knowing Peter is Spider-Man (Amazing Spider-Man Vol. 1 #257, 1984); origin and family history, relationship begins anew (Amazing Spider-Man Vol. 1 #259, 1984); Peter proposes second time (Amazing Spider-Man Vol. 1 #290, 1987); accepts proposal (Amazing

Spider-Man Vol. 1 #292, 1987); wedding (Amazing Spider-Man Annual #21, 1987); honeymoon (Spectacular Spider-Man Annual #7, 1987); Mary Jane Kidnapped (Amazing Spider-Man Vol. 1 #307, 1988); announces pregnancy (Spectacular Spider-Man Vol. 1 #220, 1995); nearly killed by hypnotized Peter (Spectacular Spider-Man Vol. 1 #228, 1995); baby stillborn (Amazing Spider-Man Vol. 1 #418, 1996); believed dead in plane explosion (Amazing Spider-Man Vol. 2 #13, 2000); found safe (Amazing Spider-Man Vol. 2 #29, 2001); leaves Peter for California (Amazing Spider-Man Annual 2001, 2001); returns to Peter (Amazing Spider-Man Vol. 2 #50, 2003)

POWER RATINGS

STRENGTH
Ability to lift weight

1 Weak: cannot lift own body weight
2 Normal: able to lift own body weight
3 Peak human: able to lift twice own body weight
4 Superhuman: 800 lbs-25 ton range
5 Superhuman: 25-75 ton range
6 Superhuman: 75-100 ton range
7 Incalculable: In excess of 100 tons

INTELLIGENCE
Ability to think and process information

1 Slow/Impaired
2 Normal
3 Learned
4 Gifted
5 Genius
6 Super-Genius
7 Omniscient

ENERGY PROJECTION
Ability to discharge energy

1 None
2 Ability to discharge energy on contact
3 Short range, short duration, single energy type
4 Medium range, medium duration, single energy type
5 Long range, long duration, single energy type
6 Able to discharge multiple forms of energy
7 Virtually unlimited command of all forms of energy

FIGHTING ABILITY
Proficiency in hand-to-hand combat

1 Poor
2 Normal
3 Some training
4 Experienced fighter
5 Master of a single form of combat
6 Master of several forms of combat
7 Master of all forms of combat

DURABILITY
Ability to resist or recover from bodily injury

1 Weak
2 Normal
3 Enhanced
4 Regenerative
5 Bulletproof
6 Superhuman
7 Virtually indestructible

SPEED
Ability to move over land by running or flight

1 Below normal
2 Normal
3 Superhuman: peak range: 700 MPH
4 Speed of sound: Mach-1
5 Supersonic: Mach-2 through Orbital Velocity
6 Speed of light: 186,000 miles per second
7 Warp speed: transcending light speed

BETTY BRANT

REAL NAME: Betty Brant
KNOWN ALIASES: Betty Brant-Leeds
IDENTITY: No dual identity
OCCUPATION: Investigative journalist; former secretary/assistant, cultist
CITIZENSHIP: U.S.A.
PLACE OF BIRTH: Philadelphia, Pennsylvania
MARITAL STATUS: Widowed
KNOWN RELATIVES: Mrs. Brant (mother, deceased), Bennett (brother, deceased), Ned Leeds (Hobgoblin, husband, deceased)
GROUP AFFILIATION: Daily Bugle staff, Jameson News Digest staff, Students of Love
EDUCATION: High-school dropout
FIRST APPEARANCE: Amazing Spider-Man Vol. 1 #4 (1963)

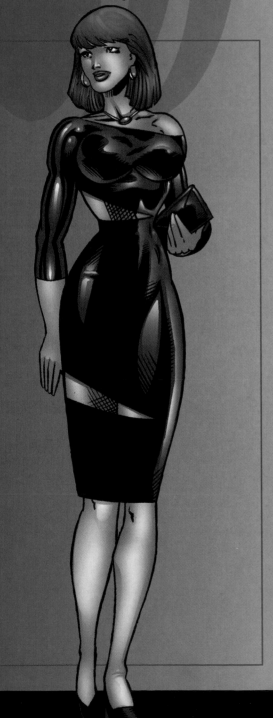

HISTORY: Raised by a single mother and often disappointed by her weak-willed brother Bennett, young Betty Brant found herself drawn to strong men. While still in high school, she dated university student Gordon Savinski, a fast-living friend of her older brother. Gordon and the Brant siblings were a chummy trio for some time, but Savinski's wild and reckless ways gradually estranged Betty and endangered Bennett. When Gordon and Bennett incurred a huge gambling debt to mobster Blackie Gaxton, Savinski callously abandoned Bennett, leaving the Brants to face the consequences. Gaxton's thugs came to the Brant home, and Mrs. Brant suffered permanent brain damage in the resultant scuffle.

Forced to grow up fast, Betty dropped out of school so she could work to pay off her mother's medical bills and her brother's gambling debts. Betty's mother had been the personal secretary to J. Jonah Jameson, the tyrannical publisher of the Daily Bugle newspaper. Perhaps out of sympathy for Betty or out of loyalty to Mrs. Brant, Jameson offered Betty her mother's job at the Bugle, and Betty accepted. Patient, hardworking and capable, Betty proved to be one of the very few secretaries who ever managed to meet Jameson's demanding standards while tolerating the publisher's prickly personality.

Over time, a mutual attraction developed between Betty and young Bugle photographer Peter Parker, secretly the costumed hero Spider-Man. Peter bore a striking resemblance to Gordon Savinski; but unlike Gordon, Parker was quiet, serious, moral, responsible—in short, he seemed safe. Peter first noticed Betty when she stuck up for Peter's alter ego during one of Jameson's anti-Spider-Man tirades. Later, Peter and Betty grew closer when they shared an intimate chat in the wrecked Bugle offices after an attack by the Vulture. Before long, they were a couple, and Betty became Peter's first real girlfriend.

Intensely danger-shy after Gordon, Betty worried incessantly about the hazards of Peter's job, which often required him to photograph criminals and super-villains in action. When the criminal Enforcers came after Betty to collect on the Brant family's remaining debts, Betty tried to protect Peter by leaving town, then tried to wipe out the last of her brother's debts by recruiting Doctor Octopus to break Blackie Gaxton out of prison. When Spider-Man intervened, Gaxton was recaptured, but not before Bennett sacrificed himself to shield Betty from a stray bullet. A devastated Betty blamed Spider-Man for the tragedy at first, and Peter decided he could never share the secret of his double identity with her. Betty returned to her job at the Bugle, but found little peace there; she was soon menaced in turn by Doctor Octopus, the Sinister Six and her old boyfriend Gordon, who had become the superhuman mob enforcer Terrier. Spider-Man defeated all these foes, but his role in her brother's death still made her wary of him.

Deeply insecure, Betty was often jealous of Peter's female friends, and she sometimes assumed that the oft-absent Peter was two-timing her, or had simply grown tired of her. Betty responded by dating Ned Leeds, a new reporter at the Bugle who only had eyes for her. For a time, Betty was romantically linked to both Peter and Ned while she tried to sort out her feelings. Eventually, a smitten Ned proposed marriage. Betty was still in love with Peter, but she craved the stability she thought Ned represented. While Betty stalled for time to make up her mind, Peter decided Betty would be better off without Spider-Man in her life and acted boorishly in an effort to drive her away altogether. Finally, seeing Peter injured after an encounter with Doctor Octopus, Betty realized she couldn't bear to love another man who lived dangerously. She left town again to think things through, and by the time she returned, she and Peter

came to the mutual realization that the romantic spark between them was gone. Happily reunited with Leeds, Betty accepted Ned's proposal.

Engaged for years, Ned and Betty finally got married despite the interference of the costumed criminal Mirage, who tried to rob the wedding guests until he was subdued by Spider-Man. Jameson sent the couple to Paris on a "working honeymoon" to establish Ned as a European foreign correspondent; however, with Ned constantly off on assignment, Betty grew lonely and bitter. Separating from Ned and returning to New York, she sought comfort with Peter, who was tempted to rekindle their old romance; but when an angry Ned arrived to fight for Betty, Peter pretended he wasn't really interested in her and declared he never wanted to see either of them again, hoping this might bring the couple back together. Stung, Betty and Ned went away together to rebuild their marriage.

Ned continued to throw himself into his work as a Bugle reporter, a situation made much worse when the criminal Hobgoblin (Roderick Kingsley) secretly brainwashed Ned into acting as his accomplice and occasional stand-in. Ned became increasingly angry, violent and unstable. Betty began cheating on him with old friend Flash Thompson, prompting Ned to frame Flash for Hobgoblin's crimes. When Flash broke out of jail and sought refuge with Betty, Ned-as-Hobgoblin attacked Flash, and Betty saw Ned unmasked during the struggle. By this time, Kingsley had come to regard Leeds as a liability, and leaked word of Ned's double identity to the underworld. Hobgoblin's criminal rival Jack O' Lantern (Jason Macendale) hired the Foreigner to kill Ned, who was murdered by the Foreigner's agents. Macendale would adopt Ned's gear to become the new Hobgoblin, though he would eventually be murdered by Kingsley. Betty, already reeling from the revelation of Ned's double life, had a complete breakdown after Ned's death. She became delusional and prone to hallucinations.

The broken Betty was easy prey for the Students of Love, a cult of brainwashed pawns led by the charismatic Teacher, a charlatan and supposed faith healer who stripped his followers of all their possessions. Spider-Man, Flash and Reverend Tolliver joined forces to free Betty, and the cult was destroyed in a fire. Deprogrammed and restored to relative mental health by Tolliver, but having lost all her belongings to the cult, Betty moved in with Flash. She reached a turning point during the demonic invasion of New York known as Inferno, when demons posing as Spider-Man and the late Ned attacked Flash's home; Betty found new inner strength and used it to save herself and Thompson from the demons, though Thompson's home was destroyed in the process. Later, when the emotion-controlling villain Mister Fear (Alan Fagan) tried to manipulate Betty into killing Spider-Man, she resisted and helped defeat Fagan; in the process, she began to understand and overcome the fear of loneliness at the root of her desperate attachments to the men in her life.

Betty and Flash drifted apart, and Betty began a long process of radically reinventing herself. Easing out of secretarial work and into reporting, Brant became an investigative journalist for the Bugle, eventually tracking the killers of her husband. Studying martial arts and marksmanship, a heavily-armed Betty even managed to hold her own against the Foreigner's forces alongside Spider-Man, uncovering more details regarding the circumstances of Ned's death in the process. Less successful was her investigation of the F.A.C.A.D.E. affair, during which the high-tech F.A.C.A.D.E. battle armor was stolen and used to murder Betty's colleague, Bugle photographer Lance Bannon. Working together, Spider-Man and Betty managed to defeat F.A.C.A.D.E. and wreck the armor, but

its wearer escaped and was never identified—though one of the suspects, industrialist Archer Bryce, managed to arouse a romantic as well as professional interest in Betty. Nothing ever came of the Brant-Bryce attraction, though, nor did anything lasting emerge from Flash's attempts to rekindle their romance. Similarly doomed was Betty's brief romantic interest in Ben Reilly, who was murdered by the Green Goblin.

Betty continues to work at the Bugle under the direction of her longtime bosses, Jameson and editor-in-chief Joe "Robbie" Robertson. Her notable friends and colleagues there have included secretary Glory Grant (who took over Betty's old job), city editor Kathyrn "Kate" Cushing and fellow reporters such as Ben Urich, Joy Mercado, Jessica Jones and young Kat Farrell, whom Betty has mentored to some extent. Brant's investigative reporting has helped crack a number of important criminal cases over the years. Her greatest and most personal triumph was exposing businessman Roderick Kingsley as the true Hobgoblin, finally clearing Ned's name in the process.

Art by Steve Ditko

HEIGHT: 5'7"
WEIGHT: 125 lbs.
EYES: Brown
HAIR: Brown

ABILITIES: Betty is a highly capable investigative reporter. She has become proficient in martial arts and marksmanship, and is well versed in a variety of firearms.

POWER GRID	1	2	3	4	5	6	7
INTELLIGENCE							
STRENGTH							
SPEED							
DURABILITY							
ENERGY PROJECTION							
FIGHTING SKILLS							

CARRION

REAL NAME: Clone of Professor Miles Warren; Malcolm McBride; Dr. William Allen

KNOWN ALIASES: None

IDENTITY: (Warren clone) No dual identity; (McBride) Publicly known; (Allen) Known to S.H.I.E.L.D.

OCCUPATION: (McBride) Former graduate student; (Allen) Former S.H.I.E.L.D. scientist

CITIZENSHIP: (McBride, Allen) U.S.A.

PLACE OF BIRTH: (Warren clone) The Jackal's lab in New York City; (McBride) Astoria, New York; (Allen) Annapolis, Maryland

MARITAL STATUS: Single

KNOWN RELATIVES: (McBride) Beatrice Martha McBride (mother)

GROUP AFFILIATION: (McBride) Former member of "Maximum Carnage"; (Allen) Former S.H.I.E.L.D. employee

EDUCATION: (Warren clone) Possessed Professor Warren's knowledge; (McBride) Graduate studies in Biology; (Allen) Ph.Ds in Biochemistry and Microbiology

FIRST APPEARANCE: (Warren clone) Peter Parker: The Spectacular Spider-Man #25 (1978); (McBride) Spectacular Spider-Man Vol. 2 #149 (1989); (Allen) Spider-Man: Dead Man's Hand #1 (1997)

HISTORY: Professor Miles Warren created a virus at the High Evolutionary's lab that was intended to turn the animal-like New Men fully human but which turned them into living corpses instead. Warren, as the insane Jackal, later modified this virus with his own genetic material and combined it with his own cell sample in a "clone casket," hoping to create a creature that could poison everyone except clones. The Jackal, however, was apparently killed and never returned to his lab. The casket remained closed until Randy Vale, a former undergraduate student of Warren's, opened it and Carrion emerged—a Warren clone/genetic virus hybrid with the Jackal's desire to gain revenge upon Spider-Man for the death of Gwen Stacy and, as he soon discovered, the "death" of Warren himself. Under Carrion's guidance using technology from Warren's lab, Vale assumed the costumed role of Darter and became a willing partner in Carrion's schemes in exchange for power. Possessing Warren's knowledge of Spider-Man's identity, Carrion offered his services to the Maggia but was rejected.

On his own, Carrion stalked Peter Parker and eventually faced Spider-Man at the Empire State University gym where he abandoned Darter and incapacitated the web-slinger with his mysterious red dust, taking him back to Warren's lab and revealing his clone origins. He injected some of Spider-Man's blood into a primitive amoebic clone ancestor of Peter Parker, creating a "Spider-Amoeba;" a large shifting organic mass with spider-powers that began crushing the chained-up wall-crawler. Darter burst in demanding that he should receive Spider-Man's powers; Carrion turned on him and killed him with the red dust but not before a stray gunshot from Darter's weapon freed Spider-Man. In the ensuing fight involving Carrion, Spider-Man, the amoeba and the White Tiger (Hector Ayala), a fire broke out, distracting Carrion and allowing Spider-Man to throw the amoeba at him. Perhaps because of its clone casket origins, the amoeba negated Carrion's genetic powers and consumed him, just before the fiery building collapsed upon them both.

Sometime later, in an effort to discredit the believed-dead Warren with the worshipful New Men who had started a Cult of the Jackal, the High Evolutionary planted a false journal that claimed Warren never cloned humans at all but rather used genetic viruses to rewrite DNA. He left a sample of the Carrion virus to "prove" the point, which was found by Malcolm McBride, a science graduate student at ESU who bore Peter Parker a grudge for losing a research grant to him. The virus infected Malcolm and another Carrion was born. The virus carried Warren's memories so Carrion initially believed he was a clone and again set out to avenge Gwen Stacy's death. However, since the memories stemmed from the time Warren modified the virus, Carrion did not know that the Professor was "dead." When Spider-Man lured him to

Warren's grave, Carrion was so astonished that the wall-crawler was able to easily defeat him. Spidey turned Carrion over to the Vault, still not knowing who he was though he soon deduced he had to be the absent Malcolm McBride. Peter kept this knowledge to himself, and began working on finding a cure for the Carrion virus, eventually enlisting Reed Richards' help. The Hobgoblin (Jason Macendale) stole Richards' notes, and learning of Carrion, freed him from a Vault transport. Then, in a bid to win Carrion's loyalty, Hobgoblin led him home where Carrion confronted Malcolm McBride's mother, Beatrice. Spider-Man interceded until ambushed by the Hobgoblin while Carrion, tormented by conflicting memories of a past life, put himself in front of a thrown pumpkin bomb to save the mother he dimly remembered. It ignited a gas main, and he and Hobgoblin fell flaming into the sewers.

Carrion rose again during the "Maximum Carnage" affair, and was adopted by Shriek as a "son" into their twisted "family." His mind was a shambles but his low-level telepathy was partially responsible for many of the riots that occurred until the device called the Alpha Magni-Illuminizor drove the Carrion virus into remission, whereupon McBride was turned over to Ravencroft Institute for observation. He had regained his memories, but the guilt over what he had done as Carrion was destroying him. Dr. Ashley Kafka mistakenly took him to see Shriek who broke her restraints and kidnapped her "son." Shriek used her abilities to re-energize the Carrion virus, turning Malcolm into Carrion once more. Carrion, however, had conflicting memories of Shriek and his real mother, so Shriek took him to see Beatrice McBride and demanded that he kill her. Carrion refused, becoming so conflicted that he turned his death touch inward, but Shriek used her powers to send the virus into remission once more. She became infected herself, but her powers left the virus inert. Malcolm, his mind in a delicate state, returned to Ravencroft. There, he was called in Judas Traveller's mock trial to accuse Peter Parker of inducing him to experiment with the Carrion virus.

Meanwhile, the revived Jackal stole the virus from Shriek's body and used it to create a new version with which he infected and killed the population of Springville, Pennsylvania. Upon the Jackal's subsequent death, S.H.I.E.L.D. assigned Dr. William Allen to study the corpse. He discovered a hidden pouch containing a sample of the virus and deliberately infected himself, becoming Carrion. Though infected with Professor Warren's memories, Allen proved strong enough to resist, learning to control crowds with his red dust and releasing his "zombie plague" on Broadway. With his son one of the victims of the plague, the Tinkerer agreed to teleport Spider-Man to Wundagore Mountain to seek help from the High Evolutionary. Though he admitted his part in the creation of the Carrion virus, the High Evolutionary dismissed this as beneath him and sent Spider-Man back. Instead Spider-Man retrieved the modified journal of Warren's research, hoping that S.H.I.E.L.D would be able to develop a cure from it. In a subsequent battle, Professor Warren's memories began to reassert themselves and fought with Allen for control of the body, which allowed Spider-Man to defeat them. The High Evolutionary aided S.H.I.E.L.D. in finding a cure for the zombie plague, but was unable to find a cure for Allen himself who still resides in stasis in a secure S.H.I.E.L.D. facility.

HEIGHT: 5'10"
WEIGHT: 175 lbs.
EYES: Yellow
HAIR: None

DISTINGUISHING FEATURES: Pallid yellow skin, odor of decay

SUPERHUMAN POWERS: Carrion can teleport over short distances leaving behind a cloud of brimstone, telekinetically control and decay organic matter (including Spider-Man's webbing), ignite fires and induce death with a touch, levitate, generate repelling energy, become intangible, and regenerate rapidly. He has low-level telepathy (stronger in Allen than the others) and is immune to certain forms of detection including Spider-Man's spider-sense. The Carrion virus is strangely non-communicable. Once it has a host, it becomes dormant and cannot be transmitted to others. Separated from a host body, however, it is extremely contagious. Despite the appearance of being "undead," the virus does not kill its host.

ABILITIES: All Carrions possessed the knowledge of Professor Miles Warren. The Warren clone demonstrated knowledge of mechanics sufficient to develop a flight suit and hand-held stun laser for Darter.

PARAPHERNALIA: All Carrions used Red Dust of Death (or Decay). Organic in nature, it causes pain, unconsciousness, or a choking death, sometimes demonstrating acidic and flesh-eating properties.

POWER GRID	1	2	3	4	5	6	7
INTELLIGENCE							
STRENGTH							
SPEED							
DURABILITY							
ENERGY PROJECTION							
FIGHTING SKILLS							

CHAMELEON

REAL NAME: Dmitri Anatoly Smerdyakov Kravinoff
KNOWN ALIASES: Dr. Ashley Kafka, Dr. Turner, J. Jonah Jameson, Torpedo, Rick Jones, Dr. Henry Pym, Peter Parker, Captain George Stacy, Dr. Robert Bruce Banner, General Thaddeus Ross, Captain America, Kraven the Hunter, Spider-Man, Professor Newton, others
IDENTITY: Secret
OCCUPATION: Ex-New York Crimelord, ex-Soviet spy
CITIZENSHIP: Russia
PLACE OF BIRTH: Russia

MARITAL STATUS: Single
KNOWN RELATIVES: Kravinoff patriarch (father, deceased), mother (unnamed), Sergei Kravinoff (Kraven the Hunter, half-brother, deceased), Vladimir Kravinoff (The Grim Hunter, nephew, deceased), Alyosha Kravinoff (Kraven the Hunter, nephew, deceased), Ned Tannengarden (nephew, deceased)
GROUP AFFILIATION: Sinister Twelve, Sinister Six
EDUCATION: Unrevealed
FIRST APPEARANCE: Amazing Spider-Man Vol. 1 #1 (1963)

HISTORY: Dmitri Smerdyakov was the illegitimate son of the patriarch of the Russian Kravinoff family and a servant. His only friend growing up was Joe Cord, an American boy who once saved his life while his half-brother Sergei, the legitimate heir, and his father treated him with contempt and brutality. This scarred Dmitri so deeply that he repressed his very identity and came to believe he had been friends with Sergei instead. His loss of self led him to become a master of disguise and a Soviet spy. Initially without super-powers, the Chameleon relied on his skills and a mixture of costumes and make-up to conceal his identity. He wore a multi-pocket disguise vest in which he kept the materials he would need to mask himself at short notice.

In his first known appearance, Chameleon impersonated Professor Newton, a government scientist, to steal half of some missile defense plans. He then sent a message to Spider-Man, electronically contacting him via his spider-sense, requesting a meeting and implying a profitable venture. Chameleon disguised himself as Spider-Man, though, and stole the second half of the plans, making his escape just as the real wall-crawler showed up. Spidey was at first framed for the theft but managed to bring Chameleon back to the police. Chameleon disguised himself as a police officer, scaring Spider-Man off by siccing the other cops on him. Spidey left the scene, thinking he had failed, not realizing that he had torn Chameleon's police uniform, allowing the cops to see the phony Spider-Man outfit underneath.

Chameleon was deported back to Russia, but returned soon after, having given up being a spy, and turned instead to a life of crime. Stymied again by the wall-crawler, Chameleon invited his half-brother, now known as Kraven the Hunter, to America to capture Spider-Man. The duo worked together, with Chameleon even dressing as Kraven to fool Spidey. Ultimately, though, both were defeated and deported by freighter where they bribed a sailor to set them loose in a lifeboat near Long Island. They came ashore right by Tony Stark's munitions factory and Kraven was quickly captured by Iron Man. Chameleon concealed his presence but decided to prove his superiority over Kraven by defeating the armored Avenger. Disguising himself as Captain America, Chameleon contacted Iron Man and convinced him that he was the real Cap and that the Cap at Avengers Mansion was really Chameleon. Iron Man and Cap fought it out until Giant-Man (Henry Pym) captured Chameleon and revealed the truth.

Chameleon quickly escaped prison and went to work for the Leader as his top lieutenant. The Leader sent him to New Mexico to learn the secrets of the Hulk. There, Chameleon impersonated General Thaddeus "Thunderbolt" Ross and Dr. Bruce Banner, stole a grenade-size gamma bomb and took Betty Ross as a hostage. Realizing he couldn't escape, Chameleon set off the bomb, which was smothered by the Hulk, dampening the blast. Though caught in the rubble, Chameleon survived and escaped, remaining in the Leader's employ until his boss' supposed death.

Chameleon next encountered Spider-Man after taking the place of Captain George Stacy who had been hired to protect a valuable art exhibit at the Midtown Museum. Peter Parker and Stacy's daughter Gwen were there and noticed that the Captain didn't seem to recognize them. After the exhibit was stolen and Stacy found drugged back at his apartment, Peter realized the Chameleon must have been involved. He persuaded Joe Robertson to plant a story in the Daily Bugle about a transfer of bonds and trapped Chameleon trying to steal them. Chameleon tried to escape through disguise but made the mistake of impersonating the one person Spider-Man knew to be a fake: Peter Parker.

The terrorist organization Hydra arranged for Chameleon's escape from prison so that he could impersonate Dr. Henry Pym and steal Pym's research combating their biological weapon Virus Nine. Pym, as Ant-Man, teamed with the Hulk and thwarted Chameleon, though it appeared at the time that Chameleon had murdered Bruce Banner. Later, Chameleon impersonated Spider-Man, attempting to free his friend Joe Cord from the New York Men's Detention Center. Accidentally striking the Hulk with his car, Chameleon quickly disguised himself as Hulk's friend Rick Jones and convinced the green goliath to break Joe out of jail. However, in a battle with police, Joe protected Chameleon from gunfire and was killed.

Designing a new costume that could instantly duplicate any clothing, Chameleon went back to crime. He was pursued after a jewel heist by Torpedo (Brock Jones) and Daredevil. His quick-changes failed to help him since Daredevil tracked him by his heartbeat. His next costume innovation used a holographic belt that stored the appearances of people he came into contact with and allowed him to take on their look. In one encounter, he managed to convince people that Spidey had attacked an old lady, leaving the wall-crawler's newly restored reputation in tatters. Later he obtained further powers by using a serum that could let him change his appearance at will. This liquid actually allowed his skin to be flexible enough to shift its appearance into any disguise Chameleon desired. He tried to kidnap a top scientist but was again thwarted by Spider-Man.

Chameleon then set his sights on ruling the New York underworld. He kidnapped J. Jonah Jameson, impersonating him in a long-term bid to influence events through the Bugle, and formed an alliance with Hammerhead. The Kingpin of Crime was embroiled in a power struggle with the werewolf Lobo Brothers. Chameleon and Hammerhead tried to instigate a full-on gang war, from which they would pick up the pieces. Chameleon, posing as Jameson, injected Spider-Man with a potion that left him unconscious for several days. Recovering, Spider-Man went after Jameson and discovered he was the Chameleon all along. Hammerhead and Chameleon's plans continued as they ambushed the Lobo Brothers and Kingpin during peace talks. After carving up the city into territories they each agreed to control, their alliance collapsed and their influence waned.

Soon after, Chameleon took the guise of Doctor Turner and persuaded Spider-Man to subject himself to a machine that supposedly would analyze his spider-powers. The machine, designed by the Tinkerer, ended up temporarily removing the wall-crawler's abilities instead. After discussing it with Mary Jane, Spider-Man decided to have his powers removed permanently. Now powerless, Spidey was attacked by Tarantula (Luis Alvarez) and Scorpion and needed the Black Cat's help to survive. Changing his mind, Spider-Man searched for Doctor Turner, eventually realizing he was actually Chameleon, by which time his powers returned naturally.

The Chameleon's next big plan was set up by the Green Goblin (Harry Osborn) before his death. The Goblin persuaded Chameleon to create two robots that would appear to be Peter Parker's dead parents in an effort to get Peter to tell them who Spider-Man really was. The Goblin already knew Spidey's identity but wanted to mess with Peter's head so he convinced Chameleon that Parker, due to all the photos he had taken, was sure to know Spidey's identity. When Spider-Man discovered the fraud, he went crazy with rage and disappointment at losing his parents again. The Chameleon escaped to Kraven's old mansion while Spider-Man hunted him down. Faced with a more fearsome and vicious Spider-Man than ever before, Chameleon's repressed memories of his unhappy childhood with Sergei returned and he fell into a coma-like state.

The Chameleon was taken to Ravencroft Institute but escaped after assuming the identity of his doctor, Ashley Kafka. He kidnapped Spider-Man and unmasked him, finally understanding why Spider-Man had been so mad after discovering the robot parents. Chameleon imprisoned Peter and convinced him he was a writer named Herbert Smith who was incarcerated in an insane asylum. Chameleon then took on the role of Peter himself but was foiled by Mary Jane, armed with a baseball bat, who knew her husband too well to fall for the impersonation. Escaping, he was shot by his nephew Alyosha Kravinoff, who said there could only be one Kravinoff in the world. Chameleon again barely survived. Later, he arranged to meet Spider-Man on top of the Brooklyn Bridge, wanting to make up for his crimes. There, he tried to commit suicide by jumping. Spider-Man blamed himself for this apparent death but Chameleon somehow survived.

Chameleon was a new addition during a gathering of the Sinister Six, formed as part of an elaborate, yet ultimately failed plot to destroy Spider-Man and gain immeasurable wealth by destroying the world's monetary system. He was later recommitted to Ravencroft. In Chameleon's twisted mind he now believes himself to be his half-brother, Kraven The Hunter. This didn't stop him from joining Norman Osborn's Sinister Twelve, however.

HEIGHT: Unrevealed
WEIGHT: Unrevealed
EYES: Brown
HAIR: Unrevealed

SUPERHUMAN POWERS: The Chameleon can instantly change his appearance and imitate others so convincingly that practically no one can tell the Chameleon and his victim apart. His natural talents are now augmented with a face-changing serum.

PARAPHERNALIA: Masks, multi-pocket disguise vest, special costume that instantly duplicates clothes, holographic belt

POWER GRID	1	2	3	4	5	6	7
INTELLIGENCE							
STRENGTH							
SPEED							
DURABILITY							
ENERGY PROJECTION							
FIGHTING SKILLS							

JEAN DeWOLFF

REAL NAME: Jean DeWolff
KNOWN ALIASES: None
IDENTITY: No dual identity
OCCUPATION: Police Captain
CITIZENSHIP: U.S.A.
PLACE OF BIRTH: New York City, New York
MARITAL STATUS: Single
KNOWN RELATIVES: Phillip DeWolff (father), Brian DeWolff (The Wraith, brother), Celia DeWolff Weatherby (mother), Carl Weatherby (stepfather)
GROUP AFFILIATION: New York City police
EDUCATION: College educated
FIRST APPEARANCE: Marvel Team-Up Vol. 1 #48 (1976)

HISTORY: Jean DeWolff was one of the first law officials to openly come out in support of Spider-Man. She was an individualist in the police force, wearing '30s-style fashions and even driving her own '30s roadster. Jean and her brother Brian were quite close but she never got along with her father, Phillip, who was an ex-police commissioner. Phillip resented having a daughter, which caused problems in his marriage to Jean's mother, Celia. Six months after Jean was born, her parents split with Brian going to live with his father and Jean with her mother. Phillip was so incensed he once even told Jean she had killed her mother just by being born.

Four years later, her mother remarried another cop—Carl Weatherby—but Jean kept DeWolff as her surname. Jean adored her new stepdad and wanted to follow in his footsteps. As she became more and more successful, her real father became annoyed that Jean had earned a police captain's job.

Brian, also a cop, had been presumed dead after being shot but Phillip stole the body and secretly had surgeons operate, giving Brian superpowers. When Phillip discovered the surgeons were criminals, he fought back, getting caught in a revitalizing ray that melded his mind to Brian's, allowing Phillip to control his son's body. Brian became The Wraith and Phillip sent him to kill Jean but was thwarted by Spider-Man and Iron Man. Doctor Strange restored Brian to health and Phillip was jailed for The Wraith's crimes.

Shortly afterwards, as Spider-Man and the Human Torch battled the Super Skrull, Jean's soft spot for Spidey began to emerge and she developed a crush on him. Jean showed a few hints of jealousy at Spider-Man's closeness to Black Cat but always remained focused on her job, even going so far as to arrange a pardon for her rival. Jean also had moments of incredible bravery—once storming into a Maggia mob party during a police raid and, later, using her car to swerve into Doctor Octopus.

Sadly, soon after, Jean was murdered by the Sin Eater who turned out to be her colleague and former lover, Sergeant Stan Carter. Carter's mind had been blighted by the death of his partner and he decided Jean must be killed because she upheld the legal system. It was only after she was killed that Spider-Man realized how attached he had become to her. Carter was eventually arrested due to the joint efforts of Spidey and Daredevil.

HEIGHT: 5'8"
WEIGHT: 135 lbs.
EYES: Green
HAIR: Strawberry blonde

ABILITIES: Jean was an accomplished police captain and an excellent markswoman.

POWER GRID	1	2	3	4	5	6	7
INTELLIGENCE							
STRENGTH							
SPEED							
DURABILITY							
ENERGY PROJECTION							
FIGHTING SKILLS							

DOPPELGANGER

HISTORY: The Doppelganger began life as a living fractal, a geometric pattern in the Dimension of Manifestations, able to assume the forms and attributes of any being, real or abstract. When the mysterious Magus set out to obtain the vast power of the Infinity Gauntlet, he contracted the ruling fractal, Prime Manifester Anthropomorpho, to transform several young fractals into monstrous versions of Earth's super heroes; the Doppelganger was one such creation, based upon Spider-Man. It and its brethren were sent to Earth to attack the heroes in the so-called Infinity War. The Doppelganger interrupted a fight between Spider-Man and the Hobgoblin, who impaled the creature upon a fence.

Following the battle, the Doppelganger was retrieved by the demonic Demogoblin, who unknowingly infused it with supernatural energy, enabling it to remain in the Earth dimension following the Magus' defeat. Demogoblin directed the Doppelganger in a grudge against Hobgoblin, whom the altruistic Spider-Man protected. The foursome's fight brought them to another battle where the supernatural heroes Ghost Rider (Dan Ketch) and Blaze were fighting a group of demonic Deathspawn and Spider-Man's murderous nemesis Venom. Both the Doppelganger and Demogoblin were subsequently pulled underground by the Deathspawn, with two Deathspawn briefly taking up silent residence within the Doppelganger's body.

The disoriented Doppelganger wandered New York for days before being attacked by the psychotic Carnage, who mistook the creature for their mutual enemy Spider-Man; however, Carnage's companion, the equally insane Shriek, took a liking to the Doppelganger, and the deranged couple introduced their new "son" to the "pleasure" of random murder. During their spree, the three were joined by Demogoblin and Carrion (Malcolm McBride); they also fought Spider-Man, the Black Cat, Cloak and Dagger, Venom, Morbius, and others. The Doppelganger became devoted to Shriek; when Carnage attacked her for rebellious behavior, it sprang to her defense, but Carnage gutted it and kicked it to the street several stories below. Carnage and the others were defeated shortly afterward, but whether the Doppelganger was truly slain remains to be seen.

REAL NAME: Unrevealed, possibly inapplicable
KNOWN ALIASES: The Spider-Man Doppelganger, Spider-Doppelganger, Mindless One
IDENTITY: Unknown to the general populace of Earth
OCCUPATION: Pawn
CITIZENSHIP: None
PLACE OF BIRTH: The Dimension of Manifestations
MARITAL STATUS: Inapplicable
KNOWN RELATIVES: Anthropomorpho (creator); Hellspawn, Moonshade, many other doppelgangers (brethren)
GROUP AFFILIATION: "Maximum Carnage," Magus' doppelgangers; operative of Demogoblin
EDUCATION: Limited mental conditioning, slight capacity for behavioral changes
FIRST APPEARANCE: Infinity War #1 (1992)

HEIGHT: 6'5"
WEIGHT: 230 lbs.
EYES: White
HAIR: None

SUPERHUMAN POWERS: The Doppelganger possessed superhuman strength, speed, and agility. It could climb walls with its claws, which could also rend most substances, as could its teeth. It could shoot razor-sharp webbing from its hands. Its innate ability to reshape its body in a virtually infinite manner enabled it to recover from all but the most severe injuries. Roughly as intelligent as a wild beast, it was incapable of speech but achieved some level of learned response and primitive emotional attachment.

POWER GRID	1	2	3	4	5	6	7
INTELLIGENCE							
STRENGTH							
SPEED							
DURABILITY							
ENERGY PROJECTION							
FIGHTING SKILLS							

Art by Mark Bagley

FLY

REAL NAME: Richard Deacon
KNOWN ALIASES: Human Fly
IDENTITY: Known to authorities
OCCUPATION: Professional criminal
CITIZENSHIP: U.S.A. with a criminal record
PLACE OF BIRTH: Newark, New Jersey
MARITAL STATUS: Single
KNOWN RELATIVES: None
GROUP AFFILIATION: None
EDUCATION: Unrevealed
FIRST APPEARANCE: Amazing Spider-Man Annual #10 (1976)

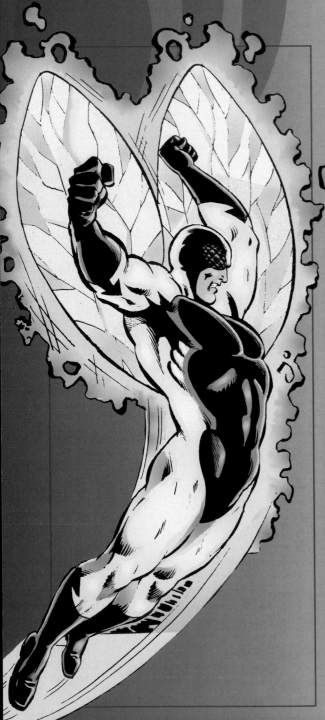

HISTORY: Richard Deacon, a small-time criminal out on parole, was shot by the police and left for dead after his unsuccessful kidnapping attempt was foiled by Spider-Man. Stumbling into the laboratory of Dr. Harlan Stillwell (whose brother Farley created the Scorpion for J. Jonah Jameson), Deacon coerced the scientist into saving his life. Overhearing an offer Jameson made with Stillwell to fund the creation of a new super hero, Deacon insisted he be the subject of the experiment. Stillwell imprinted the genetic coding of a common fly onto Deacon, empowering him and healing him of his bullet wounds. Deacon killed Stillwell and used his newfound powers to further his criminal ambitions. He first used Jameson as bait to get revenge on Spider-Man, but his inexperience was no match for the web-slinger and he was defeated.

Sometime later, the Fly attacked Spider-Man who was handcuffed to Jameson with a bomb. The Fly hurled the two from a rooftop and left them for dead. Once freed from the shackle, Spider-Man tried to stop the Fly from stealing an art exhibit, but the villain knocked him down and escaped. Soon afterwards, however, the police caught the Fly using S.H.I.E.L.D. equipment.

Traveling to San Francisco, the Fly sought out Dr. Karl Malus, a criminally inclined scientist. Malus planned to augment Deacon's powers with a blood transfusion from Spider-Woman (Jessica Drew). The Fly attacked her unsuccessfully. Malus then suggested that he kidnap her associate, Scotty MacDowell. Spider-Woman followed the Fly to Malus' headquarters and, after a brief fight, defeated him. Afterwards, Malus used some of the Fly's DNA to temporarily mutate Scotty into the similarly powered Hornet. The Fly subsequently battled Moon Knight, leaving the hero temporarily paralyzed, and again tried to seek revenge against Jameson and Spider-Man. Partnered with the Black Cat, Spider-Man once more defeated the Fly. Over time, Deacon's mutation increased; he grew antennae and became more fly-like in his behavior. After escaping from a mental institution, Deacon was killed by a Scourge of the Underworld vigilante.

HEIGHT: 5'11"
WEIGHT: 200 lbs.
EYES: Red (originally blue)
HAIR: Coarse brown (originally red)

DISTINGUISHING FEATURES: The Fly had huge, lidless, compound eyes, and transparent, membrane-like wings.

SUPERHUMAN POWERS: The Fly could lift 3 tons, had 3.5 times faster-than- average human speed and reflexes, and 3 times the endurance of an Olympic marathon runner. He could stick to most surfaces due to adhesive secretions in his digits. He could see 360 degrees around, preventing him from being surprised from behind. He could fly at 69 m.p.h. for up to 6 hours. His wings could create winds up to 190 m.p.h. and shockwaves of great concussive force.

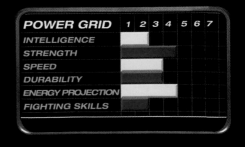

POWER GRID	1	2	3	4	5	6	7
INTELLIGENCE							
STRENGTH							
SPEED							
DURABILITY							
ENERGY PROJECTION							
FIGHTING SKILLS							

FREDERICK FOSWELL

HISTORY: Frederick Foswell was a short, slight, timid reporter for the Daily Bugle. Tired of being subservient to J. Jonah Jameson, Foswell created the masked identity of the Big Man, using built-up shoes, a padded jacket and an amplifier to disguise his voice. He then used his reporter's skills and contacts to join with the trio known as the Enforcers and unite all the New York City mobs. His disguise was so effective that even Spider-Man never figured out who the Big Man really was, but it was the web-slinger's intervention that tipped the police off to Foswell's secret and led to his arrest.

While in prison, Foswell was the cellmate of Professor Mendel Stromm. Released and vowing to go straight, Foswell was rehired by J. Jonah Jameson. Initially suspected by Spider-Man of being either the Green Goblin or the Crime Master, Foswell was actually frequenting underworld hangouts wearing a latex mask of a man with an eye patch, allowing him to create a whole new identity: the stoolie known as Patch. In his capacity as reporter and stoolie, Foswell deduced the Crime Master's identity and tipped off the police, resulting in the Crime Master's death in a shootout. He also worked with police against the Cat Burglar and told Spider-Man about a planned robbery by the Master Planner's men. He became such a trustworthy reporter that Spider-Man began tipping him off to his fights. As Patch, he became one of the first to discover that Peter Parker was Spider-Man, though he was outwitted—by a fake conversation between Peter and Spidey followed by the departure of a web-slinging web-dummy—into thinking the super hero and photographer had a secret working relationship instead.

Later, when it seemed that Spider-Man had quit and the Kingpin of Crime was reorganizing the underworld, Foswell reverted to his criminal ways. Failing to regain his place at the head of the mobs, he settled for becoming the Kingpin's first lieutenant. But when the Kingpin's men tried to kill J. Jonah Jameson, Foswell could not stand by and let his benefactor come to harm. He was gunned down by the Kingpin's men while protecting Jameson and died a hero.

The identity of the Big Man was later used by Foswell's daughter Janice, but she was tragically killed by her fiancé, the new Crime Master.

REAL NAME: Frederick Foswell
KNOWN ALIASES: Patch, the Big Man
IDENTITY: (Patch) Secret; (Big Man) Publicly known
OCCUPATION: Reporter, professional criminal
CITIZENSHIP: U.S.A. with a criminal record
PLACE OF BIRTH: Queens, New York
MARITAL STATUS: Married
KNOWN RELATIVES: Janice Foswell (daugher, Big Man, deceased), unnamed wife
GROUP AFFILIATION: Daily Bugle, the Enforcers
EDUCATION: College educated

HEIGHT: 5'5"
WEIGHT: 157 lbs.
EYES: Blue
HAIR: Brown

ABILITIES: Frederick Foswell was a superb reporter with excellent organizational skills that he used to unite the New York mobs. He was adept at disguise and an excellent marksman with handguns.

PARAPHERNALIA: As the Big Man, Foswell used lifts in his shoes, a padded suit and a voice amplifier to create the impression of a large powerful man.

POWER GRID	1	2	3	4	5	6	7
INTELLIGENCE							
STRENGTH							
SPEED							
DURABILITY							
ENERGY PROJECTION							
FIGHTING SKILLS							

Art by Tom Morgan with John Romita (inset)

FUSION

REAL NAME: Markley (first name unrevealed)
KNOWN ALIASES: None
IDENTITY: Known to authorities
OCCUPATION: Unrevealed
CITIZENSHIP: U.S.A. with a criminal record
PLACE OF BIRTH: New York City
MARITAL STATUS: Divorced
KNOWN RELATIVES: Jeremy Francis Markley (son, deceased), unnamed wife
GROUP AFFILIATION: BioTechnix
EDUCATION: College educated
FIRST APPEARANCE: Peter Parker: Spider-Man Vol. 2 #30 (2001)

HISTORY: Jeremy Francis Markley was a shy nine-year-old boy who escaped his troubles by daydreaming about Spider-Man but fell to his death trying to imitate his hero. His father, a man who achieved wealth using a mutant ability of persuasion, was devastated and blamed Spider-Man. Vowing revenge, Markley became Fusion, an apparent amalgam of every hero and criminal in the city. Carrying a mannequin and a small metal mallet to Edgar Tower, Fusion used his persuasion power to convince people that his mallet was Thor's hammer, that his arm morphed into the Hulk's arm, and that his body grew Dr. Octopus' tentacles. On the roof, Fusion convinced police that the mannequin was a hostage. Fusion made Spider-Man believe he had multiple super-powers. He tossed the mannequin off the roof, letting Spider-Man know it was a bomb. When the wall-crawler webbed it, the mannequin exploded, killing three hundred people in the building. Fusion publicly blamed Spider-Man for the deaths and challenged him to a fight at the site of Jeremy's death. There, Fusion, simulating Iron Man, Sandman, Venom and others, attacked Spider-Man. His spider-sense useless against the power of persuasion, Spider-Man thought he had been struck by a Hulk-powered punch that had broken his neck. Fusion dragged the "paralyzed" Spider-Man to his hideout where he blamed him for the Tower deaths, explaining that the bomb was built to explode only if stopped in mid-air. Spider-Man refused to accept this guilt and in his resolve discovered that his neck wasn't broken after all. Spidey's strength of will allowed him to now resist the persuasion and Fusion was forced to flee.

Fusion later turned up at BioTechnix, a company that designed prosthetic limbs containing processors that could take over the wearer's mind. Fusion apparently cowed Dr. Octopus with his powers and Ock created "lost-limb" accidents to high-ranking government personnel who were then mind-probed with BioTechnix prosthetics to locate "John Hancock," a top-secret device that traced radiation signatures, so that they could locate Spider-Man. After obtaining John Hancock, Ock, feigning submission all along, attacked and nearly beat Fusion to death. Spider-Man defeated Ock and intentionally damaged the device to discourage any tracking. Fusion faced a lengthy hospital stay and presumably a longer prison stretch for his crimes.

HEIGHT: 6'0"
WEIGHT: 190 lbs.
EYES: Brown
HAIR: Brown

SUPERHUMAN POWERS: In spite of appearances, Fusion has no great physical power. He can persuade people to perceive whatever he wishes, thereby making them react as he chooses.

PERSONAL WEAPONRY: Fusion uses a small metal mallet which he can persuade people to see as anything he wants.

POWER GRID	1	2	3	4	5	6	7
INTELLIGENCE							
STRENGTH							
SPEED							
DURABILITY							
ENERGY PROJECTION							
FIGHTING SKILLS							

HISTORY: The charming Glory Grant was pursuing a modelling career when she met Daily Bugle photographer Peter Parker, who had just moved in across the hall in her Lower West Side apartment building. Peter and Glory became fast friends; though a frequent visitor to his apartment, she remained unaware that Peter was leading a double life as the masked adventurer Spider-Man. Later, when Glory was looking for work, Peter brought her to the Bugle, where irascible publisher J. Jonah Jameson had been going through secretaries at an alarming rate since the departure of his long-time secretary Betty Brant. Glory was hesitant to apply for the job, she went ahead, encouraged by Peter and city editor Joe Robertson—and to everyone's surprise, Jonah took an immediate liking to her. The smart, pleasantly efficient Glory has gone on to become the longest-serving secretary in recent Bugle history, working for both Jameson and Robertson, who was later promoted to editor-in-chief.

As a Bugle employee and occasional associate of Spider-Man, Glory has had many brushes with danger over the years; but Grant's darkest hour by far came when she fell madly in love with lycanthropic gang boss Eduardo Lobo. Alongside his brother Carlos, Eduardo was waging a gang war against the Kingpin, and he seduced Glory with the intention of using her to access the Bugle's research files on the Kingpin. However, once he had the files, Eduardo realized he had truly fallen in love with Glory and could not bring himself to abandon her. In fact, he admitted, she was now the only thing in the world that truly mattered to him. Glory, wracked by guilt over romancing a criminal and compromising the Bugle's files, agonized over what to do next; Peter advised her to follow her heart. When the Lobos' gang war climaxed in a chaotic battle with various rival criminals, Eduardo ended up in a death struggle with Spider-Man. During the fight, Glory picked up a fallen gun (which the Kingpin's lieutenant The Arranger had loaded with silver bullets), aimed, and fired, killing Eduardo. When Spider-Man thanked her, a grief-stricken Glory revealed that she had been aiming at Spider-Man, having followed her heart as Peter suggested.

Glory regarded Spider-Man with bitter resentment thereafter, but this did not stop him from aiding her and government agent Shotgun against the late voodoo witch Calypso, who spiritually possessed Grant long enough to engineer a scheme that brought Calypso fully back from the dead. More recently, Glory has found new happiness in a romance with Randy Robertson, the son of Bugle chief Joe Robertson.

REAL NAME: Gloria Grant
KNOWN ALIASES: Glory
IDENTITY: No dual identity
OCCUPATION: Administrative assistant, Daily Bugle; former model
CITIZENSHIP: U.S.A.
PLACE OF BIRTH: Unrevealed
MARITAL STATUS: Single
KNOWN RELATIVES: Cal (uncle), Yvonne (niece), Ramon (cousin)
GROUP AFFILIATION: Daily Bugle staff
EDUCATION: Unrevealed
FIRST APPEARANCE: Amazing Spider-Man Vol. 1 #140 (1975)

HEIGHT: 5'8"
WEIGHT: 120 lbs.
EYES: Brown
HAIR: Black

ABILITIES: Glory is an organized, efficient, patient and personable administrative professional. She is a good typist with a strong working knowledge of computers.

POWER GRID	1	2	3	4	5	6	7
INTELLIGENCE							
STRENGTH							
SPEED							
DURABILITY							
ENERGY PROJECTION							
FIGHTING SKILLS							

Art by Shawn McManus

HAMMERHEAD

REAL NAME: Unrevealed
KNOWN ALIASES: Mister H
IDENTITY: Secret
OCCUPATION: Crimelord; former loan shark, enforcer, hitman
CITIZENSHIP: U.S.A. with a criminal record
PLACE OF BIRTH: Unrevealed
MARITAL STATUS: Married
KNOWN RELATIVES: Antonia (sister); unnamed wife
GROUP AFFILIATION: Sinister Twelve, Maggia; former ally of Tombstone, the Chameleon, others
EDUCATION: Unrevealed
FIRST APPEARANCE: Amazing Spider-Man Vol. 1 #113 (1972)

HISTORY: Years ago, a minor gunman for an unidentified Maggia crime family was severely beaten and, his skull literally in fragments, left to die beneath a movie poster for "The Al Capone Mob." Disfigured and delirious, he was discovered by disgraced surgeon Jonas Harrow, who, motivated by both humanitarian and experimental interests, replaced the gunman's skull and broken bones with a strong steel alloy, leaving his head broad and flattened. Upon his recovery, the gunman remembered nothing save his criminal ambitions, his mind still fixated upon the mobster poster. Rebuilding his own personality, he became a 1920s-style gangster called Hammerhead. His treatment was the earliest known instance of the criminal empowerment for which Harrow later became infamous. Determined to ascend to the underworld's peak, Hammerhead was willing to work his way to the top, and he moved from one crime family to another as his fortunes waxed and waned. His ambition and viciousness soon earned him a deadly reputation, as informants and reporters alike died for getting too close to his employers' interests. For a time he worked alongside the superhuman freelancer called Wade Wilson, later Deadpool, but little else is known of his early career.

In recent years, Hammerhead ventured into loan shark territory, and among his clientele was wrestler Crusher Hogan; in a prophetic

moment, Hammerhead was in the audience when Hogan was challenged by a masked youth soon to be known as Spider-Man. For years Hammerhead bided his time, and when the Maggia leader called the Top Man lost status after a clash with the Fantastic Four, he took control of the fallen gangster's mob and spent months reshaping it. When the Kingpin of Crime, the Maggia's greatest competitor, temporarily withdrew from New York, Hammerhead stepped into the power vacuum, as did Doctor Octopus. The pair's gangs warred in the streets until Spider-Man intervened, defeating them both. Octopus and the members of both gangs were arrested, but Hammerhead fled the country.

During his exile, Hammerhead built his fighting skills to their peak. Returning to the U.S., he and his remaining gang attacked Octopus, who fled to an advanced atomic processing plant he hoped to acquire. Despite Spider-Man's interference, Hammerhead cornered Octopus near an atomic reactor, but when he charged Octopus, he struck the reactor instead. Spider-Man and Octopus fled, barely reaching safety before the reactor exploded and devastated the island, including Hammerhead's gang, the last survivors of the Top Man's organization.

Through an unexplained space-time fluke, Hammerhead was not slain but rendered incorporeal, and he followed Octopus back to New York, briefly driving him to mental ruin. When not harassing Octopus, he materialized throughout New York and recruited new underlings, who were deeply impressed that not even an atomic explosion could end his efforts. Recovering, Octopus attempted to use a particle accelerator to eradicate Hammerhead, but this only played into Hammerhead's hands, for the accelerator instead restored him to solidity. Hunted by Octopus and Spider-Man, he fled in a helicopter, which Octopus downed over the bay, but he emerged unscathed, although he allowed his enemies to believe him dead.

Hammerhead strengthened his new Maggia family with underlings trained by the super-skilled Taskmaster and hired the inventive Tinkerer to create a strength-magnifying exoskeleton. With the

Kingpin back in power, Hammerhead sought to unite New York's Maggia families under his rule, but his summit was disrupted by the Human Torch who was following a false lead in a murder investigation. Despite his exoskeleton, Hammerhead proved no match for the Torch. When the Kingpin's interests again took him from New York, a new gang war broke out, much to the chagrin of Spider-Man and other crimefighters, but as Hammerhead planned his role, the Kingpin's right-hand man, the Arranger, had him bombed at a restaurant. Hammerhead hungered for vengeance but withdrew when the Kingpin returned to stabilize the city.

Months later, when the lycanthropic Lobo Brothers challenged the Kingpin, the shape-shifting Chameleon, pursuing the underworld crown himself, allied with Hammerhead, who followed the former spy's lead in the fray. Predictably, Spider-Man opposed all comers, but when the smoke cleared, Hammerhead was one of New York's top three crimelords. Unfortunately, he hired the infamous hitman Tombstone as his right hand, which proved his undoing; in what he fancied was a gesture of good will, Hammerhead hired the Hobgoblin (Macendale) to assassinate Tombstone's nemesis Robbie Robertson. But Tombstone had vowed that only he would slay Robertson, and when chance granted Tombstone superhuman power, he savagely beat Hammerhead, then lured Robertson into a trap. Spider-Man and other heroes intervened, enabling Hammerhead to escape, and he resumed sole rule of his organization when the Chameleon turned to other interests.

When the Kingpin was temporarily toppled, both Hammerhead and Tombstone were among those who sought his Las Vegas interests, but the vigilantes Daredevil, Nomad, and the Punisher put an end to this venture. Soon afterward, Tombstone, aspiring to Maggia heights, once more beat up Hammerhead and had him ejected from New York. Mortified, Hammerhead went abroad and undermined the interests of the assassination mogul called the Foreigner, who recruited his ex-wife, famed mercenary Silver Sable, to aid him. Hammerhead got the better of Sable and, abandoning his imagined 1920s ethics, boasted that he would rape and kill her before his Maggia peers, but his twisted fantasies were punctured when Sable defeated him. Returning to the U.S., he regained his place among the Maggia leaders, which included, to his chagrin, Tombstone.

However, when the long-absent crimelord Fortunato returned in alliance with the terrorists of Hydra, Hammerhead, incensed that such "Nazis" dared undermine New York, joined several other crimelords in a united front. They were nonetheless defeated, though the intervention of Daredevil and Ben Reilly (briefly acting as Spider-Man) disrupted Fortunato's coup. While Hydra regrouped, Hammerhead remained one of the few holdouts and formed an uneasy alliance with Spider-Man and new hero SHOC against Hydra front man Crown. Dealing Crown a crippling blow, Hammerhead was content to lay low, apparently occupying himself with, among other things, marriage to an unidentified woman. However, the Kingpin, returning to his throne, had several crimelords, including Hammerhead, attacked and left for dead.

But the Kingpin had unknowingly done Hammerhead a favor, for the attack seemingly stirred long-buried memories of a sister, Antonia, whom he learned was dying of cancer. Frantic to make up for years of amnesia, Hammerhead sought an ancient Atlantean tablet whose secrets would heal Antonia. Forcing scientist Curt Connors into his service, Hammerhead acquired the tablet and, despite Spider-Man's intervention, Connors created a serum that would bestow the desired power. However, when Connors attempted to drink the serum, Hammerhead's hireling Boomerang shattered the vial, prompting the scientist's transformation into his reptilian

alter ego, the Lizard. Eventually, all concerned converged at the hospital where Antonia lay, and when the Lizard recreated the serum, Hammerhead consumed it and achieved godlike power. In a moment of compassion, he restored Connors to his senses, but the transcendent experience so enraptured him that the power faded before he could cure Antonia. However, Spider-Man prepared a third dosage to treat her, and a grateful Hammerhead allowed himself to be arrested.

Briefly incarcerated in the power-dampening prison called the Cage, Hammerhead was soon again at liberty and, perhaps retaining a bit of godlike wisdom, launched his most ambitious scheme to date, a union of international crime families under his rule. As Hammerhead expected, the gang warfare drew Spider-Man's attention, and the crimelord obligingly manipulated the troublemakers in his organization into taking the brunt of the web-slinger's blows. He walked away from the proceedings closer to ruling status than ever, even presuming to seek financial ties with the Fantastic Four, the very team that toppled his predecessor years earlier. Although Hammerhead's rivals have often ridiculed his 1920s mannerisms, he has outlasted many such newcomers; while the Kingpin's power fluctuates and Tombstone again languishes as a henchman, he seems to be enjoying his greatest success yet.

HEIGHT: 5'10"
WEIGHT: 265 lbs.
EYES: Blue
HAIR: Black

DISTINGUISHING FEATURES: Flattened head

SUPERHUMAN POWERS: Portions of Hammerhead's skull and skeleton have been surgically replaced with a nearly unbreakable steel alloy, making him extremely resistant to physical injury; in particular, his head is virtually impervious to physical damage.

ABILITIES: Hammerhead is an exceptional athlete and hand-to-hand combatant, although his most frequent battle tactic is to charge his opponents headfirst. Although thought dim-witted by many, he possesses a keen criminal mind and is proficient in the use of most forms of firearms, especially machine guns.

PARAPHERNALIA: Hammerhead customarily carries 1920s-style Thompson submachine guns and utilizes other accoutrements of that era; at times he uses special guns which fire non-lethal stun pellets instead of bullets. On occasion he wears an exoskeleton which magnifies his strength at least tenfold and provides protection from injury and heat. His underlings use various advanced weapons as needed.

POWER GRID	1	2	3	4	5	6	7
INTELLIGENCE							
STRENGTH							
SPEED							
DURABILITY							
ENERGY PROJECTION							
FIGHTING SKILLS							

CRUSHER HOGAN

REAL NAME: Joseph Hogan
KNOWN ALIASES: None
IDENTITY: No dual identity
OCCUPATION: Custodian, former professional wrestler
CITIZENSHIP: U.S.A.
PLACE OF BIRTH: Unrevealed
MARITAL STATUS: Married
KNOWN RELATIVES: Marie Hogan (wife)
GROUP AFFILIATION: Formerly Championship Wrestling
EDUCATION: High-school dropout
FIRST APPEARANCE: Amazing Fantasy Vol. 1 #15 (1962)

HISTORY: Crusher Hogan was the top star of his wrestling league. Never interested in a staged fight, Hogan was a "shooter," a genuine athlete who knew all the body's weaknesses and was prepared to exploit them, but the crowds had fallen off and Bobby, his boss, advised him to abandon the group and join the wealthy Global Wrestling. His wife Marie also pushed him to take a job with real money but Crusher was too loyal to change. Instead, he came up with a way to bring back the audiences and save the failing league.

Taking the microphone after a match without informing Bobby of his plans, he refashioned his image into a bad guy by disrespecting the fans and offering a reward to anyone who could last three minutes in the ring with him. The promotion worked and fans lined up for tickets. Unfortunately, Crusher had borrowed the prize money from the mob and then had the misfortune to be confronted by a young man he sarcastically referred to as "a little Masked Marvel." The young man was Peter Parker in his first formal use of his spider-powers. After Peter picked him up and carried him up a pole, Crusher quickly conceded.

Presumably the gate from a full house was enough to keep the mobsters at bay but Bobby had put up his house to cover expenses and his league was dissolved. Crusher's marriage to Marie apparently ended as a result of the encounter as well. A ruined Crusher took a job as a custodian at a local gym where he regaled people like up-and-coming boxer Bobby Chance with tall tales about training Spider-Man, creating the web-shooters and providing the costume.

When gym owner Madame Fang and her enforcer Manslaughter Marsdale discovered that Bobby planned to sign a contract with someone else, they schemed to put the young boxer out of commission. Crusher overheard these plans and joined the fight on Bobby's side. It was destined to be a losing battle until Spider-Man, passing by, joined the fight and defeated Manslaughter. Afterward, Spidey played along with Crusher's stories, making the washed-up wrestler a hero in the eyes of all the gymrats.

HEIGHT: 5'10"
WEIGHT: 210 lbs.
EYES: Blue
HAIR: None

ABILITIES: In his prime, Crusher was a world-class wrestler, capable of defeating any normal opponent. Even in retirement and out of shape, Crusher is a scrapper, wielding a mean broom.

POWER GRID	1	2	3	4	5	6	7
INTELLIGENCE							
STRENGTH							
SPEED							
DURABILITY							
ENERGY PROJECTION							
FIGHTING SKILLS							

HISTORY: Cargo ship crewman Morrie Bench was accidentally knocked overboard by Spider-Man (who was battling Sub-Mariner) during the testing of a powerful new experimental underwater generator, the energies of which combined with gases from undersea volcanoes to trigger a weird mutation in Bench, who began to transform into living water. Physically and emotionally unstable, Bench dubbed himself Hydro-Man and soon attacked Spider-Man, but he evaporated after Spider-Man scattered his liquid form amidst the hot sunshine of the New York rooftops; however, the particles of Bench's body soon reintegrated, and he embarked on a long criminal career.

When Bench and rival criminal Sandman fought over the affections of barfly Sadie Frickett, the two men accidentally merged into a monstrous "mud-thing" that the police were ultimately forced to dehydrate into seemingly inert rubble. Hydro-Man and Sandman eventually managed to separate back into their original forms, but both were humiliated and traumatized by the experience. Hydro-Man did most of his criminal work in groups from that point on, perhaps seeking safety in numbers.

Both alone and as a member of teams like the Sinister Syndicate, the Frightful Four and the Assembly of Evil, Bench fought a wide array of foes, but most often clashed with Spider-Man. Hydro-Man was one of many super-criminals employed by corrupt billionaire Justin Hammer for a time, and later served in the Masters of Evil assembled by Hammer's daughter Justine, alias the Crimson Cowl; however, after Justine's arrest and the apparent death of Justin, Hammer Industries phased out its criminal enterprises and Bench, along with fellow employee the Shocker, was laid off. The Shocker and Hydro-Man then teamed up for one last crime, seeking enough money to retire, but Hydro-Man's thirst for revenge against Spider-Man led to their defeat. Trying and failing to go straight, Bench was recruited back into the Wizard's Frightful Four and, more recently, the Sinister Twelve.

REAL NAME: Morris Bench
KNOWN ALIASES: Morrie, Mud-Thing
IDENTITY: Known to the authorities
OCCUPATION: Professional criminal; former water park employee, cargo ship crewman
CITIZENSHIP: U.S.A. with a criminal record
PLACE OF BIRTH: Bronx, New York
MARITAL STATUS: Single
KNOWN RELATIVES: None
GROUP AFFILIATION: Sinister Twelve, Frightful Four, Hammer Industries, Masters of Evil, Sinister Syndicate, Assembly of Evil
EDUCATION: Unrevealed
FIRST APPEARANCE: Amazing Spider-Man Vol. 1 #212 (1981)

HEIGHT: 6'2"
WEIGHT: 265 lbs.
EYES: Brown
HAIR: Light brown

SUPERHUMAN POWERS: Hydro-Man can transform himself wholly or partially into a water-like liquid substance, the particles of which he can mentally animate and manipulate at will. By generating force from within this fluid, Bench can emit high-pressure water blasts like a fire hose. Bench mentally controls every drop of his bodily liquid; his watery form will gradually reintegrate if it has been vaporized or otherwise dispersed. He can merge with or absorb ordinary, existing water in his environment, often using it to increase his mass and volume. Recent alterations of his powers by the Wizard have enabled Bench to mentally manipulate water sources outside his own body.

POWER GRID	1	2	3	4	5	6	7
INTELLIGENCE							
STRENGTH							
SPEED							
DURABILITY							
ENERGY PROJECTION							
FIGHTING SKILLS							

JACKAL

REAL NAME: Dr. Miles Warren
KNOWN ALIASES: None
IDENTITY: Known to authorities
OCCUPATION: Biochemistry instructor
CITIZENSHIP: U.S.A.
PLACE OF BIRTH: Brooklyn, New York
MARITAL STATUS: Married
KNOWN RELATIVES: Monica Warren (wife, deceased), brother (first name unrevealed), son (first name unrevealed, deceased), daughter (first name unrevealed, deceased), alleged son
GROUP AFFILIATION: None
EDUCATION: Ph.D in biochemistry
FIRST APPEARANCE: (Professor Warren) Amazing Spider-Man Vol. 1 #31 (1965); (Jackal) Amazing Spider-Man Vol. 1 #129 (1974)

HISTORY: Miles Warren was born into a family with a proclivity for science. His brother became a science teacher at Midtown High School where Peter Parker was his favorite pupil, but Miles' talents far exceeded that. After earning his Ph.D in biochemistry, Miles traveled to Wundagore Mountain to assist the High Evolutionary in his experiments to evolve animals into human form. Whereas the Evolutionary's subjects never fully lost their animal appearance, Miles succeeded in creating two "New Men" who looked practically human. This caused some friction between Miles and the Evolutionary that accelerated when a group of New Men began to worship Miles. When Miles evolved a jackal that exhibited a Jekyll-Hyde personality and then escaped, the Evolutionary banished him from Wundagore. Miles stayed in the area where he met and married Monica, fathering two children, but he spent so much time with his research that Monica took the children and left. Unbeknownst to the Warrens, Miles' jackal-man, envious of his creator's life, had been stalking the family. He caused a car accident that killed Monica and the children. When Miles learned of this, he realized the cause and blamed the High Evolutionary. He returned to Wundagore, challenged the Evolutionary and left with the New Men faction that worshipped him, promising to make them human.

He returned every summer but spent the rest of the year in Manhattan where he had obtained a position as Professor at Empire State University. There, his brother introduced him to Peter Parker on the same day that Miles first saw and immediately fell in love with Gwen Stacy. Disturbed by his feelings, Miles convinced himself his intentions were paternal and that Gwen was like the daughter he never had, blotting out the memory of his dead children. The following semester, both Peter and Gwen were students in his biology class. Continuing his New Men research, Miles hired Anthony Serba as an assistant and had him collect cell samples from the students in his class. He created a serum from these samples and injected New Men volunteers. The serum made the New Men human but transformed them into living corpses, then killed them. Miles tried to genetically engineer duplicate bodies for the New Men, making his first excursions into cloning which he later continued at ESU with Serba. Back in New York, Miles invited Peter, his best, though occasionally distracted, student, to a science demonstration. When Peter brought Gwen Stacy along, Miles couldn't help but voice his approval. When Spider-Man appeared, Miles expressed an interest in studying him.

To Peter Parker, Miles was a professor who badgered him about not attending classes. Even after Gwen Stacy was killed by the Green Goblin (Norman Osborn, also apparently killed), Miles kept up this routine but inside he was devastated. The day after Gwen's death, Serba showed him a frog produced by their cloning experiment. Miles then gave Serba tissue samples from Gwen and Peter. When Serba discovered he was cloning humans, he came to Miles and demanded their destruction. Hushing Serba up, Miles accidentally killed him. Unhinged by his act, he became convinced someone else did the murder. When he walked past a class discussing jackals, he recalled his jackal-man and created an evil alter-ego for himself: the Jackal. He designed a green costume with electro-prod claws and began extensive athletic training. Believing Spider-Man was responsible for Gwen's death, Miles sought revenge but his evil side also yearned to be a crime boss. So, the Jackal convinced the Punisher to kill the web-slinger. He then murdered the Punisher's colleague, the Mechanic, hoping to blame the Punisher for the crime. When this failed, he arranged to bring Hammerhead, Dr. Octopus and Spider-Man together, hoping to pick up the gangland pieces, but this scheme also fizzled.

Meanwhile, Miles' clones were not developing properly, degenerating quickly into genetic waste. He hired a new assistant, Seward Trainer, and put his clones in stasis. The Jackal began spying on Peter Parker in search of a link to Spider-Man. He spotted Peter tossing a web-bundle on his apartment building roof, which contained a spare Spider-Man costume and web-shooters. Stealing this, the Jackal was almost certain Parker was Spider-Man but he wanted absolute proof. He hired the Grizzly to lure Peter into a trap. He then attached a metal harness to Peter's arm, telling him the device was a homing beacon that would explode if removed. This was a ruse to induce Peter to go to the ESU labs where he disposed of the harness. Peter then changed to Spider-Man with Miles secretly watching, confirming his suspicions.

During this time, Norman Osborn, still alive, had established himself as a criminal mastermind in Europe, leading the cabal called the Scriers. He stepped in to help Miles' cloning, via his Scrier representative. The Scrier caught Seward Trainer stealing secrets and demanded a future favor in exchange for his silence. Together, Miles, Seward and the Scrier birthed the first successful Peter Parker clone. However, the clone began to exhibit cellular degeneration. Learning this, Miles planned to kill his flawed creation but the clone escaped, later calling himself Kaine. Other failed Parker clones followed until Miles refined his technique and somehow created stable Peter Parker and Gwen Stacy clones as well as clones of himself. Miles briefly returned to his New Men, this time in his costumed identity, inspiring the Cult of the Jackal. He vowed to fulfill his promises but never returned. Back home, he used drugs and hypnosis to bend the new clones to his will, then began tormenting Spider-Man by sending the Gwen clone to Peter Parker's apartment.

Before continuing his plans, Miles combined his cells with his genetic virus to create a clone intended to destroy the human race, but the creature awakened too early to have full powers and became Carrion. Eventually, with Tarantula (Anton Miguel Rodriguez) in his employ, Jackal revealed his identity to Spider-Man, then pitted him against his Spider-Clone in a fight ending in an explosion that seemed to kill both Miles and his creation. In reality, the killed Jackal was a clone. Miles stepped out of hiding, found both Spider-Men alive and injected what he believed was the real one with a drug to simulate death. His plan was to later retrieve the body, revive him, and brainwash him into thinking he was the clone. Convinced by this, the "real" Spider-Man took the name Ben Reilly and left the city.

In reality, Miles' tests had been manipulated by Seward Trainer, following Norman Osborn's secret agenda, and Ben Reilly was the clone. Miles moved to a lab in upstate New York where he spent five years in a genetic regeneration chamber, reshaping his body to resemble his jackal-man, creating clones by long-distance and going totally insane. The High Evolutionary, thinking the Jackal dead, forced his Cult into hiding, then forged and planted a diary in Miles' handwriting to discredit his clone work by claiming the Parker and Gwen clones were Serba and a woman named Joyce Delany, who had been genetically reconstructed by the same genetic virus Miles previously tried on the New Men. The Evolutionary also planted Miles' genetic virus, which turned student Malcolm McBride into another Carrion. Believing all this, the superbeing Daydreamer transformed the Gwen clone into Joyce but she reverted back, later meeting and marrying Warren Miles, a Professor Warren clone who eventually degenerated.

As Miles' regeneration approached its completion, he summoned Ben Reilly, now known as the Scarlet Spider, and Peter Parker to his lab where he tormented them with clues about their true identities and subjected them to clones, which degenerated rapidly, even revealing a third Peter Parker whom he claimed was truly the original. His real goal was to get inside Ravencroft Institute to steal a sample of his Carrion Virus contained within the body of the villain Shriek. While Seward Trainer's switch resulted in tests proving Ben Reilly was the real Spider-Man, Miles teamed up with the third Parker, who was a combination clone/genetic construct he named Spidercide, to unleash his improved Carrion Virus on Springville, Pennsylvania, killing nearly everyone in town, a first step toward killing the entire human race and replacing them with clones. The Jackal planned to set off his next virus bomb at the Daily Bugle but faced opposition from Spider-Man, the Scarlet Spider, Mary Jane Watson-Parker and the Gwen Stacy clone. When Gwen fell off the roof, Miles' love resurfaced and he attempted to save her but fell to his own death instead. Unless, that is, he was only another clone.

An alleged son of Miles Warren, possibly the Jackal Man, became the new Jackal but was quickly defeated by Beta Flight.

HEIGHT: 5'10"
WEIGHT: 175 lbs.
EYES: Green
HAIR: Gray

SUPERHUMAN POWERS: After regeneration, Miles Warren had the strength, speed and agility of a jackal, amplified to super-human levels.

ABILITIES: Miles Warren was a genius in the fields of biochemistry, genetics, and cloning.

PARAPHERNALIA: Drug-tipped, formerly electro-prod, claws

POWER GRID	1	2	3	4	5	6	7
INTELLIGENCE							
STRENGTH							
SPEED							
DURABILITY							
ENERGY PROJECTION							
FIGHTING SKILLS							

JOHN JAMESON

REAL NAME: John Jameson
KNOWN ALIASES: Vanwolf, Skywolf, Stargod, Man-Wolf
IDENTITY: (Man-Wolf/Stargod): Secret
OCCUPATION: Employed by the Queens Dept. of Social Services; former security chief of the Ravencroft Institute, monster hunter, astronaut, test pilot
CITIZENSHIP: U.S.A.
PLACE OF BIRTH: New York, New York
MARITAL STATUS: Single

KNOWN RELATIVES: J. Jonah Jameson (father), Joan Jameson (mother, deceased), Marla Madison (stepmother), David and Betty Jameson (grandparents, presumed deceased)
GROUP AFFILIATION: Ravencroft Institute, Avengers Support Crew, NASA, USAF
EDUCATION: Master of Science degree in Aeronautical Engineering
FIRST APPEARANCE: Amazing Spider-Man Vol. 1 #1 (1963)

HISTORY: As a career test pilot and astronaut, Col. John Jameson was, according to his father J. Jonah, "made of the stuff of heroes," unlike masked menaces such as Spider-Man. However, Spider-Man has saved his son's life on numerous occasions. During his first mission orbiting Earth, Spider-Man replaced a guidance module in Col. Jameson's plummeting space capsule. In a subsequent mission in space, Jameson contacted spores from Jupiter that endowed him with superhuman strength, increased his size, and made him act more aggressively. NASA gave him a special suit from Tony Stark's lab to keep his strength in check. When it appeared that Spider-Man was responsible for a bank robbery, John was persuaded by his father to become a public hero by apprehending him. Spider-Man had the upper hand, but John sought a rematch. This time, Spider-Man neutralized the spores with a dose of high-voltage electricity, returning John to normal.

Later, Jameson was sent to the moon to collect rock samples on a top-secret mission and stumbled upon a glittering red gemstone. Once his mission was complete, he had a strange urge to obtain the gemstone from quarantine and have it made into a pendant, which he wore around his neck. The stone reacted to the moonlight on the first night of the next full moon, transforming Jameson into a savage lupine creature. The gem was actually the Godstone, the crystallized power and essence of Stargod, an ancient ruler from a dimension called Other Realm. When Stargod was dying he opened a portal to Earth's moon and channeled his energy into the jewel, which had landed there millennia before following the destruction of the collection of power gems known as the Lifestone Tree. Ancient prophecies foretold that in evil times, Stargod would be reborn to save the people of Other Realm. The energies of the Godstone transformed Jameson into the form of the Stargod, but the radiation that leaked through the portal to Other Realm was so weak that the change was only partial. Whenever the moon shone upon the Godstone, Jameson gained the form, strength, and primal fury of Stargod, but lacked his wisdom and power.

Jameson fought the transformations for months. As the Man-Wolf, he instinctively sought out and seemingly attacked his father, who was quick to suspect the creature was partnered with Spider-Man. When Jonah recognized the pendant around the Man-Wolf's neck, he knew the creature was his son. However, he could not cure him by removing the pendant, since it had grafted itself onto his skin. In a subsequent battle with the Man-Wolf, Spider-Man tore the stone from his neck and threw it into the Hudson River. The wound took months to heal, but Jameson was cured.

Unfortunately, the artificial vampire Michael Morbius recovered the stone and reverted Jameson into the Man-Wolf again, hoping to use the beast in a scheme to cure himself of his affliction. Spider-Man thwarted the effort, but both Morbius and Jameson escaped. Once again, the Man-Wolf ran rampant monthly. The police assigned special investigator Simon Stroud to the case of the Man-Wolf. Jameson fled New York to Georgia where he became entangled in a fight between S.H.I.E.L.D. and the Hate-Monger (a clone of Adolph Hitler). Nick Fury, director of S.H.I.E.L.D., escorted Jameson back to NASA, where he had been absent without leave. NASA offered

to drop the charges if Jameson agreed to perform a secret mission to investigate the communication breakdown with an orbiting space station. At the station, Jameson began his journey to discover the other-dimensional origin of his powers. He journeyed with three humanoids from Other Realm through the portal on the moon into their dimension. There, he was fully transformed into the essence of Stargod, this time maintaining his personality and intelligence. Fulfilling the prophecies, Jameson donned the costume and wielded the weapons of Stargod, ultimately managing to access his full power and help the "Realmites" defeat the tyrant Arisen Tyrk.

Using the Godstone, Jameson teleported back to Earth. Once again he found himself afflicted with lycanthropy as the stone bored itself into his throat. This time, the stone was slowly poisoning him. In hopes of a future cure, John's body was cryogenically frozen, but Jameson was thawed and mentally controlled by the dying scientist Spencer Smythe in an attempt to get revenge on Jonah and Spider-Man. Atop the Brooklyn Bridge with Spider-Man and his father, Man-Wolf reverted back to human. Smythe remotely caused John to fall backwards in agony off the bridge only to disappear. The Godstone had dimensionally teleported him away. Once again he became the Stargod and, with She-Hulk and Hellcat, saved Other Realm from gravitational collapse. Although he enjoyed being the Stargod, Jameson decided to return to Earth, losing his memory of Other Realm. Reunited with his father, he and Spider-Man sought Dr. Curt Connors to administer a biomagnetic treatment that caused John's body to reject the Godstone. With the stone crumbled into powder, he ceased transforming into the Man-Wolf. John broke up with his fiancée Kristine Saunders and spent some time at the Sherwood Nursing Home sanitarium to mentally recover from all his life's ordeals. There, before his father's second marriage, he was kidnapped by the Scorpion, but was rescued by Spider-Man.

For a time, Captain America hired Jameson to serve as pilot of his personal Quinjet, Freedom's Flight, as well as his van. While aboard the Freedom's Flight, Jameson's alias was "Skywolf;" while aboard the van, his alias was "Vanwolf." Jameson assisted Captain America during the "Bloodstone Hunt," and in his attempts to combat the drug trade during a turf war between the Kingpin and the Red Skull. At one point, Jameson was hypnotized with other members of the Avengers support crew by Mother Night and Minister Blood, and was forced to assist them in an attempt on the Avengers' lives, but the Avengers managed to halt him. Eventually he was contacted by the villain Dredmund Druid. Jameson attempted to defeat Dredmund himself, but was overpowered and temporarily transformed into a werewolf that greatly resembled his Man-Wolf form. Dredmund reassembled the Godstone and attempted to use it, but was defeated by Captain America; the stone was destroyed again. John was attracted to Captain America's girlfriend Diamondback and left his employment in shame after trying to steal a kiss.

After a time as a freelance monster-hunter, he served as security chief at the Ravencroft Institute, where he began a romantic relationship with the director, Dr. Ashley Kafka. After several problems with superpowered criminally insane inmates including Carnage, the Institute was temporarily shut down. Kafka thought she was close to healing the Chameleon of his mental illness, but was duped by the villain, enabling him to escape and kidnap her, John, and Spider-Man. With this final breach of security, Senator Roeberg fired Jameson and Kafka, hiring Dr. Leonard Samson as the new director of Ravencroft. Shortly thereafter, Mad Jack (Daniel Berkhart) implanted a command in Jameson's mind to smother his hospitalized father with a pillow, causing John to act wolf-like, though in human form. Kafka used hypnosis to undo the effects, transforming him temporarily into the Man-Wolf despite the

Art by Dean Haspiel

absence of the Godstone. Residual affects of the Godstone are apparently permanently a part of Jameson. He and Kafka broke up sometime thereafter.

John hopes to someday return to a more adventurous life. For now he is living simply as a social worker. He recently expressed some romantic interest in She-Hulk, and gave her his Jupiter suit (after a few modifications by Reed Richards) to help her manage her out-of-control strength. Currently, to end a crusade to discover Spider-Man's identity, John's father has been tricked by Peter Parker into believing his son is secretly Spider-Man.

HEIGHT: 6'2" (6'6" as Man-Wolf)
WEIGHT: 200 lbs. (350 lbs. as Man-Wolf)
EYES: Brown (red as Man-Wolf)
HAIR: Red-brown (white as Man-Wolf)

SUPERHUMAN POWERS: As the Man-Wolf, Jameson possessed superhuman strength, agility, speed, healing, and stamina as well as heightened senses. He was able to lift 4 tons under peak moonlight conditions. As Stargod, he had some degree of energy manipulation, but the full extent of his powers remains unknown. As Man-Wolf, he was not a traditional werewolf vulnerable to silver.

ABILITIES: Jameson is a skilled pilot, astronaut, and is experienced in hand-to-hand combat and a variety of weapons.

PARAPHERNALIA: As the Stargod, he wore scale mail armor, and used a broadsword, dagger, short bow and arrows.

POWER GRID	1	2	3	4	5	6	7
INTELLIGENCE							
STRENGTH							
SPEED							
DURABILITY							
ENERGY PROJECTION							
FIGHTING SKILLS							

JONAH JAMESON

REAL NAME: John Jonah Jameson
KNOWN ALIASES: J.J.J., Jolly Jonah, Flat-Top, Prune Face, others used by employees
IDENTITY: No dual identity
OCCUPATION: Owner, publisher, and executive editor of the Daily Bugle and Now Magazine; CEO of Jameson Publications; philanthropist; former publisher of Jameson News Digest, publisher of Woman Magazine, editor-in-chief, city editor, reporter, copy boy, paperboy
CITIZENSHIP: U.S.A.

PLACE OF BIRTH: New York City, New York
MARITAL STATUS: Twice married, once widowed
KNOWN RELATIVES: David (father, presumed deceased); Betty (mother, presumed deceased); Joan (first wife, deceased); John (Man-Wolf, son); Dr. Marla Madison-Jameson (second wife); Martha "Mattie" Franklin (Spider-Woman, foster daughter)
GROUP AFFILIATION: Century Club, Daily Bugle staff
EDUCATION: High-school dropout; later G.E.D. and college work
FIRST APPEARANCE: Amazing Spider-Man Vol. 1 #1 (1963)

HISTORY: The son of an abusive veteran, Jameson began his journalism career as a paperboy, then copy boy for the Daily Bugle, formerly edited by old man Jameson, whom some presume to have been his father. A sullen and bullying student, he quit school after becoming a reporter. At twenty he uncovered police corruption by supposed department hero Sam Kenner; beaten and bombed, Jameson nonetheless exposed Kenner with the help of Bugle owner William Goodman. He became a full-time Bugle reporter, including a stint as a war correspondent, criticizing most costumed heroes as glory-seeking vigilantes upstaging the common man.

Marrying his high school sweetheart Joan, Jameson rose to editor-in-chief and became renowned for supporting civil rights and opposing organized crime. When Goodman's heirs put the Bugle up for sale, Jameson tapped his last dollar and made the newspaper his own. He worked hard to support his wife and their son John, eventually becoming a millionaire member in New York's elite Century Club; although earning a reputation as a notorious miser, he supported many charities and often helped employees in true need. Still a reporter at heart, he ventured to Korea for a story but was crushed when Joan was killed by a masked gunman in his absence; this and other self-perceived failures contributed to his distrust of masked heroes and the heroic ideal.

In recent years, when the superhuman performer Spider-Man became a crimefighter, Jameson vowed to expose him as a publicity-seeking scofflaw, and not even the rescue of John from a space flight disaster dissuaded him. He relied on photos from Peter Parker, not knowing he was employing Spider-Man himself. Jameson heralded the Spacemen as superior heroes, but this gambit failed when Spider-Man exposed them as criminals; support for Mysterio yielded similar results. Despite his many achievements, Jameson's harsh self-analysis weighed upon him, for his hatred of Spider-Man was motivated by fear that he was indeed the selfless hero Jameson could never be.

Jameson hired Dr. Farley Stillwell to mutate investigator Mac Gargan into the Scorpion to defeat Spider-Man, but the debacle left Stillwell dead and the insane Scorpion hating Jameson. Plagued by guilt, the publisher confessed his actions to his friend Norman Osborn. Scientist Spencer Smythe soon offered Jameson the first of many Spider-Slayer robots, with which he battled Spider-Man to a standstill before the web-slinger escaped. Jameson rallied New York against the Kingpin's crime wave; abducted for his insolence, he remained defiant before being rescued by Spider-Man.

Months later, Osborn, the Green Goblin, seemingly died in battle with Spider-Man; Jameson suspected Spider-Man of outright murder, hiring Luke Cage to bring the wall-crawler in, but desisted when John became the Man-Wolf. Jameson's obsession paled before concern for his son, but his own safety became an issue when he was attacked by the Grizzly, a violent wrestler he had blacklisted a decade before. Spider-Man rescued Jameson but

chided him for the grudge; in response, Jameson hired Daniel Berkhart to harass Spider-Man as Mysterio's supposed ghost. When this failed, he contracted Farley Stillwell's brother Harlan to mutate a new operative, but fugitive Rick Deacon usurped the process and became the criminal Fly, killing Stillwell and becoming an enemy of Spider-Man and Jameson alike. Jameson mysteriously received photos depicting Spider-Man with the body of Peter Parker; the photos, sent by Osborn's drug-maddened son Harry, were actually of a clone. Jonah nevertheless kept them quiet but stepped up his traditional campaigns. He approached Dr. Marla Madison to construct her own Spider-Slayer but met no better success. Finally confronting Parker, whom he imagined had been slain and replaced by Spider-Man, Jameson believed his story of faked photography. His relationship with Madison turned romantic, and he proved his principles anew by denouncing the terrorists of the People's Liberation Front. The PLF responded by hiring the Hitman (Burt Kenyon), but even in the face of death Jameson ridiculed his abductors, who were defeated by Spider-Man and the Punisher.

Meanwhile, Smythe, whose obsession had outgrown even Jameson's, learned he was dying and resolved to take Jameson and Spider-Man with him to the grave. He mesmerized the Man-Wolf into abducting Jameson and fighting Spider-Man; Jameson believed John dead when he saw his son teleported away. Smythe suddenly shackled Jonah and Spider-Man with a bomb, dying afterward. Jameson broke down, admitting his obsession had harmed him far more than its subject, but Spider-Man deactivated the bomb, leaving Jameson devastated at his confession. Scientist Jonas Harrow targeted Jonah, driving him mad, but his tenacity challenged even Harrow, and after being rescued by Spider-Man, Jameson was soon his typically paranoid self. Months later, John resurfaced alive, barely remembering his extradimensional adventures, and Jameson was overjoyed with his son's cure.

Longtime colleague Ian Fate resurfaced as a sorcerer in the company of the monstrous Man-Thing; naively expecting Jameson to help reshape the world, Fate lashed out when refused, but while Spider-Man fought the Man-Thing, Jameson calmed Fate and set him on a more peaceful path. Jameson himself returned to basics by investigating waterfront extortion, interrogating no less than the Kingpin and risking his life to uncover the perpetrators, albeit with unexpected assistance from Spider-Man. Perhaps in unconscious gratitude, Jameson's subsequent scheme to discredit Spider-Man with impostors proved half-hearted at best.

The Hobgoblin, secretly Jameson's Century Club crony Roderick Kingsley, learned Osborn's secrets and tried to blackmail Jameson over the Scorpion's mutation. Spider-Man ended this scheme, but the conscience-stricken Jameson publicly revealed his guilt anyway, then married Marla Madison. Soon afterward, he hired the alleged mutant hunters X-Factor and the mercenary Wild Pack to bring in Spider-Man but, more at peace than he had been in years, he seemed content to restrict his castigations to the printed page. However, his vendetta literally took new form when the Chameleon imprisoned and impersonated him, bringing anti-Spider-Man sentiments to new heights. Inevitably rescued by Spider-Man, he found a new crisis awaiting him, for Thomas Fireheart, secretly the mercenary Puma, acquired the Bugle to build up Spider-Man's reputation. Jameson sought solace in his lifelong convictions, denigrating neo-Nazi Eric Hartmann in print; when Hartmann's forces invaded the Bugle, for once Jameson played the rescuer when he downed Hartmann before the madman could shoot the intervening Spider-Man.

Fireheart eventually returned the Bugle to Jameson, but his control was wrested away by Norman Osborn, alive after all. Jameson nonetheless investigated the mutant-hunting Operation: Zero Tolerance. Hoping to placate the publisher, the android-human Bastion offered him the outlaw X-Men's secrets, but Jameson refused, as his distaste for prejudice outweighed even his dislike of costumed heroes. The X-Men defeated Bastion, but Jameson was scarcely short of enemies when Osborn hired Daniel Berkhart, who had joined Mysterio's cousin Maguire Beck in the identity of Mad Jack, to force Jameson to sell the Bugle. Soon afterward, when Venom was ordered to put a scare into him, the madman mistook his instructions for a kill order, and even Jameson winced at the beating Spider-Man took in his defense.

Jameson regained the Bugle when Osborn went mad in a mystic ritual, which also empowered teenager Mattie Franklin, who became a new Spider-Woman and was, ironically, entrusted to the care of the Jamesons. A different legacy hounded Jameson as 0Spencer Smythe's even madder son Alistair threatened Jameson's family before receiving his latest defeat. Berkhart and Beck, now Mysterio and Mad Jack, abducted Jameson but were outwitted by Spider-Man and Daredevil. Unencumbered by gratitude, he sought to capitalize on the revelation of Daredevil's secret identity but was undercut when reporter Ben Urich refused to participate. Jameson hired superhuman investigator Jessica Jones to break a similar story on Spider-Man, but Jones merely put his money to work for charity, making her later rescue of Mattie from drug dealers all the more biting.

Even Jameson began to face his vendetta's futility, and his invective grew sparse. After fresh humiliation in a libel trial, he agreed to a new Bugle feature with a theoretically objective focus on super heroes, co-managed by Urich and Jones, but he was stunned by seeming proof that his son John had, inexplicably, been Spider-Man all along. Jameson's hatred of Spider-Man can only intensify when he inevitably learns the truth.

POWER GRID	1	2	3	4	5	6	7
INTELLIGENCE							
STRENGTH							
SPEED							
DURABILITY							
ENERGY PROJECTION							
FIGHTING SKILLS							

KAINE

REAL NAME: None
KNOWN ALIASES: Peter Parker
IDENTITY: Secret
OCCUPATION: Assassin
CITIZENSHIP: None
PLACE OF ORIGIN: The Jackal's laboratory, New York City
MARITAL STATUS: Single
KNOWN RELATIVES: Miles Warren (The Jackal, creator); Peter Parker (Spider-Man, original); Ben Reilly, Jack, Guardian, Spidercide, uncountable unnamed clones (fellow clones)
GROUP AFFILIATION: None
EDUCATION: Possesses memories of Peter Parker's college education
FIRST APPEARANCE: Web of Spider-Man #119 (1994)

HISTORY: Kaine was the first of the Jackal's experiments in cloning that did not immediately degenerate into raw genetic waste. After some time, however, slow genetic deterioration became apparent. The Jackal became disgusted by yet another failure and planned to kill his creation, forcing the rejected clone to flee. The clone came to call himself Kaine and eventually adopted a costume that slowed his deterioration and hid his skin, but reproduced the web-like scars that run all over his body. Even as his DNA deteriorated, Kaine grew taller and stronger than the original Spider-Man.

Kaine's anger grew with his strength. Most of all he hated Ben Reilly, whom he, like the Jackal, believed to be the original Spider-Man. Believing Peter to be a successful clone, Kaine took it upon himself to aid him. This ambition eventually led Kaine to murder the Grim Hunter and Dr. Octopus (Otto Octavius).

Kaine followed Ben around the world, working occasionally as a high-priced assassin. In Salt Lake City, Kaine killed Detective Louise Kennedy, after learning that she was in league with the local mob. Detective Jack Raven eventually tracked fingerprints back to the original Peter Parker in New York City. Peter was exonerated only after he threatened to make his secret identity known and Kaine confessed to the crime in another effort to preserve Peter's happiness. After Ben was "revealed" to be the original Spider-Man, Kaine escaped from police custody but was killed by Spidercide, a shape-shifting clone of Spider-Man. The Jackal put Kaine's body in a clone regeneration pod, where it was revived some time later.

Still attempting to crush Reilly's spirit, Kaine used Elizabeth Tyne (who was living under the assumed name of Janine Godbe after shooting her abusive father), the love of Ben's life since they had met in Salt Lake City. After Ben took the role of Spider-Man, Kaine lured Janine back to New York and attempted to kill himself and them. Their love inspired him to relent, and both Kaine and Janine surrendered to the police. Kaine later escaped from prison and was last seen in Greece. His current whereabouts are unknown.

HEIGHT: 6'4"
WEIGHT: 250 lbs.
EYES: Brown
HAIR: Brown

SUPERHUMAN POWERS: In addition to Spider-Man's strength and speed, Kaine has enhanced sticking powers that allow him to rip down walls and to burn with his hands, administering the "mark of Kaine." His amplified spider-sense gives him limited precognition.

PARAPHERNALIA: Razor claws on the back of his hands

POWER GRID	1	2	3	4	5	6	7
INTELLIGENCE							
STRENGTH							
SPEED							
DURABILITY							
ENERGY PROJECTION							
FIGHTING SKILLS							

Art by Sal Buscema

MADAME WEB

HISTORY: Though Cassandra Webb suffered from a lifetime of blindness and many years of neurological deterioration due to myasthenia gravis, she compensated with her profound psychic abilities, establishing herself as a medium. Using these powers, Madame Web discovered Peter Parker's secret identity when Spider-Man rescued one of her students who had been kidnapped during a scam at the Daily Globe newspaper. Later, Madame Web helped Spider-Man prevent an assassination attempt against a political candidate. When Black Tom Cassidy sent the Juggernaut to kidnap Web so he could use her powers for his criminal activities, she foresaw the attack and called Spider-Man for help. He was unable to stop the Juggernaut, who left Madame Web in a state of severe shock after he unknowingly removed her from her chair, which provided her vital life functions.

After being in a coma and suffering short-term memory loss, she appeared to temporarily forget Spider-Man's identity. She again contacted him for help since she had foreseen her own impending death. Believing that joining Norman Osborn in an arcane ritual called the Gathering of the Five would save her life, she asked Spider-Man to retrieve one of the five required artifact fragments. Each of the five participants would receive either knowledge, power, immortality, insanity, or death. Spider-Man succeeded, and in the course of the ceremony, Madame Web apparently received death. Actually, she received immortality, and found herself much younger and healthier. Soon after, Doctor Octopus created a Spider-Woman using Cassandra's granddaughter, Charlotte Winter, whose siphoning powers absorbed the abilities of the other Spider-Women Jessica Drew, Julia Carpenter, and Mattie Franklin. To capture Charlotte, Madame Web gathered the spider women into a team. Charlotte was defeated, but later siphoned Madame Web's telepathy, re-aging her in the process. With the help of Spider-Man and Franklin, Madame Web determined how to drain Charlotte's power, leaving Witter unconscious in a dormant state. Madame Web, now youthful again, performed psychic surgery to sever her link to Charlotte and removed Charlotte and Mattie's memories of Spider-Man's identity. Madame Web continued to assist Mattie during the rest of her time as Spider-Woman.

REAL NAME: Cassandra Webb
KNOWN ALIASES: None
IDENTITY: Publicly known
OCCUPATION: Professional medium
CITIZENSHIP: U.S.A.
PLACE OF BIRTH: Salem, Oregon
MARITAL STATUS: Widowed
KNOWN RELATIVES: Jonathan Webb (husband, deceased), Charlotte Witter (granddaughter)
GROUP AFFILIATION: Leader of Spider-Woman team
EDUCATION: Unknown
FIRST APPEARANCE: Amazing Spider-Man Vol. 1 #210 (1980)

HEIGHT: 5'6"
WEIGHT: 110 lbs.
EYES: Pale gray
HAIR: Black

SUPERHUMAN POWERS: Madam Web possesses psychic abilities including telepathy, clairvoyance, and prescience. She can also perform astral projection and appear to others in spirit form.

PARAPHERNALIA: Madam Web used to be cybernetically linked to a spiderweb-like life support system to attend to her bodily needs. The system could shift upright or recline, and provided robotic arms to substitute for her arms.

POWER GRID	1	2	3	4	5	6	7
INTELLIGENCE							
STRENGTH							
SPEED							
DURABILITY							
ENERGY PROJECTION							
FIGHTING SKILLS							

MINDWORM

REAL NAME: William Turner
KNOWN ALIASES: None
IDENTITY: Publicly known
OCCUPATION: None
CITIZENSHIP: U.S.A. with a criminal record
PLACE OF BIRTH: New York
MARITAL STATUS: Single
KNOWN RELATIVES: Mother and father (both deceased)
GROUP AFFILIATION: None
EDUCATION: High-school equivalent from orphanage
FIRST APPEARANCE: Amazing Spider-Man Vol. 1 #138 (1974)

HISTORY: An experimental government lab infected a residential community causing William Turner to be born a mutant with an enlarged head and sharp, piercing eyes. Young William could sense thoughts and feelings but he was also a psychic parasite who unknowingly drained his mother until she eventually died. His terrified father fled and was killed by a speeding car. He was sent to an orphanage where a bully routinely beat him until William did something to damage his attacker's brain. From then on, William worked hard to develop a powerful body as well as honing his powerful brain.

Upon leaving the orphanage, William sought a secluded spot where he could drain emotions from his neighbors without being detected. Now calling himself the Mindworm, William chose an abandoned house in Far Rockaway and leeched nourishment off the community for years—drawing residents, zombie-like, around his home. But Peter Parker's visit to Flash Thompson's apartment alerted Spider-Man to Mindworm's presence. With Spider-Man resistant to his mental powers, Mindworm resorted to using a crushing bear hug, but his comments about "hearing" Spidey's mind prompted the web-slinger to clap his hands over Mindworm's ears, severing his link with his victims. Feeling devastatingly alone, Mindworm was taken into custody by the police.

Denied the emotional nourishment of others' minds, Mindworm was hospitalized. Though appearing comatose he actually was working to focus his mental strength to gain revenge on Spider-Man from a distance. Instead, he had a dream that was so psychically potent it drew the sleeping Peter Parker inside it as well. With the wall-crawler's help, Mindworm realized that his feelings stemmed from his guilt over his parents' deaths. Now understanding his anguish, he regained the use of his body and turned his back on his vampiric past. Unfortunately, William slipped into robbery and, caught by Spider-Man, was sent to Ravenscroft Institute and later the Cage. Out of prison and mentally ill, William took to alcohol and lived on the streets where Spider-Man found him telepathically broadcasting his misery throughout an entire city block. Unsure of how to help, Spider-Man delayed too long, and William was murdered by some street thugs.

HEIGHT: 6'1"
WEIGHT: 210 lbs.
EYES: Brown
HAIR: Brown

SUPERHUMAN POWERS: Mindworm was a mutant with the ability to leech thoughts and emotions from those around him. This power eventually drained a victim to death. The Mindworm originally linked to brains to feed and fight off loneliness but he could also read minds, unleash mental force waves and illusions, inflict brain damage, invade dreams, draw people to him and mentally command them.

POWER GRID	1	2	3	4	5	6	7
INTELLIGENCE							
STRENGTH							
SPEED							
DURABILITY							
ENERGY PROJECTION							
FIGHTING SKILLS							

Art by Talent Caldwell

MORBIUS

HISTORY: Nobel Prize-winning biochemist Dr. Michael Morbius discovered he was dying, a rare disorder dissolving his blood cells. Not wanting to distress his fiancée Martine, Morbius began secretly working on a cure. With the aid of his partner Emil Nikos, Morbius attempted using distilled fluids from bats to stay his disease. While experimenting with such serums on board his yacht, Morbius had Nikos run an electrical shock through his system. The combination profoundly changed Michael's body, transforming him into something resembling a vampire. Now driven by a blinding hunger for blood, Morbius slew Nikos, but stopped short of draining his friend's body. Fearful that he would strike at Martine next, Michael tried ending his life by jumping into the sea, but self-preservation led him to escape the water's embrace.

Morbius' subsequent attacks on innocents brought him into conflicts with Spider-Man, the Lizard, and the Human Torch. His adventures led to other worlds and dimensions, including the dimension of the Cat People and a planet orbiting Arcturus. He traveled the country, foiling the plots of the coven Demon-Fire and its master, Apocalypse (Kazarian). He also encountered the otherworldly Caretakers, destroying their Children of the Comet, intended to replace humanity, as well as the Brotherhood of Judas vampire cult.

Martine's search for her fiancée had not ended, and she convinced him to return to her after he had encountered Jack Russell, the Werewolf. Using the last of Michael's Nobel Prize monies, Martine purchased the Mason House, located just outside Boston. Though reputedly haunted, Martine felt that it would afford them privacy while Morbius sought a cure. CIA agent Simon Stroud, seeking a killer vampire in Boston, came to view Morbius as the prime suspect. While Morbius discovered that he had a psychological need to drink blood from living victims, Stroud invaded the Mason House and arrested Martine. While the police questioned his fiancée, Morbius discovered his new home was a portal to a world ruled by the demonic entity Helleyes. Stroud, still in pursuit of Morbius, worked with him to escape Helleyes, discovering the demon's weakness and fleeing Mason House.

During their time away, Martine had been attacked by the killer vampire and transformed into a pseudo-vampire like Morbius. She was eventually cured of her condition when Morbius created an antidote that was a derivative of his own blood. Frustrated at both his inability to cure himself and the perpetual danger to Martine, Morbius ended their relationship. Once more on his own, the Living Vampire had more confrontations with Spider-Man, and even a short-lived alliance with the Ghost Rider (John Blaze), Man-Thing and Werewolf. This "Legion of Monsters" unwittingly slew the benevolent Starseed before going their separate ways. Morbius later used the Living Eraser's palm bands to flee Earth entirely, hoping to avoid feeding on more innocents. He became the unwilling host to an extradimensional being known as the Empathoid, who forced him back to Earth and into conflict with Spider-Man once more. After being freed from the alien's control, Morbius resumed his search for a cure.

Eventually, Morbius clashed with Spider-Man atop a Long Island mansion. He was struck by a bolt of lightning while draining Spider-Man's blood, catalyzing its radioactive elements and reversing much of his vampiric condition. He no longer required the blood of others to survive, but he retained a physiological need to drink it. Fleeing to Los Angeles, Morbius found work in a neuroradiology lab at the University of California. While working on a serum to cure himself of his continued craving for blood, Morbius met Jennifer Walters, the She-Hulk. Morbius gave Walters his serum, curing her of a

REAL NAME: Doctor Michael Morbius
KNOWN ALIASES: The Living Vampire, formerly Morgan Michaels
IDENTITY: Publicly known
OCCUPATION: Former biochemist, former hematologist
CITIZENSHIP: Citizen of unknown European country; criminal record in the U.S.A.
PLACE OF BIRTH: Unknown
MARITAL STATUS: Single
KNOWN RELATIVES: Martine Bancroft (ex-fiancée)
GROUP AFFILIATION: Midnight Sons, the Nine, Legion of Monsters
EDUCATION: Ph.D in Biochemistry
FIRST APPEARANCE: Amazing Spider-Man Vol. 1 # 101 (1971)

degenerative disease and allowing her to control her transformations into She-Hulk. Walters later served as Morbius' defense attorney during his trial for the murders he'd committed as a pseudo-vampire. The jury, convinced that Morbius had been unable to control his urges, convicted him only of involuntary manslaughter and sentenced him to five years in prison, to be served after completing his cure. After succeeding, Morbius went to prison willingly and was soon paroled for good behavior. Moving back to Los Angeles, Morbius aided Jack Russell in his attempts to control his Werewolf transformations. He also assisted the West Coast Avengers, who sought him out for information on the Cat People.

Eventually, however, the urges returned and Morbius slowly regressed into pseudo-vampirism. Failing to get the help he desired from Doctor Strange, Morbius allowed himself to fall in with the Subhumans, a group of homeless people living in the Morlock Tunnels. These people brought him victims, which led to another confrontation with Spider-Man. Sickened to discover that the victims upon whom he'd fed were innocents, Morbius once more fled into the night. By this time, the Ghost Rider (Dan Ketch) and John Blaze had begun pursuing Morbius, in preparation for the coming war with the demonqueen Lilith and her children, the Lilin. He was reunited with Martine, who had also decided to help Michael once more. She had contacted Dr. David Langford, who had created a new serum from Morbius' notes. Unbeknownst to Martine, Langford was employed by Dr. Paine who wanted to kill Morbius so that he might lay claim to and profit from his research. One of Lilith's children, Fang, added his own blood to the serum, transformed it, and it altered Morbius on the cellular level. Blinded by pain, Morbius sought out an old friend, Dr. Jacob Weisenthal, for help. When Martine was slain by Langford after discovering his plans, Morbius went berserk and slew Langford in turn. Realizing that he felt no guilt for this murder, Morbius swore to Ghost Rider that he would only drink the blood of the guilty in the future.

With Weisenthal's help, Morbius refined his serum, combining it with dialysis treatments and periods spent in a hyperbaric chamber. Now able to return himself to a normal appearance, Morbius adopted the identity of Dr. Morgan Michaels and worked in the hematology department of St. Jude's. He also began a relationship with a co-worker, Mandy Tyler. While some aspects of his life seemed to be stabilizing at last, Morbius found himself battling Dr. Paine, the Basilisk, Simon Stroud and his vampiric "son," Vic Slaughter. Blaming himself for Slaughter's transformation from mercenary to undead killer, Morbius fought him alone and alongside the Nightstalkers. Morbius asked Nightstalker Frank Drake to use his necrotechnology on him, hoping it would cure his condition. Demoralized over this failure, Morbius was easy prey for Lilith's control during the so-called Midnight Massacre. He was slain by a Darkhold-empowered Blade, but was soon reborn.

Bolstered by the return of his friend Jack Russell to his life, Morbius continued seeking a cure. Dr. Strange informed him that he was now a soulless being, which brought about further depression. Using a page of the Darkhold himself, Morbius revived Martine, but found she was now the host for a Lilin named Parasite. The dark part of his soul tainted by Fang's blood began to emerge, as well, calling itself Bloodthirst and attempting to alter Morbius in both body and mind. The Werewolf and the Ghost Rider (Ketch) both sought to capture him, but in the end it was Morbius himself who drove the demon out. Martine was slain yet again, but an immortal named Embyrre resurrected her spirit. The couple was denied happiness, however, as Martine was now emotionless and increasingly frustrated with the fact that Morbius would not allow her the peace of death. After battles with Deathlok (Michael Collins), the Wraith, and Bloodthirst

(now in his own body), Morbius met the young Lena Ivana. Rescuing her from a life of forced prostitution, the two began a tumultuous romance. Still distraught over his failed relationship with Martine and his ongoing existence as a living vampire, Morbius killed himself, only to be revived by Weisenthal, who had created a serum to reanimate his friend.

Morbius then began a period of wandering, leaving behind his life as Morgan Michaels. He crossed paths with Blade in New Orleans, during Ulysses Sojourner's plot to unite the East Coast vampires under his rule, and later fought X-Man and Spider-Man. A few weeks later, Morbius sought out Dr. Andrea Jansen's help in finding a cure, only to discover that she was in league with Hydra and the villain Crown. Morbius seemingly sacrificed himself to destroy Crown, but was actually taken prisoner and experimented upon. After Crown's transformation into the vampiric Hunger, Morbius was freed by Blade and Spider-Man. Nearly mindless with bloodlust, Morbius bit Blade and fled the scene. Months later, Morbius attempted to feed on a paralyzed young man named Joey Beal, but was foiled by Spider-Man. The Living Vampire continues to search for a cure, hoping to somehow regain the humanity he lost so long ago.

Art by Isaac Cordova

HEIGHT: 5'10"
WEIGHT: 170 lbs.
EYES: Blue
HAIR: Black

SUPERHUMAN POWERS: Morbius' unique form of pseudo-vampirism gives him enhanced strength, regeneration, minor hypnotic powers, the ability to float on air currents, and limited control over the physical properties of his body. His bite is also capable of transforming others into pseudo-vampires.

ABILITIES: Morbius is one of the world's foremost experts on biochemistry and blood-related diseases.

PARAPHERNALIA: Morbius sometimes wears leather bodysuits for further protection.

POWER GRID	1	2	3	4	5	6	7
INTELLIGENCE							
STRENGTH							
SPEED							
DURABILITY							
ENERGY PROJECTION							
FIGHTING SKILLS							

HISTORY: Quentin Beck found his calling when his uncle gave him an old movie camera. Despite his widowed father making fun of him, he grew up to become a successful stunt man and special effects designer in Hollywood. That changed when he became frustrated and felt he wasn't getting the recognition he deserved. First he teamed up with the Tinkerer to steal industrial and military plans, with Beck donning an alien costume to throw potential snoopers off the track and leading a group of supposed extraterrestrials. Later, an article in the Daily Bugle gave Beck the idea of pretending to be Spider-Man and framing him for crimes, then becoming a hero and bringing Spider-Man to justice. Beck studied Spider-Man for weeks and was able to duplicate his powers, apart from spider-sense, mechanically. After a few robberies posing as the web-slinger, which added more grist to the mill for J. Jonah Jameson's vendetta, Beck, as Mysterio, trounced an unsuspecting Spider-Man. When they next met, Beck fought and apparently beat Spider-Man, then boasted how he had achieved it all. Spider-Man taped the confession and cleared his name. Despite the clever gadgetry Beck built in to the Mysterio costume, Spider-Man managed to defeat him.

Beck next joined up with Doctor Octopus when he formed the Sinister Six but the group had no better luck in defeating Spider-Man. Then Beck posed as Doctor Ludwig Rinehart, a psychiatrist visiting from Europe. Using illusions, Beck convinced Spider-Man that he was going mad and could only be cured if he revealed his secret identity. As Spider-Man was about to do just that, Jonah Jameson and Flash Thompson burst in, Jonah having been told that Rinehart was a fraud. This unexpected arrival spoiled Mysterio's scheme and Beck was soon returned to prison. Now unemployed, and with a criminal record, Beck planned a way to take revenge against Spider-Man and Jameson by staging a car crash where Spider-Man was the cause, and Jameson supposedly died. In reality, the "body" was an automaton, and the real Jameson was placed in a special-effects version of Hell. Emboldened by the seeming success of his plan, Beck found the courage to call a childhood friend, Betsy Schneider, and they started dating. After Spider-Man rescued Jameson, Betsy admiringly told Beck that they could make lots of money off his story. Beck became enraged, certain she was only using him. Later, he proposed marriage to Betsy, but she had changed her mind about him.

In yet another plan of revenge, Beck teamed up with the Wizard against Spider-Man and the Human Torch; after that failed, he bided his time in jail until he was able to escape. He then devised a series of elaborate traps in an abandoned amusement park, convincing Spider-Man that he was only six inches high. Back in prison, Beck had an epiphany of sorts; he realized that master criminals spent more time avoiding capture and battling foes than they did accumulating wealth and gaining power. He devised a quiet, long-term plan, a nursing home scam whereby he would trick the infirm into signing all their wealth over to him. To this end, he made use of his cellmate, Daniel Berkhart, taking him into his confidence, teaching h i m all his secrets and training him to replace him as Mysterio, even as he engineered his own "death." Berkhart was released, looking for revenge on behalf of his "buddy" Beck, and was hired by Jameson to pretend to be the ghost of Mysterio and capture Spider-Man. He

REAL NAME: Quentin Beck; Daniel "Danny" Berkhart
KNOWN ALIASES: (Beck) Nicholas Macabes, Rudolph Hines, Gerdes, Doctor Ludwig Rinehart; (Berkhart) Jack O'Lantern, Mad Jack
IDENTITY: Known to authorities
OCCUPATION: (Beck) former stunt man and special effects designer; (Berkhart) former criminal
CITIZENSHIP: U.S.A with a criminal record
PLACE OF BIRTH: (Beck) New York, New York; (Berkhart) unrevealed
MARITAL STATUS: Single
KNOWN RELATIVES: (Beck) Henrietta Beck (mother, deceased), Elmore Beck (father), Vincent (uncle) Maguire Beck (cousin)
GROUP AFFILIATION: (Beck) Sinister Six; (Berkhart) Sinister Seven, Sinister Six
EDUCATION: (both) High-school level
FIRST APPEARANCE: (Beck) Amazing Spider-Man Vol. 1 #13 (1964); (Berkhart) Amazing Spider-Man Vol. 1 #141 (1975)

Art by Staz Johnson

plagued Spider-Man with illusions, even as Peter Parker, by planting an image-inducer on the wall-crawler's costume. Spidey later used the inducer to track down and confront a nervous Berkhart. When Spider-Man wasn't fooled by the ghost routine, Berkhart lost his temper and was easily overcome.

Later, Beck assumed the identity of Doctor Rinehart and ran his scam at the Restwell Nursing Home on Long Island. He amassed eight million dollars in three years but ran afoul of the Burglar who had killed Peter's Uncle Ben. The Burglar had broken into the Parker home years before in search of a treasure hidden in the 1930s by the gangster Dutch Mallone and now sought more information from Aunt May who was a resident of the nursing home. The Burglar held "Rinehart" prisoner, inducing the "Doctor" to help. Beck figured he could dispose of the Burglar once he learned the treasure's location so he faked May's death from a heart attack to allow the Burglar to take her from the nursing home without Peter knowing. Spider-Man, however, recognized Beck and confronted him after battling numerous illusions. Eventually, Beck escaped to work on other, safer scams, among them a scheme to undermine Spider-Man's confidence by making him the cause of an innocent bystander's death.

These plans failed but Mysterio continued with others including an encounter with Spider-Man in which the web-slinger was confused by the appearance of the Mysterio-like Chief Examiner who tapped his power to use against the Black Fleet (Starblasters) assaulting his homeworld. Following struggles against the She-Hulk and Power Pack, Beck rejoined the Sinister Six but bailed out when he realized that Dr. Octopus (Otto Octavius) was using the group for his own ends. Later, the other five met, intending to get revenge on Doctor Octopus but Octavius anticipated such an attack and instead had another proposition for them involving the appropriation of Hydra's satellite control station. The others reluctantly accepted, though Beck secretly planned to take over once they had obtained their goal. During a heated battle with a number of different heroes, Beck made his play, causing the heroes to fight each other, but he was knocked unconscious by Deathlok (Michael Collins), who literally saw through the illusions.

Now unhinged, possibly due to exposure to his own hallucinogenic mist, Beck posed as Mr. Gerde, Dr. Octopus attorney (after the multi-armed criminal's apparent death) and forged a videotaped will, that used Octavius' relative Elias Hargrove as a pawn along with the remainder of the Sinister Six. Using misdirection and Spider-Man, Beck stole a data disk containing details on underworld figures. He needed Hargrove to get the right code, but Hargrove had worked out that the tape was a fake. Before he could coerce Hargrove, the Scarlet Spider stopped Beck. Beck set off the booby-trapped data disk, but the Scarlet Spider managed to escape with Hargrove just before the building exploded, with Beck apparently caught in the blast.

In a new scheme, Beck assumed the identity of Rudolph Hines and set up a new network, "Mystery Vision," which sent addictive subliminal signals to viewers mesmerized in front of their TVs. With ratings soaring, Beck also plotted to use an unsuspecting Spider-Man (Ben Reilly) as part of his programming. He tricked Spider-Man into wearing receivers, but when Ben realized what was happening he was able to trace the source of the transmissions and put the transmitter out of action. With no special signal, the network's ratings plummeted, and Beck's fame was over. While in prison after another failed union with the Sinister Six, he learned he was dying as a result of prolonged exposure to his special effects chemicals. On release he planned his swan song. But the Ben Reilly Spider-Man was not the one he knew, so he decided to destroy Daredevil

instead. Buying information from the Kingpin, he proceeded to drive Daredevil insane, both with drugs and by harming or killing those close to him. Beck's final attempt to goad Daredevil into killing him failed, and he apparently committed suicide by shooting himself in the head.

Upon learning of Beck's death, Berkhart again took up the Mysterio identity, giving his Mad Jack identity to his protégé Maguire Beck, Quentin's cousin. He joined in with the Sinister Seven, ostensibly to get vengeance on Doctor Octopus, but in reality to use them for his own ends. He and Electro gained control of Senator Stewart Ward, who had been permeated with a strange energy. Before they could make use of him though, they had to deal with Venom, who was hunting down the rest of the Sinister team members. Berkhart abandoned the group and instead kidnapped those who had the most contact with Spider-Man, subjecting them to an artificial scenario in which Flash Thompson was a super hero in an attempt to learn Spider-Man's identity. Flash finally broke free of the illusion but Berkhart escaped. Most recently, Berkhart was involved with Maguire in a plan to kill Spider-Man, Daredevil, Joe Smith and Betsy Schneider. His current whereabouts are unknown, though he has been spotted in New York.

HEIGHT: (Beck) 5'11"; (Berkhart) 5'10"
WEIGHT: (Beck) 175 lbs.; (Berkhart) 160 lbs.
EYES: (Beck) brown; (Berkhart) blue
HAIR: (Beck) black; (Berkhart) brown

ABILITIES: Beck was a master of make-up, physical stunt work, mechanical and visual special effects. He knew basic psychiatry and could employ hypnotism successfully. He also learned a great deal of applied chemistry, especially the use of hallucinogens, and electronics. Beck was a meticulous planner and organizer, and a skilled actor who kept himself in top physical form. Berkhart learned these skills from Beck.

PARAPHERNALIA: Beck's original Mysterio costume contained boots with chemical smoke ejectors to produce a concealing mist, magnetic plate springs allowing him to leap heights, an acid spray in his gloves, enabling him to dissolve Spider-Man's webbing, and a one-way helmet with a built-in sonar device that jammed Spider-Man's spider-sense and allowed Mysterio to see through his mist. In subsequent encounters, he improved on his costume, adding a "psychedelic power" to his helmet, knock-out gas, an electrically-charged cloak, hypnogens in his cloaking mist, and electric bolts from his gloves. Beck used a tranquilizer dart gun, an electro-magnetic disrupter beam, automatons, holographic projectors, and a stolen Digital Imagery Transmission chip. Beck was not above using out-of-work actors with criminal tendencies as part of his plans. Berkhart used Beck's equipment but also employed a sensory-deprivation tank to enhance the effect of his hallucinogens.

POWER GRID	1	2	3	4	5	6	7
INTELLIGENCE							
STRENGTH							
SPEED							
DURABILITY							
ENERGY PROJECTION							
FIGHTING SKILLS							

LIZ OSBORN

HISTORY: The daughter of a restaurant and hotel owner, Liz Allan came from a family of privilege. She and Peter Parker were childhood friends, but once in high school she became part of the "popular crowd" (along with boyfriend Flash Thompson and buddies Jason Ionello, Sean "Tiny" McKeever, Seymour O'Reilly, and Sally Avril) who were often picking on him. However, when everyone thought that Peter was foolishly impersonating Spider-Man to rescue Betty Brant from Dr. Octopus, Liz recognized Peter's bravery—and actually developed a crush on him. Liz's flirting with him irked Flash so greatly that it led the rivals to a boxing match and a prom-night dare on the unprotected edge of a bridge.

After graduation, Liz left Flash and the old crowd behind. She became a nurse's aid, privately tending to her stepbrother, Mark Raxton, the Molten Man. The Molten Man went out of control, and Liz sought Peter for some levelheaded advice. Liz joined Peter's inner circle of friends where she met Harry Osborn, who had returned from psychiatric care after becoming the Green Goblin. Liz and Harry began dating following Harry's heroics at Betty's wedding and the two fell in love. Liz was arrested trying to steal chemicals from her hospital workplace to help the Molten Man deal with his fiery condition. Ashamed, and fearful of damaging her boyfriend's reputation, Liz left Harry. Later, after tackling the Green Goblin (Bart Hamilton) with Spider-Man, Harry returned home to find Liz waiting for him. With Harry's new responsibilities at Osborn Industries, the couple left for the New Jersey suburbs and married, seeking a peaceful life.

That peace was short-lived thanks to both Molten Man and Hobgoblin (Roderick Kingsley) threatening the Osborn family. After a difficult labor brought on by the trauma of facing the Hobgoblin, Liz gave birth to a son, Norman Harold Osborn, and asked Peter and Mary Jane to be the godparents. When the Parkers were evicted, Harry and Liz took them in as tenants. Harry began to lose mental stability again and returned to menacing Spider-Man as the Green Goblin. Liz drifted into a state of denial, unable to cope with her husband's madness. Tragically, Harry was poisoned by an experimental Goblin formula, leaving Liz a young widow. Following Harry's death, Liz took over his responsibilities within Osborn Industries. During this time, she endured the kidnapping of her son by robotic Goblinettes left behind by Harry. "Normie" was rescued by Spider-Man and the reformed Molten Man. Upon her father-in-law's return from the "dead," Liz lost control of the company. She dated Foggy Nelson for a short time until Mysterio intervened in the relationship. She remains one of Peter Parker's oldest friends.

REAL NAME: Elizabeth Allan Osborn
KNOWN ALIASES: None
IDENTITY: No dual identity
OCCUPATION: Independent means; former executive of Osborn Industries, nurse's aid
CITIZENSHIP: U.S.A. with a criminal record for attempted robbery
PLACE OF BIRTH: Queens, New York
MARITAL STATUS: Widowed
KNOWN RELATIVES: Wilson Allan (father), Doris Raxton (mother), Norman Harold Osborn (son), Harold "Harry" Osborn (Green Goblin, husband, deceased), Norman Osborn (Green Goblin, father-in-law), Mark Raxton (Molten Man, stepbrother)
GROUP AFFILIATION: Osborn Industries
EDUCATION: Graduate of Midtown High School and Certified Nurse's Aid program
FIRST APPEARANCE: Amazing Fantasy Vol. 1 #15 (1962)

HEIGHT: 5'9"
WEIGHT: 135 lbs.
EYES: Blue
HAIR: Blonde

ABILITIES: Liz Osborn is an accomplished nurse's aid and businesswoman.

POWER GRID	1	2	3	4	5	6	7
INTELLIGENCE							
STRENGTH							
SPEED							
DURABILITY							
ENERGY PROJECTION							
FIGHTING SKILLS							

Art by Sal Buscema

QUEEN

REAL NAME: Adriana "Ana" Soria
KNOWN ALIASES: None
IDENTITY: Secret, known only to high-ranking American officials
OCCUPATION: None; former American soldier
CITIZENSHIP: U.S.A.
PLACE OF BIRTH: Unknown
MARITAL STATUS: Single
KNOWN RELATIVES: None
GROUP AFFILIATION: None
EDUCATION: Unrevealed
FIRST APPEARANCE: Spectacular Spider-Man Vol. 3 #15 (2004)

HISTORY: During the Second World War, Ana Soria was the first female Marine in combat. In the late stages of the war, the Americans feared they were not powerful enough to contain the Japanese or the Soviets. Using Captain America as a model, they continued with super-soldier experimentation on genetically likely subjects, none of whom were properly informed. Already a mutant, Ana was lined up with several officers on the island of Bikini Atoll, where they were blasted with the radiation of nuclear weapons in order to release latent powers. Most were killed, but Ana survived, warping into a human-insect hybrid. However, when the experiments did not produce obvious results, the program was shut down and Ana was thrown into a military asylum, her mind fractured. Worse, Captain America, with whom Ana had a close relationship, was believed killed at the end of the war, which only encouraged the U.S. government to abandon her. In the 1950s, however, Ana escaped and went into hiding.

Recently, Ana surfaced in New York, still youthful and calling herself "the Queen". She demonstrated complete control over anyone possessing the so-called "insect gene," Spider-Man among them. While her human drones built her a nest in a New York highrise, Ana chose Spider-Man as her mate. She forced a fateful kiss on the web-slinger that unleashed an enzyme into his body. When he resisted, she began executing civilians, then used her powers to immobilize him. Spider-Man was only saved when Captain America knocked Ana off the building. Surviving the fall, Ana moved her operations underground to a secret lab, where she had held the doctor responsible for her transformation since abducting him years before, and waited for the arrival of Spider-Man who was slowly mutating due to her kiss. Initially growing extra eyes, extra arms and fangs, Spider-Man was drawn to and defeated by the Queen before completely morphing into a giant spider. Ana expected the spider to give birth to her offspring but once the transformation was complete the spider died instead. Distraught, Ana destroyed the lab and left without witnessing Peter Parker's rebirth from the spider's womb, with a few extra spider-like powers. Ana still held New York hostage, threatening to detonate a bomb that would exterminate all human life within 600 miles. Spider-Man disarmed the bomb and an unrelated explosion seemingly killed Ana.

HEIGHT: 5'10"
WEIGHT: 125 lbs.
EYES: Brown
HAIR: Black

SUPERHUMAN POWERS: Ana can lift up to one ton and can control the motor functions of all insects and humans possessing the "insect gene." She is telekinetic and possesses a destructive sonic scream that can be focused with great precision.

ABILITIES: Ana was a dedicated soldier in the U.S. military, and possessed a high degree of combat training in both weaponry and fighting skills.

POWER GRID	1	2	3	4	5	6	7
INTELLIGENCE							
STRENGTH							
SPEED							
DURABILITY							
ENERGY PROJECTION							
FIGHTING SKILLS							

HISTORY: Ben Reilly was the most genetically stable of the many clones of Spider-Man created by Professor Miles Warren. After many failed attempts, Warren succeeded in creating a clone that did not suffer cellular degeneration. The Jackal pitted this clone against Spider-Man in a deathtrap involving a bomb and Ned Leeds. The Jackal on scene, a clone of Warren, repented and saved Ned, dying as a result. With both Spideys unconscious, the real Jackal emerged, found who he thought was the real Spider-Man, and injected him with a drug to simulate death. The other Spider-Man awoke and dropped the "dead" body in a smokestack, where the Jackal implanted it with clone memories. However, his assistant, Seward Trainer, himself coerced by the Green Goblin (Norman Osborn), had deceived the Jackal: the Spider-Man the Jackal recovered was the clone after all.

Reviving and returning home, the clone discovered the other Peter already there. Now believing himself the imposter, the clone named himself after "Uncle" Ben and "Aunt" May Reilly Parker and spent the next five years wandering. He also met and was befriended by Seward Trainer. Ben anonymously called to check up on Aunt May occasionally, but did not return to New York until he heard that she had been hospitalized.

Back in New York, Ben adopted a new costume and was dubbed the Scarlet Spider. His return triggered the release from stasis of the Jackal, who raised the possibility that Peter, not Ben, was the clone. When Seward Trainer, following up his earlier deception of the Jackal, announced that Ben was indeed the original Spider-Man, Ben assured Peter he had no intention of taking back his life. Together, Peter and Ben stopped the Jackal's plan to unleash the Carrion virus on the world.

Originally distrustful of each other, the two Spiders developed an uneasy alliance that slowly grew to strong friendship. As Peter considered the impending responsibility of fatherhood, he relinquished the title of Spider-Man to Ben. But Ben created his own life, bleaching his hair and working at a coffee shop. As Spider-Man, Ben slightly modified the classic costume. Believing to the end that he was the real Spider-Man, Ben was killed by the Green Goblin (Norman Osborn), sacrificing his life to save Peter from the impaling spike of the Goblin's glider. Ben's body degenerated into dust immediately after his death.

ASSUMED NAME: Benjamin Reilly
KNOWN ALIASES: Spider-Man, the Scarlet Spider, Spider-Man's clone
IDENTITY: Secret
OCCUPATION: Server at the Daily Grind coffee shop; former teaching assistant, septic system telemarketer, waiter/bodyguard at the Club Noir, many others
CITIZENSHIP: None
PLACE OF ORIGIN: The Jackal's laboratory, New York City
MARITAL STATUS: Single
KNOWN RELATIVES: Peter Parker (Spider-Man, "brother"); Miles Warren (The Jackal, creator); Kaine, Jack, Guardian, Spidercide, uncountable unnamed clones (fellow clones)
GROUP AFFILIATION: The New Warriors
EDUCATION: Possesses Peter's memories of attending university
FIRST APPEARANCE: Amazing Spider-Man #149 (1975)

HEIGHT: 5'10"
WEIGHT: 165 lbs.
EYES: Hazel
HAIR: Brown (bleached blond)

SUPERHUMAN POWERS: Ben shared Peter Parker's spider-powers, including superhuman strength, speed, agility, and the ability to cling to surfaces. Ben's spider-sense was the same as Peter's, except that it could not be overridden by Venom.

PARAPHERNALIA: Web-shooters, impact webbing, stingers

POWER GRID	1	2	3	4	5	6	7
INTELLIGENCE							
STRENGTH							
SPEED							
DURABILITY							
ENERGY PROJECTION							
FIGHTING SKILLS							

JOE ROBERTSON

REAL NAME: Joseph Robertson
KNOWN ALIASES: Robbie
IDENTITY: No dual identity
OCCUPATION: Editor-in-Chief, Daily Bugle; former convict, city editor, reporter
CITIZENSHIP: U.S.A. with a criminal record (pardoned)
PLACE OF BIRTH: Harlem, New York
MARITAL STATUS: Married
KNOWN RELATIVES: Martha (wife), Patrick Henry (son, deceased), Randolph (Randy, son), Samuel Robertson (father, deceased), Alice Robertson (mother, deceased), Amanda (Mandy, ex-daughter-in-law)
GROUP AFFILIATION: Daily Bugle staff, Jameson News Digest staff
EDUCATION: Columbia School of Journalism graduate
FIRST APPEARANCE: Amazing Spider-Man Vol. 1 #51 (1967)

HISTORY: Joe Robertson was born to be a journalist. As a student at Harlem High School, he worked for the school paper, becoming its editor during his senior year and winning a scholarship to the Columbia School of Journalism. Hardworking and dedicated, "Robbie" was a fearless reporter—until he ran afoul of one particular subject, fellow Harlem student Lonnie Thompson Lincoln, nicknamed Tombstone. A massive albino taunted by his peers because of his appearance, the brutal Lonnie considered Robbie a friend of sorts since Robbie was one of the few who never mocked him; however, when Lonnie began using his considerable strength to extort money from classmates, Robbie prepared a story for the Harlem High paper exposing Lonnie's activities. Ambushing Robbie after school, Tombstone beat him bloody until Robbie agreed to kill the story, which never saw print. Lonnie saw this as a cordial understanding between friends, but Robbie was disgusted with himself and determined never to compromise his ethics again.

Putting the Tombstone incident behind him, Joe graduated from Harlem, attended Columbia, got his degree, and landed a job several years later as a night-desk catcher with a Philadelphia newspaper. He also married his girlfriend, Martha, but Robbie's old secret would soon come back to haunt his new life. When a telephone tipster told Robbie he knew who had killed local crimelord Ozzy Montana, Robbie set up a secret waterfront meeting; but he found his informant dead in the grip of Tombstone, who had become a mob hitman with a penchant for snapping necks. Robbie fled and kept quiet about the whole incident, fearful of what Tombstone might do to him or his wife if he talked. Joe realized he had never fully recovered from his early encounters with Tombstone, and that the killer had a strange sort of hold over him.

Trying to forget his Tombstone failures, Robbie threw himself back into his journalism career. He and Martha moved back to Manhattan, where Joe became a reporter for the Daily Bugle. Over the next twenty years, Robbie rose through the ranks to become the Bugle's city editor and one of the city's most respected journalists. He formed a close friendship with the Bugle's publisher and editor-in-chief, J. Jonah Jameson, supplying a calming yin to Jameson's raging yang. Though a good newspaperman at heart with a strong social conscience, Jameson has often allowed his personal biases to compromise his journalistic perspective, but Robbie's counterbalancing views have kept the Bugle's news coverage relatively fair (unlike many of Jameson's editorials). Jameson and Robertson have sharply differing views on super heroes in general and Spider-Man in particular. Jameson tends to regard costumed vigilantes with suspicion and contempt, and is consumed by a jealous loathing of Spider-Man, not knowing the hero is secretly young Bugle photographer Peter Parker. Robbie has a more objective view of New York's super heroes, judging them by their actions, and has aided Spider-Man and other heroes on many occasions. Robbie has also been something of a fatherly mentor to Peter Parker, and has often seemed aware of Peter's dual identity; but he has never voiced, exploited or acted on this knowledge, and has even protected Peter's secret on occasion, such as when he steered Bugle reporter Ken Ellis away from learning the truth.

Robertson and Spider-Man first worked together when Robbie helped Spider-Man capture the criminal Chameleon. Later, when Robbie exposed corrupt politician Sam Bullitt, Spider-Man and Iceman teamed up to rescue Robertson from a vengeful Bullitt's thugs. Robbie went on to target another corrupt politician, mayoral candidate Richard Raleigh, and Spider-Man saved Robertson from Raleigh's savage super-agent, the Smasher, who later killed Raleigh himself.

Robbie's family life often ran less smoothly than his professional life. His firstborn son, Patrick, died while still an infant. His second son, Randy, grew to adulthood, but often fought bitterly with his father over their differing beliefs. An anti-establishment radical, Randy was a key player in student protest movements at Empire State University, where Robbie sometimes intervened as both father and reporter. Ultimately deciding to pursue social work as a career rather than journalism, Randy transferred to the University of Pittsburgh, where he met and married a white Jewish woman named Amanda, much to Robbie's discomfort. Randy eventually moved back to New York and found employment as a social worker, and Robbie gradually accepted his son's mixed marriage, though Randy and Amanda later broke up. In recent times, Randy has been dating Glory Grant, long-time secretary to Jameson and Robertson at the Daily Bugle.

Jameson's obsessive hatred of Spider-Man drove him to unusual lengths over the years, including the funding of several projects designed to capture, humiliate or destroy the hero. One such project created the mad super-criminal known as the Scorpion. Jameson kept his involvement secret for years, but after the Hobgoblin (Roderick Kingsley) tried to blackmail him using this information, Jameson made a full public confession and stepped down as the Bugle's editor-in-chief, promoting Robertson to replace him. While Jameson has remained a very hands-on presence in the Bugle as its publisher, Robertson has proved very successful and effective in his new role as the paper's chief editor. He has been a friend and mentor to reporters and columnists such as Betty Brant, Kate Cushing (his successor as city editor), Kat Farrell, Ned Leeds, Joy Mercado, Leila Taylor and Ben Urich.

Then, at the height of Robbie's success, Tombstone brought his whole world crashing down. After years of rising through the ranks of organized crime as a Philadelphia mob enforcer, Tombstone began working for New York crime boss Wilson Fisk, the Kingpin. Consumed by guilt over having helped make Tombstone's many murders possible with his silence, Robbie confronted Tombstone with a gun, intending to take him into custody and tell the police everything. Lonnie overpowered Joe and seriously injured him, seemingly breaking his back. By this time, Robbie had left an audiotape with Peter Parker, confessing his role as an accessory in Tombstone's criminal career. But when Tombstone menaced the crippled Robertson in the hospital, Joe began to have second thoughts about going to the police. Berated by Parker and reporter Ben Urich for his weakness, and supported by Randy, Robbie finally worked up the courage to face his fears. He rapidly regained his mobility through physical therapy, and made a full confession of his Tombstone secrets to his Bugle colleagues and the public. Robbie offered to resign his editorial post, but Jameson refused to accept his resignation. Lonnie, meanwhile, had been captured by Spider-Man, who was baffled by Tombstone's admission that he spared Robertson's life because he still regarded Robbie as his friend.

The public and Robertson's colleagues seemed prepared to forgive his mistakes, but a corrupt Kingpin-connected judge sent Robbie to prison for his indirect role in Tombstone's crimes. To make matters worse, Tombstone fixed it so that he and Robbie ended up in the same federal prison, where Lonnie and his cronies could continue to haunt his old friend. Robertson befriended a massive convict known as Bruiser, who acted as his bodyguard for a time, but Bruiser was ultimately taken unawares and beaten to death. Later, Tombstone broke out of prison, taking Robbie with him as a hostage. When Spider-Man intervened, Tombstone had the hero at his mercy and was about to kick him off an airborne helicopter, but Robbie tackled Tombstone first, sending himself and Lonnie hurtling toward

Earth. Incredibly, they survived the fall and landed in a riverbed on Amish farmland, where Tombstone forced the Amish folk to treat the seriously injured Robbie, then challenged Robertson to a duel to settle their differences. Robertson was taking a beating until he finally struck back by stabbing Tombstone with a nearby pitchfork. Badly wounded and shocked that his "friend" Robbie would do this to him, Tombstone staggered off alone, and Robbie turned himself in to the authorities; however, the late Bruiser's brother, attorney Stuart McPhee, used his connections to secure Robertson a Presidential pardon. Robbie was released from prison and reclaimed his post at the Bugle.

Tombstone soon resurfaced and Robertson confronted him again, this time shooting Lonnie; as a result of this encounter, Tombstone was accidentally exposed to an experimental gas that made him superhumanly powerful. Pleased with this outcome, even grateful, Lonnie gave up his vendetta against Robertson and told Robbie their debts were settled, though Tombstone remains active as a dangerous super-criminal. Robertson, meanwhile, has remained a mainstay of the Daily Bugle. When Thomas Firehart (alias Puma) engineered a hostile takeover of the paper as part of a misguided scheme to improve Spider-Man's reputation, Robbie was among the Bugle veterans who joined Jonah in publishing the new Jameson News Digest until Jameson regained control of the Bugle and they all returned to their old positions. Later, when corrupt industrialist Norman Osborn seized control of the Bugle, Robbie resigned in protest, but returned after Jameson squeezed Osborn out. More recently, Robbie has finally made some headway in moderating the anti-super-hero views of Jameson, and they have hired retired super hero Jessica Jones to collaborate with Ben Urich on a superhuman affairs column called The Pulse. In addition to his Spider-Man connection, Robertson maintains cordial relations with various other New York superheroes — notably the Falcon (Sam Wilson), whom he considers a friend. Robertson and Bugle columnist Leila Taylor recently helped Captain America and the Falcon subvert rogue U.S. naval operations supervised by Admiral Jimmy Westbrook in cooperation with the Rivas drug cartel. During these events, Robbie also helped Cap realize how Falcon's personality had been drastically altered for the worse by the Scarlet Witch, urging Cap's intervention.

HEIGHT: 6'1"
WEIGHT: 210 lbs.
EYES: Brown
HAIR: White

ABILITIES: Robbie is a veteran editor, manager and reporter, well respected for his wisdom, courage and integrity. He is renowned for his saintly patience, sly wit and relentless work ethic. He has some experience with hand-to-hand combat and firearms, but is unskilled and reluctant in these areas, and seldom has to rely on violence. A lifelong pipe-smoker, Robbie is seldom seen without his trademark pipe.

POWER GRID	1	2	3	4	5	6	7
INTELLIGENCE							
STRENGTH							
SPEED							
DURABILITY							
ENERGY PROJECTION							
FIGHTING SKILLS							

JOE SMITH

REAL NAME: Joseph "Joe" Smith
KNOWN ALIASES: Guy Named Joe, Crimson Bat
IDENTITY: Secret
OCCUPATION: Child care assistant, learning support worker; former actor, stuntman, wrestler, boxer
CITIZENSHIP: U.S.A.
PLACE OF BIRTH: Unrevealed
MARITAL STATUS: Married
KNOWN RELATIVES: Betsy Schneider (wife), Liz (ex-wife), Joe, Jr. (son, deceased)
GROUP AFFILIATION: None
EDUCATION: High-school equivalent
FIRST APPEARANCE: Amazing Spider-Man Vol. 1 #38 (1966)

HISTORY: A born loser with big dreams, Joe failed at boxing and professional wrestling. His manager, Tommy Tomkins, made him a TV fantasy film extra; wearing an alien costume, Joe accidentally gained power in an electrified pool of chemicals. The dazed Joe went on a rampage, seeking vengeance on those who had mocked him. Joe held his own against Spider-Man, but eventually his head cleared and his powers faded. Exonerated due to presumptive temporary insanity, Joe's performance led to a new job. Allegedly starring in a weekly TV series, Joe actually played the lead in the low-budget science fiction potboiler *The Alien and the Ozone*. His unspectacular performance interrupted by Mysterio, Joe saw his chance to shine again. He confronted Mysterio to free kidnapping victim Betsy Schneider; powerless, he lasted only five seconds, with Spider-Man saving his life. Joe rescued Betsy and then literally pulled the plug on Mysterio's power source, enabling Spider-Man to quickly defeat him. Joe and Betsy had a brief romance, after which he starred as the Crimson Bat, meeting and marrying studio script girl Liz.

The Crimson Bat was cancelled after three years, and the typecast Joe was unemployed. His son, Joe Jr., had severe birth defects, leaving him mentally handicapped and fragile. Devastated, Liz left Joe, but Joe never gave up, taking his son for special care despite being in financial straits. Joey eventually died, triggering in Joe a post-traumatic stress flashback. His powers re-emerged, again affecting his mind, driving him to seek vengeance on benefit-cutting bureaucrats. These assaults led Captain America to learn Joe's history, and he managed to subdue and reach Joe, convincing him his son's death was not his fault. Regaining his mind, Joe surrendered and was given medical care. Medications restored Joe's sanity, and he was released on time served plus community service. Working at a children's center, Joe found his true calling. When the center was vandalized, the powerless Joe donned his costume in a failed attempt to intimidate the culprits. However, his actions inspired the neighborhood to drive off the gang. Joe later decked small-time criminal Red Bear, who stole from an art gallery and knocked over an old woman. Reunited with and married to Betsy Schneider, they were abducted by Mysterio (Danny Berkhart) and Mad Jack (Maguire Beck) who targeted all who had crossed the various incarnations of Mysterio. Joe helped capture Mad Jack, possibly regaining his power in the process. Betsy decided to write stories about her new hero: A Guy Named Joe.

HEIGHT: 6'1"
WEIGHT: 225 lbs.
EYES: Blue
HAIR: Reddish-brown

SUPERHUMAN POWERS: Joe intermittently demonstrates superhuman strength and durability, often accompanied by dazed and aggressive behavior.

ABILITIES: Joe has limited experience and skill in boxing and wrestling.

POWER GRID	1	2	3	4	5	6	7
INTELLIGENCE							
STRENGTH							
SPEED							
DURABILITY							
ENERGY PROJECTION							
FIGHTING SKILLS							

HISTORY: Mutated by the bite of an irradiated spider, Peter Parker's failure to stop a burglar led to his Uncle Ben's death. Having learned that with great power comes great responsibility, he became Spider-Man. Recently Peter was made to question his powers by the mysterious Ezekiel, who shared the same abilities and said they derived from magic. Ezekiel had stolen his powers through a mystical ceremony and needed to sacrifice Spider-Man to keep them. When his ritual joined their minds, however, Ezekiel realized Spider-Man was the worthy hero and sacrificed himself.

Back home, Spider-Man fought the two adult children of his ex-love, Gwen Stacy. Years before, Gwen had slept with Norman Osborn and given birth to twins, Gabriel and Sarah. After his own "death," Osborn found the pair, who were aging rapidly due to their genetic inheritance of the Goblin formula. Osborn told them that Peter was their father and had killed their mother but Spider-Man eventually made them face the truth.

Osborn also revealed Spider-Man's identity to Mac Gargan, the Scorpion, and had him kidnap Aunt May. Osborn had been publicly revealed as the Green Goblin and jailed after murdering journalist Terri Kidder. He knew big businesses had been conspiring since the 1950s to create super-villains and, as a potential whistle-blower, was an easy target in prison. Osborn wanted Peter to break him out in return for May's freedom but, when Peter did, a battle erupted with the Sinister Twelve, including Gargan himself—now a new Venom after bonding with the alien symbiote. Around this time, Spider-Man met The Queen who had powers allowing her to control the world's insects, eventually causing Spider-Man to mutate into a giant spider. She planned to detonate a bomb that would kill everyone except those with the insect gene but Peter returned to his human form and stopped her, albeit with enhanced powers. Recently, Spider-Man joined the new Avengers. No matter his change in powers or group membership, Spider-Man is always one of the world's greatest heroes.

REAL NAME: Peter Benjamin Parker
KNOWN ALIASES: Formerly Hornet, Dusk, Ricochet, Prodigy, Black Marvel, Captain Universe, others
IDENTITY: Secret, known to certain government officials
OCCUPATION: Freelance photographer, science teacher
CITIZENSHIP: U.S.A.
PLACE OF BIRTH: New York City
MARITAL STATUS: Married
KNOWN RELATIVES: Richard Parker (father, deceased), Mary Parker (mother, deceased), Benjamin Parker (uncle, deceased), May Parker (aunt), Will Fitzpatrick (grandfather), Mary Jane Watson-Parker (wife), May Parker (daughter, deceased), Benjamin Reilly (Scarlet Spider, clone, deceased), Kaine (clone), other clones (deceased)
GROUP AFFILIATION: The Avengers
EDUCATION: College educated (science major), doctorate studies in biochemistry (incomplete)
FIRST APPEARANCE: Amazing Fantasy Vol. 1 #15 (1962)

HEIGHT: 5'10"
WEIGHT: 170 lbs.
EYES: Hazel
HAIR: Brown

SUPERHUMAN POWERS: Peter can cling to most surfaces, can now lift 15 tons, and is roughly 15 times more agile than a regular human. His spider-sense has increased from giving him an early warning to include a psychic alignment with his environment, specifically to insects. He can create organic webs limited by his body's health and nutrition.

ABILITIES: Peter is an accomplished scientist, inventor and photographer.

PARAPHERNALIA: Spider-tracers that he can follow with his spider-sense; the spider-signal

POWER GRID	1	2	3	4	5	6	7
INTELLIGENCE							
STRENGTH							
SPEED							
DURABILITY							
ENERGY PROJECTION							
FIGHTING SKILLS							

Art by Mike Deodato Jr.

SPIDER-MOBILE

FIRST APPEARANCE: Amazing Spider-Man Vol. 1 #130 (1974)

HISTORY: At a time when Spider-Man was wanted by the police, advertising agency Carter and Lombardo decided that he would be the ideal person to promote the new non-polluting engine of their client, Corona Motors. Spider-Man turned them down when initially approached, as he thought it was a dumb idea, but later changed his mind when an eviction notice for non-payment of rent came in. Spider-Man agreed to the plan for a thousand dollars cash in advance, only to learn he had to design and build the car as well. Not having the right engineering skills, he enlisted the Human Torch's help. Two months later, the Spider-Mobile was finished in a dune buggy design, most probably based on the Meyers Manx.

Spider-Man was still not enamored with the idea, calling it a "Four-wheeled Fiasco" and other like endearments. On its first test run, it performed better than Spider-Man, who caused havoc with his driving. He revealed to Torch that he had never needed a driver's license. Later, intending to deliver it to Carter and Lombardo for the remainder of his advance, Spider-Man used the Mobile to defeat Hammerhead's henchmen, and it survived a direct hit from Hammerhead himself. The Spider-Mobile was left in its camouflaged state for a few months, before Spider-Man used it once again, this time to help him in his search for the Jackal. Instead, he ran into the police, then Mysterio, and as a result of one of Mysterio's illusions, ended up driving it off a pier in the mistaken belief the pier was an alley. The Mobile ended up at the bottom of the Hudson River.

Events caught up with Spider-Man, and it wasn't until several months later, when he saw an ad in the Bugle threatening to sue him if he didn't return the Spider-Mobile, that he attempted to salvage the vehicle. The only sign of it, however, was a side-view mirror. Not too long after, Spider-Man was attacked by the vehicle, modified by the Tinkerer for an undisclosed client. Spider-Man was able to defeat his foe and recover a now wrecked Spider-Mobile. He then kept his part of the deal with Carter and Lombardo, and delivered the car, 14 stories above Madison Avenue. Spider-Man recently had another brief encounter with the car, or a perfect replica of it, from the Cooper-Hewitt National Design Museum. The Spider-Mobile is a part of his past that Spider-Man would rather forget.

Art by Paul Smith

TOP SPEED: 125 mph
ENGINE RATING: 1650cc
SPECIAL FEATURES: A spider-signal mounted centrally on the roll bar; web-cannons mounted behind swivel headlamps; an ejector seat. The body was made of a tough steel alloy and painted to resemble Spider-Man's costume. A switch enabled the buggy to be automatically camouflaged to resemble an inconspicuous '50s Chevrolet Fleetline. Modifications made later by the Tinkerer added the ability to drive it by remote control; special tires; an electron gyroscope which allowed it to drive up walls.

Art by Ross Andru

SPIDER-SLAYERS

FIRST APPEARANCE: Amazing Spider-Man Vol. 1 #25 (1965)

HISTORY: The Spider-Slayers are robots originally designed by Spencer Smythe to capture and destroy Spider-Man. Smythe read J. Jonah Jameson's many anti-Spider-Man editorials, and offered his services to the publisher. Jameson quickly dismissed the solicitation until Peter Parker, thinking the robot to be a laughable, easy means to sell photographs to the Bugle, appealed to Jonah's ego and convinced him to use the robot. Parker lived to regret his underestimation of the Spider-Slayer and the legacy of subsequently more powerful models built by Spencer, his son, Alistair, and even Jameson's current wife, Marla Madison.

VERSION I: A biped with extensible legs developed by Spencer Smythe, with funding from J. Jonah Jameson, which featured a near-inexhaustible power supply and a web-resistant oily coating, it was remote-controlled via an embedded video feed. A screen and loudspeaker displayed the face and voice of the operator. The robot tracked Spider-Man with a "hyper-sensitive Geiger-type apparatus" and unleashed auto-sensing steel tendrils to trap him. Spider-Man was unable to break free of the steel bindings while Jameson, controlling the robot, taunted him. However, he was able to defeat it by removing its chest plate with his fingertip suction and manipulating the electronics to set himself free. Later, the Reanimator salvaged the discarded Slayer. He activated it and other robots when Wolverine tracked him down. The Version I was quickly destroyed by Wolverine's claws. Spider-Girl also faced a Version I Spider-Slayer when she traveled from her alternative future timeline to her father's high-school days. She dodged the Slayer, allowing Spider-Man to defeat the robot in the same manner as he did originally.

VERSION II: The so-called "Invincible Spider-Slayer" was humanoid in shape. Larger and more powerful than its predecessor, its controls were far more sensitive, and it was built to track anything with a spider's scent. Like Version I, Version II also bore the face of the robot's controller, J. Jonah Jameson. Capable of climbing walls and armed with a "destructo-beam," Version II was slow—but seemingly unstoppable. While Jameson only wanted to trap Spidey, Smythe wanted him dead, so he took over the controls from Jameson. Spider-Man defeated the Slayer by confusing it with many spiders. Unaware of the multiple arachnids, Smythe increased the Slayer to full power, causing it to short-circuit and explode.

VERSION III: A giant steel spider, Version III was also funded by Jameson. Capable of shooting steel webbing, climbing walls,

and striking with uncanny speed, the robot was faster, stronger, and deadlier than Spider-Man himself. It also featured a nullifier capable of blocking Spider-Man's spider-sense. This prototype possessed the power to defeat the web-slinger, but Smythe had other plans for it. As New York City's scientific advisor, he had persuaded the mayor to establish a network of video cameras throughout Manhattan. Jameson thought the Slayer he was guiding to capture Spider-Man was malfunctioning, but Smythe actually had taken control of the unit and led it into the lab housing the camera network's master control unit. When the robot stole the device and returned to Smythe, Spider-Man was left to take the blame.

VERSION IV: With unlimited access to the city's video cameras from the computer element stolen by Version III, Smythe found himself able to get away with virtually any crime. Smythe attracted four major local gang lords and suggested criminal uses for the camera network. When Spider-Man pretended to be unmasked in front of the cameras, mocking Smythe, the mobsters demanded that Smythe take care of the wall-crawler first before making any deals. Smythe then called upon Version IV—a full-sized iteration of Version III. This creature was so large that its inventor could ride inside it. Equipped with an ethyl-chloride spray that weakened the web-slinger, the Slayer captured Spider-Man. While the mobsters went to rob a bank, assisted by the camera network, Spider-Man took advantage of Smythe's distraction and broke free of the Slayer's coils. Spidey sabotaged the Slayer with his webbing and by rearranging its controls before capturing the gangsters. Smythe arrived in the Slayer, but was trapped inside when the malfunctioning machine ensnared itself.

VERSION V: With Smythe now marked as a criminal, Jameson enlisted his future wife, Empire State University electro-biologist Dr. Marla Madison, to create a new Spider-Slayer. Version V was modeled after Version II, but was larger. A psycho-cybernetic helmet, not physical controls, operated it. The robot also featured an impulse-beam, a web-like filament spray, and grappling and cutting devices housed in its chest plate. Spider-Man trapped it underneath a heavy statue.

VERSION VI: The final Spencer Smythe Slayer, Version VI, was another small, spider-shaped robot, very similar to Version III. Smythe was dying from the radioactivity he had received from manufacturing the previous Spider-Slayers. Mentally controlled by Smythe as part of the professor's final revenge on Jameson and the wall-crawler, Version VI successfully enabled Spider-Man's capture by leaping off a roof and taking Spidey with it. Spider-Man was knocked unconscious and kidnapped by Smythe, but the Slayer was destroyed by the fall. Smythe left Spider-Man and Jameson shackled together with a time bomb before his demise. The two escaped moments before the bomb exploded.

VERSION VII: Spencer Smythe's son, Alistair, took up the role of Spider-Slayer engineer. Employed by the Kingpin as an inventor, Alistair's first effort at making Spider-Slayers was Version VII, an eight-legged flying saucer that was equipped with a no-stick surface, laser beams and metal, whip-like arms. Mistaking Mary Jane Watson for Spider-Man, he captured her and her aunt, Anna Watson. Mary Jane stalled Smythe, while the Spider-Slayer dangled her over Manhattan. Spider-Man rescued Mary Jane and lured the Slayer into power lines at a train yard, short-circuiting it and crippling Alistair.

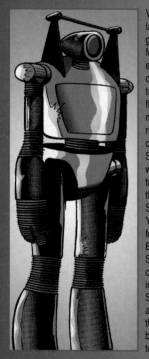

VERSION VIII: Alistair Smythe later sought revenge with a giant biped Spider-Slayer featuring a non-stick surface, ethyl-chloride gas with a chemical additive for remote tracking, extensible limbs, a flexible neck, suction boots, and magnetic field generation. The robot carried Alistair in its chest cavity. Alistair's first battle with Spider-Man in the Version VIII was thwarted by a courageous tractor operator who damaged the Slayer. Peter Parker left the Spider-Slayer at large in New York when Mary Jane pleaded for him to join her in Pittsburgh. But Alistair followed, tracking Spider-Man through a tracer chemical he had sprayed on him in their previous battle. When the Slayer threatened Mary Jane again, Spider-Man smashed through the chest plate with his bare hands and extracted the terrified operator.

VERSION IX-XVIII: Alistair escaped from an asylum for the criminally insane, forcing other brilliant inmates to join him, including Max Young, a former assistant to Mendel Stromm. Smythe, calling himself the Ultimate Spider-Slayer, had scientists encase his body in a carapace that boosted his strength and allowed him to walk again.

After using hand-sized mini-Spider-Slayers as scouts (Version IX) to prepare the scene, Alistair launched a series of vicious Slayers: a six-armed monstrous Slayer (Version X), a flying bird-like Slayer (Version XI), and a heavily armed humanoid Slayer (Version XII). Young then unleashed his amoeboid Slayer (Version XIII), which was destroyed during a battle with the Scorpion. This was followed

by a giant multi-faced Slayer (Version XIV) that reflected all three of his split personalities. Version XIV eventually destroyed itself. Alistair's final offensive consisted of a black widow Slayer (Version XV), a tarantula Slayer (Version XVI), and a scorpion Slayer (Version XVII) that together merged into the Triple Spider-Slayer (Version XVIII). Spider-Man electrocuted it after the Black Cat used her claws to cut through the insulation.

VERSION XIX: Alistair later attacked Spider-Man with a robot army consisting of a replica of every Spider-Slayer ever created. This was the warm-up for Version XIX, a massively powerful, four-armed humanoid Slayer set to attack J. Jonah Jameson. Simultaneously, many psi-empathic Version IX mini-Slayers were dispatched, after reading Spider-Man's brain waves, to target those Peter loved most. But again, threatening Spider-Man's family proved to be Alistair's downfall: Spider-Man wrecked the Version XIX robot with his bare fists, thereby shutting down every mini-Slayer.

HISTORY: Norman Osborn once helped rescue Police Captain George Stacy and his daughter, Gwen, from a kidnapping by the Kingpin's men at one of Osborn's chemical factories. Gwen visited Norman to thank him. Finding him despondent yet powerfully alluring and charismatic, Gwen felt both sympathetic and attracted to Osborn. The two had a spontaneous affair, leaving Gwen pregnant with twins. Gwen fled to Europe where she secretly carried to full term in only seven months, giving birth to twins Sarah and Gabriel. Osborn arranged to provide for the twins in Paris, while Gwen returned home and reunited with Peter Parker. Gwen argued with Norman that she should raise the children, assuming that Peter's love would enable him to overlook her infidelity and marry her. Gwen confided only in Mary Jane Watson, who had overheard the argument and promised to keep her secret. Osborn planned to raise the children as his heirs to the Goblin legacy and, as the Green Goblin, knocked Gwen off the Brooklyn Bridge to her death during a battle with Spider-Man. She never lived to tell Peter Parker about her children.

The twins were raised in Paris under the supervision of Osborn's hired servants, and "Uncle Norman" himself from time to time. Due to the Goblin Formula in their father's blood, Sarah and Gabriel were gifted with a superhuman physiology, but stricken with rapid aging. Osborn had them privately tutored and physically trained to maximize their potential. He lied to the twins, telling them that Parker was their father who abandoned them and that Spider-Man killed their mother. Osborn instructed them that their goal in life was to get vengeance upon both Spider-Man and Peter Parker.

The twins suffered from terrible headaches from their rapid growth. They turned to barbiturates to stave off the pain. To escape their confinement from Osborn's estate, and make some money to buy their painkillers, the twins turned to crime, delivering illegal drugs for a crook named Bruce. Bruce's operation was taken over by a local drug lord named Monsieur Dupres, connected to a criminal organization called the Black Hand. They had no choice but to work for Dupres.

When Osborn was finally exposed publicly as the Green Goblin and jailed, the twins (now physically aged to about 18 years) mailed Peter a page from one of Gwen's unsent letters from a time when she traveled to Europe between college semesters shortly before her death. Visiting Gwen's grave, the twins, faces concealed, attacked Spider-Man and later made threats against his family. Peter had the letter analyzed by police detective Lamont for latent handwriting impressions of a second page that revealed Gwen had given birth to the twins. Peter took a sample of Gwen's DNA from her grave and compared it with the twins' DNA left on the letter's adhesive. He proved that Gwen was indeed the twins' mother. Sarah attacked Spider-Man at the genetics lab where he was able to unmask her before she escaped and saw that she was a dead ringer for Gwen. Mary Jane read the letter and revealed to Peter the secret she promised to keep all these years.

Spider-Man lured Gabriel and Sarah to the top of the Brooklyn Bridge. There he told them the truth about their real father, and confirmed his suspicions that they were dying from the accelerated aging. Sarah believed Spider-Man, noting that he had tested for Gwen's maternity, not his own paternity. Gabriel called Spider-Man a liar and attacked, firing a gun and prompting the police down below the bridge to fire back at the three. Spider-Man kicked Gabriel into the East River, while Sarah was shot. Spider-Man quickly carried her to the hospital.

REAL NAMES: Gabriel and Sarah Stacy
KNOWN ALIASES: The Gray Goblin (Gabriel), none (Sarah)
IDENTITY: Secret
OCCUPATION: None
CITIZENSHIP: France
PLACE OF BIRTH: Paris, France
MARITAL STATUS: Single
KNOWN RELATIVES: Gwen Stacy (mother, deceased), Norman Osborn (Green Goblin, father), Harold "Harry" Osborn (Green Goblin, half-brother, deceased), George and Helen Stacy (grandparents, deceased), Ambrose Osborn (grandfather, deceased), Arthur Stacy (uncle once removed), Nancy Stacy (aunt once removed, deceased), Paul and Jill Stacy (cousins once removed)
GROUP AFFILIATION: None
EDUCATION: Privately educated
FIRST APPEARANCE: Amazing Spider-Man #509 (2004)

Gabriel survived the fall and fled through the sewers to a place Osborn had instructed them to go after exacting revenge upon Parker. There, male and female Goblin suits awaited, while a pre-recorded message from Osborn informed Gabriel that he was to inherit his legacy. Osborn offered Gabriel a serum that would complete the effects of the Goblin formula already in his genetic code. He would become more powerful, and slow or halt the advanced aging. Accepting his father's offer, Gabriel injected himself with the serum, gaining a superhuman physiology even greater than his father and becoming the Gray Goblin. Like Osborn, Gabriel had been rendered mentally unstable, facing a future of paranoia, psychosis and memory loss.

Meanwhile, Sarah lay dying in the hospital. Though her accelerated healing mended the bullet wound, her body rejected the donated blood. Spider-Man realized his blood could be a match. He gave a large transfusion to her that left him weakened, but Sarah was saved. On his inherited glider, the Gray Goblin attacked the recuperating Spider-Man in the hospital. When Sarah discovered the two battling, she chose to save Spider-Man, shooting her brother's glider with a security guard's revolver. The glider exploded sending Gabriel crashing into the harbor. He washed up upon a beach alive but apparently with amnesia.

Sarah fled back home to Paris. In what appeared to be a suicide attempt, she was hospitalized for a pill overdose. Since he was named as her contact in case of an emergency, Peter flew to Paris. Sarah said the overdose was an accident, and explained her regular consumption of painkillers. Sarah, infatuated with Peter, attempted to manipulate him into loving her in return. Mentally, Sarah was not well; she was both emotionally immature for her apparent age as well as occasionally delusional, perhaps a result of inheriting her father's own instability.

Previously, to escape Dupres and their restrictive life in Paris, Gabriel had kept almost a million and a half dollars of the drug money. After Gabriel disappeared as the Gray Goblin, Dupres put out a contract on Sarah to draw out her brother. While Sarah spent time with Peter in France, Dupres attacked her. She used her abilities to defend herself, making light of the attacks to conceal her shady past from Peter. After Peter foiled a sniper's attack on her, Sarah confessed the story of her addiction and drug dealing, but kept secret that she had been caring for her intermittently amnesiac brother at the estate. Gabriel began to forget that Sarah was his sister and became sporadically violent. When Mary Jane came to the Stacy estate to find Peter, a crazed Gabriel mistook her for Sarah. Meanwhile, Sarah decided to confront Dupres to end his attacks. An Interpol agent named Francois Benoit followed Sarah as he investigated Dupres. While Spider-Man rescued Mary Jane, Gabriel fled on a Goblin-glider. Spider-Man urged Benoit to pursue Sarah at Dupres' complex. Sarah single-handedly overcame Dupres' defenses and guards. When Spider-Man and Benoit arrived, Sarah was aiming a gun at Dupres. Spider-Man convinced her to trust him and lower the weapon. She left Dupres to the police, and accepted an offer by Benoit to be trained and cared for by Interpol as a superhuman agent.

Art by Mike Deodato Jr.

SARAH

HEIGHT: 5'6"
WEIGHT: 125 lbs.
EYES: Blue
HAIR: Blonde

SUPERHUMAN POWERS: Sarah was born with heightened intelligence, speed, reflexes, and endurance, along with superhuman strength, and regenerative ability. She can lift (press) 5 tons.

POWER GRID	1	2	3	4	5	6	7
INTELLIGENCE							
STRENGTH							
SPEED							
DURABILITY							
ENERGY PROJECTION							
FIGHTING SKILLS							

GABRIEL

HEIGHT: 6'0"
WEIGHT: 180 lbs.
EYES: Brown
HAIR: Reddish-brown

SUPERHUMAN POWERS: Gabriel was born with heightened intelligence and agility, along with superhuman strength and healing rate. Upon injecting himself with the Goblin serum, his superhuman abilities increased to levels greater than the original Green Goblin. He can lift (press) 15 tons and has gained superhuman toughness, rendering his skin nearly bulletproof.

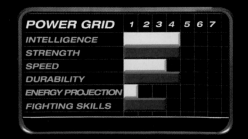

POWER GRID	1	2	3	4	5	6	7
INTELLIGENCE							
STRENGTH							
SPEED							
DURABILITY							
ENERGY PROJECTION							
FIGHTING SKILLS							

MENDEL STROMM

HISTORY: Mendel Stromm was sickly growing up, but discovered a love of gadgetry and robots that helped him get through an unhappy childhood. As an adult, he became Norman Osborn's business and scientific partner in the early days of Osborn Industries until he was caught embezzling and Norman had him arrested. On his release from prison ten years later, Stromm wanted revenge on Osborn and sent robots to destroy his livelihood. Spider-Man stopped the robots and captured Stromm, saving him from being shot by Osborn, only to see him apparently die from a heart attack. Stromm's robots reappeared soon after which led to the discovery of the Robot-Master, a robot duplicate of Stromm, who had transferred his memories to it shortly before his "death." It was quickly disposed of by Spider-Man. Years later, Norman Osborn became curious about the unexpected effects of the Green Goblin formula of which Stromm had developed the prototype. He had Stromm exhumed and discovered him alive, due to the formula, although his body was a withered husk. Revived, Stromm, now Gaunt, was given a promise of rejuvenation if he carried out Osborn's plans to ruin Peter Parker. Stromm blackmailed Seward Trainer into developing a regenerator, and hired the Hobgoblin (Jason Macendale), Arcade, and Cell-12 in a succession of attempts to either harm or kill Ben Reilly and others.

Successfully rejuvenated, Stromm, clad in robot armor and calling himself the Robot-Master, attempted to kill Reilly himself, but failed. As a consequence of his failure, Osborn zapped him with a concussive blast and left him for dead. He came to with loss of memory. While wandering aimlessly, he stumbled across his original hideout and began making toy robots for hospitalized children until mention of Osborn's name brought back Stromm's thirst for revenge, and he became unhinged before Spider-Man stopped him. At Ravencroft, Dr. Kafka discovered that he had no memory of the previous nine years. Obsessed with terminating Spider-Man, he attempted a new technique, interfacing his brainwaves with a computer that would enable him to control robots by mind power alone. The computer started to take over Stromm's mind, decapitating him, and seizing control of New York's computer infrastructure. With the help of Peter Parker's hacker friend Shea Tinker, Spider-Man introduced a recursive virus into the Machine, which sent Stromm and the Machine into standby, until Spider-Man could figure out a way to help Stromm permanently without killing him. Stromm is still currently in this suspended state.

REAL NAME: Professor Mendel Stromm
KNOWN ALIASES: Robot-Master, Gaunt
IDENTITY: Known to authorities
OCCUPATION: Former scientist and robotics engineer, business partner
CITIZENSHIP: U.S.A. with a criminal record
PLACE OF BIRTH: Unrevealed
MARITAL STATUS: Single
KNOWN RELATIVES: None
GROUP AFFILIATION: None
EDUCATION: Ph.D
FIRST APPEARANCE: Amazing Spider-Man Vol. 1 #37 (1966)

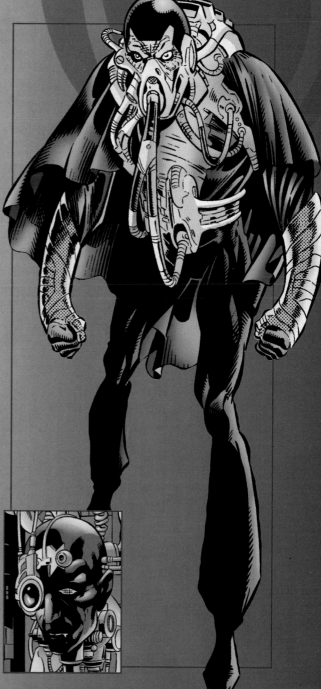

HEIGHT: 5'10"
WEIGHT: 150 lbs.
EYES: Blue
HAIR: None

ABILITIES: Stromm is a chemist and robotics expert.

PARAPHERNALIA: Robots, strength-augmenting environmental suit with gas dispenser, robotic armor with arm cannons and blades, and particle grenades hooked up to a computer guidance system

POWER GRID	1	2	3	4	5	6	7
INTELLIGENCE							
STRENGTH							
SPEED							
DURABILITY							
ENERGY PROJECTION							
FIGHTING SKILLS							

Art by Mark Bagley with Mark Buckingham (inset)

REAL NAME: Eugene Thompson
KNOWN ALIASES: Flash; has impersonated Stilt-Man, Hobgoblin, Spider-Man
IDENTITY: No dual identity
OCCUPATION: Unemployed; former Oscorp employee, gym teacher, soldier, college football player
CITIZENSHIP: U.S.A. with a criminal record
PLACE OF BIRTH: Forest Hills, Queens, NY
MARITAL STATUS: Single
KNOWN RELATIVES: Harrison (father), Rosie (mother), Jessie (sister)
GROUP AFFILIATION: Alcoholics Anonymous, Oscorp staff, U.S. Army, Spider-Man Fan Club
EDUCATION: High-school graduate, some college courses and military training
FIRST APPEARANCE: Amazing Fantasy Vol. 1 #15 (1962)

HISTORY: Handsome and naturally athletic, young Eugene Thompson seemed to have a bright future ahead of him, but hidden darkness in his family set the stage for what became a life of wasted potential. His father, popular policeman Harrison Thompson, had a secret drinking problem, and it was all the Thompson family could do to hold him together at times. Alternating between anger and despair, the self-loathing Harrison took out his frustrations on his family, often treating Eugene abusively. Eugene, in turn, became a neighborhood bully, taking out his own frustrations on weaker and less popular children. One of his earliest and longest-running targets was Peter Parker, a bookish boy who later became the masked adventurer Spider-Man.

Despite his often-obnoxious personality, football prodigy Eugene became one of the most popular (and most conceited) students at Midtown High School, where his speed on the football field earned him the lifelong nickname "Flash." His wide circle of friends included Sean "Tiny" McKeever, Jason Ionello, Seymour O'Reilly, Charlie and numerous female admirers such as Sally Avril and Liz Allan, who was Flash's steady girlfriend for some time. The more popular Flash became, the more he mocked the shy Peter Parker; however, as Parker (secretly emboldened by his new spider-powers) became more confident, he began to stand up to Flash more often, and even took on Flash in a boxing match that ended with Flash being kayoed by a spider-strength jab that most onlookers misinterpreted as a lucky sucker punch. Flash continued to ride Peter despite this setback, and Peter generally tolerated Flash's abuse since he didn't want to risk revealing his super-powers or seriously injuring Thompson. Gradually impressed by Peter's maturity and sick of Flash's bullying, Liz dumped Flash and began showing strong romantic interest in Peter, which only made Thompson hate Parker all the more.

Shortly after Spider-Man first appeared, Flash declared himself the wall-crawler's biggest fan, never dreaming that his hero was the same "Puny Parker" he so often tormented. As annoyed as Peter was by Flash in general, he was secretly touched and impressed by Thompson's enduring loyalty to Spider-Man. Flash founded the Forest Hills chapter of the Spider-Man Fan Club and took it upon himself to defend the oft-maligned Spider-Man's reputation, sometimes in reckless and foolish ways. When Flash impersonated Spider-Man in an attempt to teach Parker some respect for the hero, Flash was mistaken for the real thing and imprisoned by Doctor Doom until the true Spider-Man rescued him. Later, when a humiliating encounter with the Green Goblin (Norman Osborn) had the whole city calling Spider-Man a coward, Thompson donned a Spider-Man costume and tackled some cheap crooks in an effort to restore Spidey's reputation, but all he got for his trouble was a beating. Shortly thereafter, when another Spider-Man impersonator tried to tarnish the hero's name with a string of petty crimes, Flash unmasked the culprit as his own friend Jason Ionello, who wrongly blamed Spider-Man for the recent death of their mutual friend Sally Avril during Spider-Man's battle with the Black Knight. Flash also repeatedly denounced the many anti-Spider-Man tirades by Daily Bugle publisher J. Jonah Jameson, and one angry confrontation between Thompson and Jameson caused the unwitting pair to foil a plot against Spider-Man by Mysterio.

When Flash and Peter graduated from Midtown High, both were awarded full scholarships to Empire State University (for athletic and academic achievement, respectively). By this time, relations between the two had begun to thaw ever so slightly, and both soon became part of a circle of friends that included fellow students Gwen Stacy, Harry Osborn (son of Norman) and Mary Jane Watson. By the time Flash left college to join the army, he and Peter parted as

friends. During his tour of duty, Flash was stationed in Southeast Asia, where he stumbled across a hidden temple whose residents—notably the beautiful Sha Shan—nursed a wounded Flash back to health; however, after American forces mistakenly shelled the temple despite Flash's efforts to protect it, Flash left the army to return to America, where temple survivors who mistakenly blamed him for the tragedy made attempts on his life. With the aid of Spider-Man, Flash lived to convince the temple survivors of his innocence, and was briefly reunited with Sha Shan. Later, Sha Shan returned to America as Sister Sun, the reluctant bride of cult leader Brother Power (Achmed Korba), himself a pawn of the evil Man-Beast. Sha Shan ultimately turned on Korba, and the Man-Beast was thwarted through the combined efforts of Spider-Man, Razorback and Flash. Korba having died in the battle, Sha Shan became Flash's lover and lived with him for some time.

Later, Flash's old friend Betty Brant was struggling to cope with her failing marriage to reporter Ned Leeds, who had secretly been brainwashed into serving as a pawn and occasional stand-in for the criminal Hobgoblin (Roderick Kingsley). Betty sought comfort in the arms of Flash, and soon the two were having a secret affair. Sha Shan realized this and walked out on Flash after a violent argument. The unstable Ned suspected the truth as well, and Flash unwittingly provoked matters further when he insulted the Hobgoblin on television. The Hobgoblin responded by framing Flash as the supposed Hobgoblin, sending Flash to prison, where he would have been killed by the vigilante Scourge if not for the intervention of Spider-Man. Escaping jail, Flash sought refuge with Betty Brant but was attacked by the Hobgoblin, who fled after Betty saw him unmasked as Leeds. Shortly thereafter, word of Ned's double identity leaked out and Leeds was murdered by assassins hired by his rival Jason Macendale, who used Ned's gear to become the new Hobgoblin. Aiding Spider-Man in battle with the new Hobgoblin, Flash suffered an arm injury that ended any hope of restarting his old sports career, but he was cleared of all charges related to the Hobgoblin case and set free.

Ned's death sent Betty into a nervous breakdown, and she fell under the influence of a sinister cult known as the Students of Love. Flash, Spider-Man and Reverend Tolliver joined forces to liberate Betty and deprogram her. Having lost all her worldly possessions to the cult (which was destroyed in a fire), Betty took up residence with Thompson until the demonic invasion of New York known as Inferno, when demons posing as Spider-Man and the late Ned attacked Flash's home; the demons were defeated, but Thompson's home was destroyed in the process. Shortly thereafter, Betty and Flash decided they were better off as friends rather than lovers and parted amicably. By now, Peter Parker had married Mary Jane Watson, and Harry Osborn had married Flash's old flame Liz Allan, and odd-man-out Flash was determined to find a new love of his own. For a while, he dated the glamorous adventurer Felicia Hardy, alias the Black Cat. Formerly Spider-Man's lover and partner, Felicia dated Flash mostly to irritate Peter at first, but found herself genuinely falling for Thompson over time; however, Flash ultimately broke up with her since he felt he could never fit into her exotic lifestyle.

Directionless, lonely and increasingly bitter, Flash developed a drinking problem like his father before him, leading to a car crash that got Flash arrested again and cost him his job as a school gym teacher. By this time, Flash had begun blaming much of his troubles on his family in general and his father in particular, but a violent confrontation with his father finally forced Flash to realize that he had become the same sort of self-deluded wreck his father was, and that only he could take responsibility for fixing his life. Flash sobered up and started trying to turn his life around, though without much

Art by Humberto Ramos

success in terms of either romance or career. His luck seemed to change when wealthy industrialist Norman Osborn offered him a good job with his Oscorp company. Osborn had actually done this as part of an elaborate plot against his enemy Peter Parker in hopes of turning Flash against Spider-Man, though Flash remained loyal to his boyhood idol despite Osborn's influence. Later, when Osborn stepped up his attacks on Parker, he staged a car crash that sent an Oscorp truck crashing into Midtown High with Thompson at the wheel, and made it look as if Flash had been driving drunk. Rendered comatose by the accident, Flash eventually revived, but was broken in mind and body, wheelchair-bound and trapped in a speechless haze. He is regularly visited by old friends such as Peter Parker and Liz Allan Osborn (now Harry's widow), who used her wealth to provide Flash with an apartment and full-time medical care. Whether Flash will ever recover remains to be seen.

HEIGHT: 6'2"
WEIGHT: 185 lbs.
EYES: Blue
HAIR: Reddish blond

ABILITIES: A natural all-around athlete, Flash was a capable unarmed combatant thanks to his boxing background and his military experience, and was a well-trained soldier during his army days. Flash was also a gifted football player in his youth. Since his recent accident, Flash has been a mental and physical wreck, confined to a wheelchair and stuck in a speechless stupor.

POWER GRID

	1	2	3	4	5	6	7
INTELLIGENCE							
STRENGTH							
SPEED							
DURABILITY							
ENERGY PROJECTION							
FIGHTING SKILLS							

TOXIN

REAL NAME: Patrick "Paddy" Mulligan
KNOWN ALIASES: None
IDENTITY: Secret
OCCUPATION: Police officer
CITIZENSHIP: U.S.A.
PLACE OF BIRTH: New York City
MARITAL STATUS: Separated
KNOWN RELATIVES: Gina Mulligan (wife), Edward Mulligan (son), Carnage (symbiote parent), Venom (symbiote grandparent), Mr. Mulligan (father), Mrs. Mulligan (mother)
GROUP AFFILIATION: Ally of Spider-Man and Black Cat
EDUCATION: College educated
FIRST APPEARANCE: Venom vs. Carnage #1 (2004)

HISTORY: Born into a long line of Irish New York police officers, Patrick Mulligan was living his family's dream. Recently married to a loving woman named Gina, the couple had a baby on the way, and his NYPD career was going perfectly. However, Patrick didn't expect a chance encounter with the psychotic Carnage, who was enraged at his own impending asexual pregnancy. Carnage implanted Patrick with his "other," and left the new Symbiote to incubate within him. At the same time, Venom argued with Carnage over the Symbiote offspring. Carnage insisted on killing it, but Venom was concerned that as the 1,000th Symbiote of their line, "Toxin" could potentially become psychotic as a result of genetic breakdown. Carnage tracked his offspring to Patrick's apartment, and threw Gina down a stairwell. Spider-Man was able to save Gina, while Black Cat managed to distract Carnage.

Patrick continued his life, haunted by his encounter with Carnage. He soon discovered that he was much faster and stronger than before, and was easily able to subdue Black Cat before she could escape his questioning. However, Carnage interrupted the conversation, attacking Patrick and the Cat. Patrick became Toxin, saving Cat. Though unnerved by his transformation, Patrick decided that his new powers could be used for good. Teaming up with Spider-Man to stop an armed robbery, Patrick found himself filled with murderous urges. He struggled to keep himself together, telling Spider-Man that he was only "joking" about eating the robbers' brains.

Mulligan later used his powers to save Spider-Man and Black Cat from Venom and Carnage, beating them both single-handedly. He realized that he had much in common with Spider-Man and made the web-slinger his role model. Realizing his presence was putting Gina and newborn Edward in serious danger, Pat left them behind, offering Gina little explanation. Patrick now walks the New York streets alone as Toxin, hoping to as much as he can from Spider-Man.

HEIGHT: 6'2"
WEIGHT: 215 lbs.
EYES: Blue
HAIR: Brown

SUPERHUMAN POWERS: Toxin possesses the power to stick to walls and create "tendrils" to swing between buildings. Toxin can project elongated claws or "snares" from his costume in the same manner as Carnage. His symbiotically induced strength is greater than that of Venom and Carnage combined. Toxin can also use the symbiote to simulate any type of clothing. Presumably, Toxin possesses the same vulnerability to fire and intense sonic attacks from which all other symbiotes suffer.

POWER GRID	1	2	3	4	5	6	7
INTELLIGENCE							
STRENGTH							
SPEED							
DURABILITY							
ENERGY PROJECTION							
FIGHTING SKILLS							

Art by Clayton Crain

CHARLIE WEIDERMAN

HISTORY: Charlie Weiderman was the one student at Midtown High School more bullied than Peter Parker. Even Peter took advantage of Charlie to score some points with the in-crowd before guilt led him to make friends with his scorned classmate, but Charlie, beaten by his father at home and humiliated at school, only sought revenge. First, he ingested a homemade version of Captain America's super-soldier formula, which only landed him in the hospital; later, he tried to pull a knife on his tormentors. When Charlie slashed his classmates' tires and lied about it, Ben Parker told him never to come see Peter again.

As an adult, Charlie still searched for vindication. His father died and left him enough money to help fund the creation of a porous polymer compound that could completely cover a soldier and protect him from harm. Charlie eventually realized that his "skinsuit" would have to be composed of the energy-absorbing metal Vibranium to protect the wearer from any impacts. Charlie talked Peter into a letter of recommendation that swayed industrialist Tony Stark, aware of Spider-Man's true identity, into authorizing a large grant. When Peter saw Charlie's hasty shortcuts involving the volatile Vibranium, however, he wanted to pull the plug on the project. Frantic, Charlie rushed the procedure and the Vibranium blew up, encasing him in a skinsuit that bestowed the metal's properties on him.

Attempting to duck responsibility, maddened by the chemicals in his suit and by Peter's insistence that he turn himself in, Charlie went on a rampage, locating and killing Rich and Sheila, a young married couple who had both ridiculed him back in high school, fighting Spider-Man, and planning to kill Aunt May and Mary Jane. Unable to track down the Parkers, Charlie settled for destroying Peter's apartment and the family home in Forest Hills. Recalling that the fluid Vibranium could be made solid by the use of extreme pressure, Spider-Man forced Charlie into an atmospheric chamber at Stark International, causing the skinsuit to harden, immobilizing him inside. Although doctors can penetrate the suit enough to take care of Charlie's bodily needs, he remains trapped within, perhaps for the rest of his life.

REAL NAME: Charles "Charlie" Weiderman
KNOWN ALIASES: "Weinerman," "Whiney-Man"
IDENTITY: Known to authorities
OCCUPATION: Inventor, High School "punching bag"
CITIZENSHIP: U.S.A.
PLACE OF BIRTH: Queens, New York
MARITAL STATUS: Single
KNOWN RELATIVES: Father (deceased), Mother (presumed deceased)
GROUP AFFILIATION: None
EDUCATION: College educated
FIRST APPEARANCE: Amazing Spider-Man #515 (2005)

HEIGHT: 5'7"
WEIGHT: 140 lbs.; (with skinsuit) 173 lbs.
EYES: Blue
HAIR: Blond

SUPERHUMAN POWERS: Charlie has superhuman strength sufficient to lift an SUV and go toe-to-toe with Spider-Man. The madder he gets, the stronger he gets. His Vibranium skinsuit is fireproof; can absorb impact, rendering him virtually invulnerable; and can vibrate at frequencies that allow him to split diamonds and slough off Spider-Man's webbing.

POWER GRID	1	2	3	4	5	6	7
INTELLIGENCE							
STRENGTH							
SPEED							
DURABILITY							
ENERGY PROJECTION							
FIGHTING SKILLS							

BIBLIOGRAPHY

BETTY BRANT

First Appearance: Amazing Spider-Man Vol. 1 #4 (1963)
Origin: Untold Tales of Spider-Man #12 (1996)
Significant Issues: Grew closer to Peter (Amazing Spider-Man Vol. 1 #7, 1963); first date with Peter (Untold Tales of Spider-Man #3, 1995); Bennett killed (Amazing Spider-Man Vol. 1 #11, 1964); began dating Ned Leeds (Amazing Spider-Man Vol. 1 #18-19, 1964); ended romance with Peter for good (Amazing Spider-Man Vol. 1 #41, 1966); married Ned (Amazing Spider-Man Vol. 1 #156, 1976); driven mad by Ned's death (Amazing Spider-Man Vol. 1 #289, 1987); fought demons (Spectacular Spider-Man Vol. 2 #148, 1989); fought Mister Fear (Web of Spider-Man #63, 1990); exposed Hobgoblin (Spider-Man: Hobgoblin Lives #1-3, 1997)

CARRION

First Appearance: (Warren Clone): Peter Parker: The Spectacular Spider-Man #25 (1978); (McBride): Spectacular Spider-Man Vol. 2 #149 (1989); (Allen): Spider-Man: Dead Man's Hand #1 (1997)
Origin: (Warren Clone): Peter Parker: The Spectacular Spider-Man #31 (1978); (McBride): Spectacular Spider-Man Vol. 2 #149 (1989); (Allen): Spider- Man: Dead Man's Hand #1 (1997)
Significant Issues: Revealed identity to Peter (Peter Parker: The Spectacular Spider-Man #30, 1979); created Spider-Amoeba, consumed by it (Peter Parker: The Spectacular Spider-Man #31,1979); McBride discovered virus, infected by it (Spectacular Spider-Man Vol. 2 #149, 1989); seemingly sacrificed himself to save mother (Spectacular Spider-Man Vol. 2 #163, 1990); rose during Maximum Carnage (Spectacular Spider-Man Vol. 2 #201, 1993); virus in remission, sent to Ravencroft (Spectacular Spider-Man Vol. 2 #203, 1993); kidnapped by Shriek (Amazing Spider-Man Vol. 1 #390, 1994); turned powers on himself when confronted with choice between mothers (Amazing Spider-Man Vol. 1 #393, 1994); Allen exposed himself to virus, infected people with "zombie plague," given into S.H.I.E.L.D.'s custody (Spider-Man: Dead Man's Hand #1, 1997)

CHAMELEON

First Appearance: Amazing Spider-Man Vol. 1 #1 (1963)
Origin: Amazing Spider-Man Vol. 1 #1 (1963); Amazing Spider-Man Vol. 1 #389 (1994)
Significant Issues: Teamed with Kraven the Hunter (Amazing Spider-Man Vol. 1 #15, 1964/Sensational Spider-Man Annual #1, 1996); impersonated Captain America (Tales of Suspense Vol. 1 #58, 1964); employed by the Leader (Tales to Astonish Vol. 1 #62, 1964); disguised himself as Peter Parker (Amazing Spider-Man Vol. 1 #80, 1970); worked for Hydra (Incredible Hulk Vol. 1 #154, 1972); death of Joe Cord (Marvel Team-Up Vol. 1 #27, 1974); used serum to change his appearance at will (Amazing Spider-Man Vol. 1 #307, 1988); kidnapped J. Jonah Jameson (Web Of Spider-Man #50, 1989); made Spider-Man lose his powers (Amazing Spider-Man Vol. 1 #341 1990); unveiled as the creator of Peter's fake parents (Amazing Spider-Man Vol. 1 #388, 1994); had a breakdown when faced with a vengeful Spider-Man (Amazing Spider-Man Vol. 1 #389, 1994); found out Spider-Man's identity (Spectacular Spider-Man Vol. 2 #242, 1997); shot by his nephew (Spectacular Spider-Man Vol. 2 #245, 1997); tried to commit suicide (Webspinners: Tales Of Spider-Man #11, 1999)

JEAN DEWOLFF

First Appearance: Marvel Team-Up Vol. 1 #48 (1976)
Origin: Marvel Team-Up Vol. 1 #49 (1976), Peter Parker, The Spectacular Spider-Man #107 (1985)
Significant Issues: Found out her brother was The Wraith (Marvel Team-Up Vol. 1 #50, 1976); arranged a pardon for Black Cat (Amazing Spider-Man Vol. 1 #227, 1982); murdered (Peter Parker, The Spectacular Spider-Man #107, 1985)

DOPPELGANGER

First Appearance: Infinity War #1 (1992)
Origin: Quasar #38 (1992)
Significant Issues: First battled Spider-Man (Spider-Man #24, 1992) with Demogoblin, battled Spider-Man, Hobgoblin, Ghost Rider, and others (Web of Spider-Man #95-96/Spirits of Vengeance #5, 1992-1993); joined forces with Carnage and Shriek, "Maximum Carnage" (Spider-Man Unlimited Vol. 1 #1, 1993); defended Shriek, apparently slain by Carnage (Spider-Man #37, 1993)

FLY

First Appearance: Amazing Spider-Man Annual #10 (1976)
Origin: Amazing Spider-Man Annual #10 (1976)
Significant Issues: Attacked Spider-Man and J. J. Jameson (Amazing Spider-Man Vol. 1 #192, 1979); defeated by Spider-Woman (Spider-Woman Vol. 1 #30, 1980); left Moon Knight temporarily paralyzed (Moon Knight Vol. 1 #35, 1984); further mutations (Peter Parker, The Spectacular Spider-Man #86,1984); killed by Scourge (Amazing Spider-Man Vol. 1 #276, 1986)

FREDERICK FOSWELL

First Appearance: Amazing Spider-Man Vol. 1 #10 (1964)
Origin: Amazing Spider-Man Vol. 1 #10 (1964)
Significant Issues: As the Big Man (Amazing Spider-Man Vol. 1 #10, 1964); out of prison, rehired at Bugle (Amazing Spider-Man Vol. 1 #23, 1965); first appearance as Patch (Amazing Spider-Man Vol. 1 #26, 1965); revealed as cellmate of Mendel Stromm (Amazing Spider-Man Vol. 1 #37, 1966); returned to crime (Amazing Spider-Man Vol. 1 #50, 1967); died a hero (Amazing Spider-Man Vol. 1 #52, 1967)

FUSION

First Appearance: Peter Parker: Spider-Man Vol. 2 #30 (2001)
Origin: Peter Parker: Spider-Man Vol. 2 #32 (2001)
Significant Issues: Killed three hundred people (Peter Parker: Spider-Man Vol. 2 #30, 2001); appeared to break Spidey's neck (Peter Parker: Spider-Man Vol. 2 #31, 2001); power figured out by Spider-Man (Peter Parker: Spider-Man Vol. 2 #32, 2001); beaten nearly to death by Dr. Octopus (Peter Parker: Spider-Man Vol. 2 #40, 2002)

GLORY GRANT

First Appearance: Amazing Spider-Man Vol. 1 #140 (1975)
Significant Issues: Threw party to furnish Peter's apartment (Amazing Spider-Man Vol. 1 #163, 1976); became Jameson's secretary (Peter Parker: The Spectacular Spider-Man #2, 1977); tragic affair with Eduardo Lobo (Spectacular Spider-Man Vol. 2 #146 & 149-154/Web of Spider-Man #47-48 51 & 55, 1989); faced Calypso (Spider-Man Annual '97, 1997)

HAMMERHEAD

First Appearance: Amazing Spider-Man Vol. 1 #113 (1972)
Origin: Amazing Spider-Man Vol. 1 #114 (1972)
Significant Issues: Fought gang war with Doctor Octopus (Amazing Spider-Man Vol. 1 #113-115, 1972); blasted out of phase with Earth dimension (Amazing Spider-Man Vol. 1 #130-131, 1974); haunted Octopus, restored to corporeal state (Amazing Spider-Man Vol. 1 #157-159, 1976); fought Human Torch (Fantastic Four Vol. 1 #233, 1981); first allied with Chameleon (Web of Spider-Man #51, 1989);allied with Spider-Man and SHOC against Hydra (Peter Parker: Spider-Man Vol. 1 #80, 1997); acquired Atlantean tablet, opposed by Spider-Man, briefly obtained godlike power (Spider-Man: Lifeline #1-3, 2001); manipulated Spider-Man into fighting his rivals (Peter Parker: Spider-Man Vol. 2 #50, 2003)

CRUSHER HOGAN

First Appearance: Amazing Fantasy Vol. 1 #15 (1962)
Origin: Tangled Web #14 (2002)
Significant Issues: Created three-minute wrestling scheme (Tangled Web #14, 2002); defeated by Spider-Man (Amazing Fantasy Vol. 1 #15, 1962); fought alongside Spider-Man against Madame Fang and Manslaughter (Amazing Spider-Man Vol. 1 #271, 1985)

HYDRO-MAN

First Appearance: Amazing Spider-Man Vol. 1 #212 (1981)
Origin: Amazing Spider-Man Vol. 1 #212 (1981)
Significant Issues: Clashed, merged with Sandman (Amazing Spider-Man Vol. 1 #217-218, 1981); co-founded Sinister Syndicate (Amazing Spider-Man Vol. 1 #280-281, 1986); joined Frightful Four (Fantastic Four Vol. 1 #326-333, 1989); fired by Hammer Industries, partnered with Shocker (Peter Parker: Spider-Man Vol. 2 #51-52, 2003); rejoined Frightful Four, powers altered by Wizard (Fantastic Four #514-516, 2004)

JACKAL

First Appearance: (Professor Warren) Amazing Spider-Man Vol. 1 #31 (1965); (Jackal) Amazing Spider-Man Vol. 1 #129 (1974)
Origin: Scarlet Spider Unlimited #1 (1995); Amazing Spider-Man Vol. 1 #149 (1975); Spider-Man: The Osborn Journal #1 (1997)
Significant Issues: Worked at Wundagore Mountain (Scarlet Spider Unlimited #1, 1995); first expressed admiration for Gwen (Amazing Spider-Man Vol. 1 #53, 1967); devastated by Gwen's death (Amazing Spider-Man Vol. 1 #149, 1975); first appearance as Jackal (Amazing Spider-Man Vol. 1 #129, 1974); created Peter Parker clone (Web of Spider-Man #117, 1994); apparent deaths of Jackal and Spider-Clone (Amazing Spider-Man Vol. 1 #149, 1975); Jackal alive, tried to switch Spider-Man and clone identities (Spider-Man: The Osborn Journal #1, 1997); Gwen clone married "Warren Miles" (Web of Spider-Man #125, 1995); Jackal alive and genetically restructured (Amazing Spider-Man Vol. 1 #399, 1995); created Spidercide (Spectacular Spider-Man Vol. 2 #222, 1995); murdered Springville, Pennsylvania (Spider-Man: Maximum Clonage Alpha #1, 1995); died saving Gwen Stacy clone (Spider-Man: Maximum Clonage Omega #1, 1995)

JOHN JAMESON

First Appearance: Amazing Spider-Man Vol. 1 #1 (1963)
Significant Issues: Rescued by Spider-Man (Amazing Spider-Man Vol. 1 #1, 1963); fought Spider-Man in Jupiter suit (Amazing Spider-Man Vol. 1 #42, 1966); discovered the Godstone, first becomes Man-Wolf (Amazing Spider-Man Vol. 1 #124-125, 1973); Morbius reattaches Godstone (Giant Size Super Heroes #1, 1974); travelled to Other Realm, first became Stargod (Marvel Premiere #45, 1978); first cured of lycanthropy (Peter Parker, The Spectacular Spider-Man Annual #3, 1981); became security chief at Ravencroft (Web of Spider-Man #114, 1994); fired from Ravencroft (Spectacular Spider-Man Vol. 2 #246, 1997)

J. JONAH JAMESON

First Appearance: Amazing Spider-Man Vol. 1 #1 (1963)
Origin: Spectacular Spider-Man Vol. 2 #80 (1983); Web of Spider-Man #52 (1989); Spider-Man's Tangled Web #20 (2003)
Significant Issues: Financed Scorpion's mutation (Amazing Spider-Man Vol. 1 #20, 1965); met Spencer Smythe, operated first Spider-Slayer (Amazing Spider-Man Vol. 1 #25, 1965); sought to help John Jameson deal with Man-Wolf condition (Creatures on the Loose #30-37, 1974-1975); targeted by Hitman (Amazing Spider-Man Vol. 1 #174-175, 1977); abducted by Man-Wolf, targeted by Spencer Smythe (Amazing Spider-Man Vol. 1 #189-192, 1979); hired Spider-Man impostors (UK Spider-Man Annual, 1983); blackmailed by Hobgoblin, confessed to role in Scorpion's mutation (Amazing Spider-Man Vol. 1 #249-251, 1984); married Dr. Marla Madison (Amazing Spider-Man Annual #18, 1984); imprisoned and impersonated by the Chameleon (Web of Spider-Man #50, 1989); learned John Jameson was supposedly Spider-Man (Marvel Knights: Spider-Man #8, 2005)

KAINE

First Appearance: Web of Spider-Man #119 (1994)
Origin: Spider-Man #61 (1995)
Significant Issues: Killed Detective Louise Kennedy (Spider-Man: The Lost Years #3, 1995); killed Dr. Octopus (Otto Octavius) (Spectacular Spider-Man Vol. 2 #221, 1995); revealed himself to be a clone of Peter Parker (Spider-Man #60, 1995); confessed to the murder of Det. Kennedy (Spectacular Spider-Man Vol. 2 #226, 1995); killed by Spidercide (Spectacular Spider-Man Vol. 2 #227, 1995); revived from the Jackal's containment pod (Scarlet Spider Unlimited #1, 1995); surrendered to the police (Spider-Man: Redemption #4, 1996)

MADAME WEB

First Appearance: Amazing Spider-Man Vol.1 #210 (1980)
Significant Issues: Attacked by Juggernaut (Amazing Spider-Man Vol.1 #229-#230, 1982); Gathering of the Five (Peter Parker: Spider-Man Vol.1 #96, 1998/Spectacular Spider-Man Vol. 2 #262, 1998); gift of "immortality" revealed (Amazing Spider-Man Vol. 2 #6, 1999); defeated Charlotte Witter (Spider-Woman Vol.3 #9, 2000)

MINDWORM

First Appearance: Amazing Spider-Man Vol. 1 #138 (1974)
Origin: Amazing Spider-Man Vol. 1 #138 (1974)
Significant Issues: Drew Spider-Man into his dream (Peter Parker the Spectacular Spider-Man #35, 1979); killed by street thugs (Spectacular Spider-Man Vol. 3 #22, 2005)

MORBIUS

First Appearance: Amazing Spider-Man Vol. 1 #101 (1971)

Origin: Amazing Spider-Man Vol. 1 #101 (1971)

Significant Issues: Fought Spider-Man and the Lizard (Amazing Spider-Man Vol. 1 #101-102, 1971); clashed with Spider-Man and Human Torch (Marvel Team-Up Vol. 1, #3-4, 1972); reunited with Martine (Giant-Size Werewolf by Night #1, 1974); tracked by Stroud (Adventures into Fear #27-31, 1975); disease went into remission (Peter Parker, The Spectacular Spider-Man #38, 1980); opposed Spider-Man in the sewers of New York City (Spider-Man #13-14, 1991); infected with Lilin blood, death of Martine (Morbius #1, 1992); Martine returned as host for Parasite (Morbius #13, 1993); became involved with Lena, committed suicide, reborn (Morbius #25-32, 1994-1995); captured by Crown (Peter Parker: Spider-Man Vol. 1 #77-80, 1997); battled Spider-Man over the life of a crippled boy (Spectacular Spider-Man Vol. 3 #14, 2004)

MYSTERIO

First Appearance: (Beck) Amazing Spider-Man Vol. 1 #13 (1964); (Berkhart) Amazing Spider-Man Vol. 1 #141 (1975)

Origin: Amazing Spider-Man Vol. 1 #13 (1964)

Significant Issues: First joined Sinister Six (Amazing Spider-Man Annual #1, 1964); posed as Ludwig Rinehart (Amazing Spider-Man Vol. 1 #24, 1965); proposed to Betsy Schneider (Webspinners: Tales of Spider-Man #1, 1999); Beck apparently dead, Berkhart became Mysterio (Amazing Spider-Man Vol. 1 #141, 1975); Beck ran nursing home scam (Amazing Spider-Man Vol. 1 #193, 1979); Beck committed suicide (Daredevil Vol. 2 #7, 1999); Berkhart took over Mysterio identity (Amazing Spider-Man Vol. 2 #6, 1999)

LIZ OSBORN

First Appearance: Amazing Fantasy Vol. 1 #15 (1962)

Significant Issues: Senior prom (Webspinners: Tales of Spider-Man #7-9, 1999); graduation from Midtown High School (Amazing Spider-Man Vol. 1 #28, 1965); relationship to Molten Man revealed (Amazing Spider-Man Vol. 1 #132-133, 1974); first date with Harry (Amazing Spider-Man Vol. 1 #157, 1976); birth of Normie (Amazing Spider-Man Vol. 1 #263, 1985); death of Harry (Spectacular Spider-Man Vol. 2 #200, 1993)

QUEEN

First Appearance: Spectacular Spider-Man Vol. 3 #15 (2004)

Origin: Spectacular Spider-Man Vol. 3 #18 (2004)

Significant Issues: Became victim of U.S. government experimentation and thrown in prison (Spectacular Spider-Man Vol. 3 #18, 2004); apparently killed in subterranean explosion (Spectacular Spider-Man Vol. 3 #20, 2004)

BEN REILLY

First Appearance: Amazing Spider-Man Vol. 1 #149 (1975)

Origin: Amazing Spider-Man Vol. 1 #149 (1975)

Significant Issues: Fought Peter, apparently killed (Amazing Spider-Man Vol. 1 #149, 1975); returned to New York (Web of Spider-Man #117, 1994); adopted Scarlet Spider costume (Web of Spider-Man #118, 1994); "revealed" to be the original Spider-Man by Seward Trainer (Spectacular Spider-Man Vol. 2 #226, 1995); given charge of New York when Peter and MJ moved to Portland (Spectacular Spider-Man Vol. 2 #229, 1995); adopted new Spider-Man costume (Sensational Spider-Man #0, 1995); killed by the Green Goblin (Peter Parker: Spider-Man Vol. 1 #75, 1996)

JOE "ROBBIE" ROBERTSON

First Appearance: Amazing Spider-Man Vol. 1 #51 (1967)

Origin: Spectacular Spider-Man Vol. 2 #139 (1988)

Significant Issues: First met Jameson (Amazing Spider-Man Vol. 1 #-1, 1997); covered campus protest involving Randy (Amazing Spider-Man Vol. 1 #68-70, 1969); helped Spider-Man trap Chameleon (Amazing Spider-Man Vol. 1 #80, 1970); exposed Sam Bullitt, saved by Iceman and Spider-Man (Amazing Spider-Man Vol. 1 #91-92, 1970-1971); past with Tombstone revealed, turned on Tombstone (Spectacular Spider-Man Vol. 2 #139-142, 1988); jailed with and fought Tombstone, pardoned (Spectacular Spider-Man Vol. 2 #150-157, 1989); worked with Cap and Falcon (Captain America and the Falcon #1-6 & 8, 2004)

JOE SMITH

First Appearance: Amazing Spider-Man Vol. 1 #38 (1966)

Origin: Amazing Spider-Man Vol. 1 #38 (1966), Captain America Vol. 1 #246 (1980)

Significant Issues: Saved Betsy from Mysterio (Webspinners: Tales of Spider-Man #1-3, 1999); rampaged after son's death (Captain America Vol. 1 #246, 1980); inspired neighborhood against vandals (Amazing Spider-Man Annual #28, 1994); opposed Mysterio and Mad Jack (Spider-Man: Mysterio Manifesto #1-3, 2001)

SPIDER-MAN

First Appearance: Amazing Fantasy Vol. 1 #15 (1962)

Origin: Amazing Fantasy Vol. 1 #15 (1962)

Significant Issues: Death of Ezekiel (Amazing Spider-Man #508, 2004); discovered Gwen slept with Norman Osborn (Amazing Spider-Man #512, 2004); developed new powers including organic webbing (Spectacular Spider-Man Vol. 3 #20, 2004); learned Mac Gargan kidnapped Aunt May (Marvel Knights: Spider-Man #9, 2005); Peter's apartment and Parker family home destroyed (Amazing Spider-Man #518, 2005)

SPIDER-MOBILE

First Appearance: Amazing Spider-Man Vol. 1 #130 (1974)

Origin: Amazing Spider-Man Vol. 1 #126 (1973)

Significant Issues: Driven off pier (Amazing Spider-Man Vol. 1 #141, 1975); modified by the Terrible Tinkerer (Amazing Spider-Man Vol. 1 #159, 1976); used as weapon against Spider-Man (Amazing Spider-Man Vol. 1 #160, 1976)

SPIDER-SLAYERS

First Appearance: Amazing Spider-Man Vol. 1 #25 (1965)

Significant Issues: Version I (Amazing Spider-Man Vol. 1 #25, 1965); Version II (Amazing Spider-Man Vol. 1 #58, 1968); Version III (Amazing Spider-Man Vol. 1 #105, 1972); Version IV (Amazing Spider-Man Vol. 1 #106, 1972); Version V (Amazing Spider-Man Vol. 1 #167, 1977); Version VI (Amazing Spider-Man Vol. 1 #191, 1979); Version VII (Amazing Spider-Man Annual #19, 1985); Version VIII (Amazing Spider-Man Vol. 1 #291, 1987); Version IX-XVIII (Amazing Spider-Man Vol. 1 #371-373, 1992-1993); Version XIX (Amazing Spider-Man Vol. 2 #20-21, 2000)

STACY TWINS

First Appearance: Amazing Spider-Man #509 (2004)

Origin: Amazing Spider-Man #512 (2004)

Significant Issues: Began threats against Peter Parker (Amazing Spider-Man #509, 2004); Sarah received blood transfusion from Parker, Gabriel became the Gray Goblin (Amazing Spider-Man #514, 2004); Sarah lured Parker to France (Spectacular Spider-Man Vol. 3 #23, 2005)

MENDEL STROMM

First Appearance: (as Mendel Stromm) Amazing Spider-Man Vol.1 #37 (1966); (as Gaunt) Spectacular Spider-Man Vol. 2 #233 (1996); (as Robot-Master) Spectacular Spider-Man Vol. 2 #240 (1996)

Origin: Spider-Man Unlimited #17 (1997); Spider-Man: The Osborn Journal #1 (1997); Peter Parker: Spider-Man Vol. 2 #27 (2001)

Significant Issues: Apparently died of heart attack (Amazing Spider-Man Vol. 1 #37, 1966); robot with Mendel's memories (Peter Parker, The Spectacular Spider-Man #68, 1982); first attempt at rejuvenation failed (Amazing Spider-Man Vol. 1 #412, 1996); rejuvenation successful, became Robot-Master (Spectacular Spider-Man Vol. 2 #240, 1996); apparently killed by Norman Osborn (Amazing Spider-Man Vol. 1 #418, 1996); re-emerged as the Robot-Master (Peter Parker: Spider-Man Vol. 2 #27, 2001); placed in indefinite suspension (Peter Parker: Spider-Man Vol. 2 #28, 2001)

FLASH THOMPSON

First Appearance: Amazing Fantasy Vol. 1 #15 (1962)

Origin: Spectacular Spider-Man Vol. 2 #-1 (1997)

Significant Issues: Menaced by Doctor Doom (Amazing Spider-Man Vol. 1 #5, 1963); boxed with Peter (Amazing Spider-Man Vol. 1 #8, 1964); founded Spidey fan club (Amazing Spider-Man Vol. 1 #17-18, 1964); graduated high school (Amazing Spider-Man Vol. 1 #28, 1965); first met Sha Shan (Amazing Spider-Man Vol.1 #108-109, 1972); framed by Hobgoblin, name cleared (Amazing Spider-Man Vol. 1 #276-277 & 289, 1986-1987); battled alcoholism, family feud (Spectacular Spider-Man Vol. 2 #248-250, 1997); caught in car crash staged by Green Goblin (Peter Parker: Spider-Man Vol. 2 #45, 2002)

TOXIN

First Appearance: (as Patrick "Paddy" Mulligan) Venom vs. Carnage #1 (2004); (as Toxin) Venom vs. Carnage #2 (2004)

Origin: Venom vs. Carnage #1-4, 2004

Significant Issues: Impregnated with symbiote offspring by Carnage (Venom vs. Carnage #1, 2004); left Gina and Edward to follow Spider-Man (Venom vs. Carnage #4, 2004)

CHARLIE WEIDERMAN

First Appearance: Amazing Spider-Man #515 (2005)

Origin: Amazing Spider-Man #515 (2005)

Significant Issues: Bullied at Midtown High (Amazing Spider-Man #515, 2005); brought knife to school, slashed tires of bullies' cars (Amazing Spider-Man #516, 2005); experiment exploded (Amazing Spider-Man #515, 2005); murdered Rich and Sheila (Amazing Spider-Man #517, 2005); destroyed Peter's apartment and Parker family home, immobilized by Spider-Man (Amazing Spider-Man #518, 2005)

POWER RATINGS

INTELLIGENCE
Ability to think and process information

1 Slow/Impaired
2 Normal
3 Learned
4 Gifted
5 Genius
6 Super-Genius
7 Omniscient

STRENGTH
Ability to lift weight

1 Weak: cannot lift own body weight
2 Normal: able to lift own body weight
3 Peak human: able to lift twice own body weight
4 Superhuman: 800 lbs-25 ton range
5 Superhuman: 25-75 ton range
6 Superhuman: 75-100 ton range
7 Incalculable: In excess of 100 tons

SPEED
Ability to move over land by running or flight

1 Below normal
2 Normal
3 Superhuman: peak range: 700 MPH
4 Speed of sound: Mach-1
5 Supersonic: Mach-2 through Orbital Velocity
6 Speed of light: 186,000 miles per second
7 Warp speed: transcending light speed

DURABILITY
Ability to resist or recover from bodily injury

1 Weak
2 Normal
3 Enhanced
4 Regenerative
5 Bulletproof
6 Superhuman
7 Virtually indestructible

ENERGY PROJECTION
Ability to discharge energy

1 None
2 Ability to discharge energy on contact
3 Short range, short duration, single energy type
4 Medium range, duration, single energy type
5 Long range, long duration, single energy type
6 Able to discharge multiple forms of energy
7 Virtually unlimited command of all forms of energy

FIGHTING ABILITY
Proficiency in hand-to-hand combat

1 Poor
2 Normal
3 Some training
4 Experienced fighter
5 Master of a single form of combat
6 Master of several forms of combat
7 Master of all forms of combat

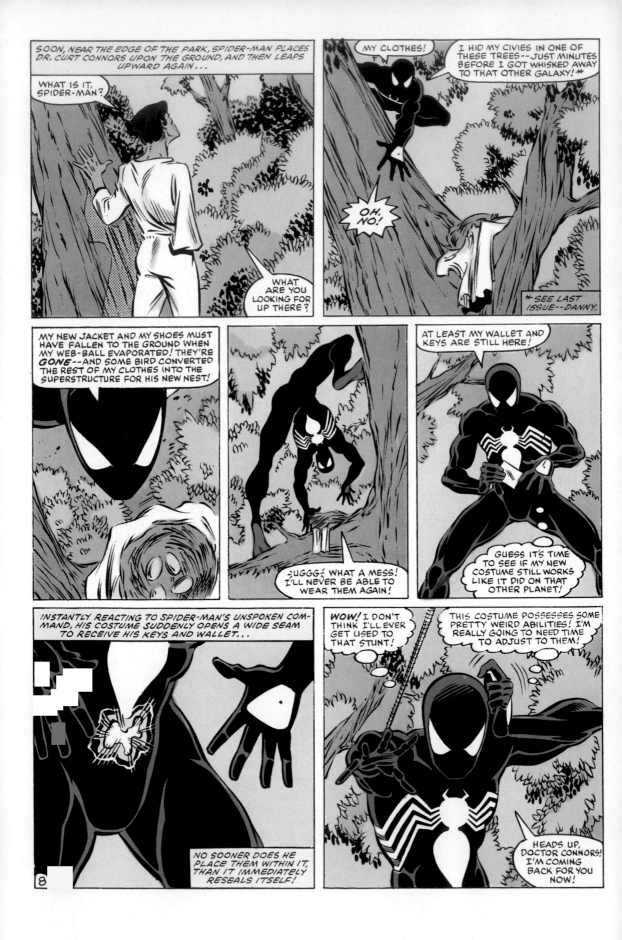

--YOUR FRIENDLY NEIGHBORHOOD SPIDER-MAN!

EDITOR'S NOTE: YOU GUESSED IT, TRUE BELIEVER! THIS IS JUST OUR SNEAKY WAY OF GIVING YOU A BONUS PIN-UP OF THE WEB-HEAD IN HIS NIFTY, NEW COSTUME! HOPE YOU LIKE IT --

DANNY!

NEXT ISSUE! SPIDER-MAN FACES THE THREAT OF A DARING, NEW VILLAIN! PLUS-- AUNT MAY FINALLY LEARNS THAT PETER HAS DROPPED OUT OF COLLEGE! DON'T MISS...